Leaky Aqueducts, Battle Pigeons, and Mystery Cults

More Frequently Asked Questions
About the Ancient Greeks and Romans

Garrett Ryan

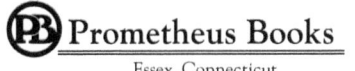 Prometheus Books

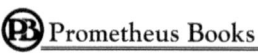 Prometheus Books

An imprint of The Globe Pequot Publishing Group, Inc.
64 South Main Street
Essex, CT 06426
www.globepequot.com

British Library Cataloguing in Publication Information Available

Library of Congress Cataloging-in-Publication Data

ISBN 9781493098378 (cloth)
ISBN 9781493090600 (paperback)
ISBN 9781493090617 (electronic)

Contents

Part VII: What If?

Preface

$\mathcal{T}$his is my third book answering questions about the ancient Greeks and Romans.* As in the first two books, the questions cover a wide range of topics. Some explore daily life ("Were there pigeons on the streets of Rome?"). Others tackle practicalities of engineering ("How much weight could a Roman bridge carry?"), nuances of belief ("How different were the Greek and Roman gods?"), and a few of the ways in which our world is indebted to antiquity ("How Roman is the Times New Roman font?"). Although the chapters are organized thematically, they can be read in any order. Whichever way you choose to peruse, please don't skip the footnotes. I saved some of the best stuff for last.

---

* The first book was *Naked Statues, Fat Gladiators, and War Elephants*. The second was *Insane Emperors, Sunken Cities, and Earthquake Machines*. Although neither is required reading, I heartily recommend both.

I

THE CITY OF ROME

Were There Pigeons on the Streets of Rome?

$\mathscr{T}$he domestic pigeon infests cities around the globe, flocking and fluttering in every inconvenient place. Unless reminded by aerial bombardment, few of us spare a thought for this least beloved of birds. For thousands of years, however, pigeons have been cherished as pets, bred for speed, and deployed in war.

A mosaic showing pigeons drinking from a basin, found in Hadrian's villa at Tivoli and now displayed in the Capitoline Museums. *Wikimedia Commons*

The pigeon is a descendent of the rock dove (*Columba livia*), which originated in the Middle East and North Africa. It was domesticated around ten thousand years ago, millennia before the chicken. Docile, delicious, and plump—and a prolific producer of field-fertilizing droppings—pigeons conquered Italy long before the Romans did. Roman agricultural writers raved about them, providing detailed advice on how to build columbaria (dovecotes). In these tower-shaped structures, sometimes large enough to house five thousand birds, pigeons were provided with piped water, troughs of seeds, and rows of nesting niches made from reused pots. Emperor Severus Alexander reportedly kept no fewer than twenty thousand pigeons in the palace aviaries, maintained by slaves who sold the eggs and squabs for profit.[1]

At a time when most Roman families lived on less than one thousand sestertii a year, a breeding pair of pigeons cost around two hundred. Birds noted for their plumage or swiftness might be sold for as much as forty thousand. Such pedigreed pigeons were pampered pets; a Roman poet rhapsodized on the theme of his girlfriend's favorite bird. Pigeons, nestled in the hands of the deceased, appeared frequently on tombstones. A pigeon lover in Syria had a monumental dovecote built atop his mausoleum.[2]

Pigeons brought to a remote place will automatically fly back to their nests. This homing instinct makes them excellent messengers. As recently as the early twentieth century, they were used to carry letters in many parts of the world; by some accounts, New Zealand's Great Barrier Pigeongram Service was the first airmail.* There is no evidence that Roman pigeons carried letters under normal circumstances. In times of war, however, they were routinely sent across enemy lines. When Decimus Brutus, one of Caesar's assassins, was besieged in Mutina, the commander of an army sent to relieve him had letters tied to the necks of pigeons and ordered the birds released as close as possible to Mutina's walls. Instinctively seeking the highest perches in sight, the pigeons flew to the towers and temple roofs

---

* There were three rival companies: the Great Barrier Pigeongram Agency, the Great Barrier Pigeongram Service, and the Original Great Barrier Pigeongram Service. Fowl play was rampant.

of the city. After his men captured the first batch of birds, Decimus Brutus ordered seed scattered to lure incoming pigeons, which kept him informed until the siege was lifted.[3]

Off the battlefield, pigeons were admired for their elaborate courtship ritual, which involves touching beaks in what looks like a kiss. They mate for life and seem affectionate to their partners; Pliny the Elder primly observed that adultery was unknown among pigeons. Thanks to their apparently amorous nature, pigeons became emblems of Venus,* who was often shown with a bird perched in her hand. Christians in the Roman catacombs used pigeons to represent the soul and eternal peace.[4]

Many Romans—whether senators with sprawling mansions or day laborers living in tenements—kept dovecotes on their roofs. Because the birds were allowed to range freely, they frequently became feral. The satirist Juvenal mentions pigeons nesting among the roof tiles of Rome's apartment buildings. Nobody seemed to mind. To the poor, feral pigeons must have been a useful source of eggs and meat. And for everyone, they had the appeal of the familiar. "My pigeon" was a term of endearment. A gladiator known as "Pigeon" was cheered in the arena. Welcome or not, the birds were always there, strutting through the Forum, posing on statues, spectating in the Colosseum—innumerable, inescapable, and indispensable.[5]

---

* The birds of the love goddess are usually described as doves. But the most familiar variety of "dove"—the kind you see on greeting cards—is nothing more or less than a large domestic pigeon, bred to have white plumage.

· 2 ·

Were Apartments Expensive?

$\mathcal{T}$he vast majority of Rome's million or so inhabitants lived in the apartment buildings known as *insulae*. According to one ancient count, there were no fewer than 46,602 *insulae* in Rome—and only 1,790 private homes. Like modern apartments, *insulae* ranged in quality from luxurious to squalid. The best units were rented by senators and wealthy freedmen. As a young man, the future dicta- tor Sulla lived in an apartment,* and even after he became emperor, Augustus sometimes slept in the apartments of his freedmen. On the other end of the scale, the migrant workers who flooded into Rome during the summer lived in cell-like rooms stacked on the roofs of ramshackle tenements.[1]

The ground floor of an *insula* was normally reserved for shops. In a world without elevators or reliable plumbing, the most desirable apartments were directly above. The cheaper units were higher up. Although the emperors limited the maximum height of apartment buildings to seventy (later sixty) feet, these regulations seem to have been honored in the breach. One apartment building, the *Insula Felicula*, was so tall that it became a tourist attraction.[2]

Although virtually all of Rome's *insulae* have disappeared, doz- ens survive in Ostia, the port at the Tiber's mouth. Most of Ostia's

---

* Sulla paid three thousand sestertii for an apartment on the first floor; a freedman rented one on the second floor for two thousand. Many years later, Sulla—now the mas- ter of Rome—nearly executed his former upstairs neighbor. Sulla was far from the only famous figure to squat in a Roman apartment. The exiled Egyptian king Ptolemy VI was forced to share a room with a painter to make his rent.

A street of *insulae* at Ostia. *Author's photo*

insulae date to the second century and were built of brick-faced concrete. Their interiors were divided into apartments of varying size. The standard layout was centered on a hall-like room known as the *medianum*, with spaces used for dining or entertaining on either end. One wall of the *medianum* had windows facing a street or courtyard. A series of small, usually windowless bedrooms opened from the opposite side.[3]

Perhaps the most remarkable apartment buildings in Ostia are the so-called Garden Houses, built during the reign of Hadrian. This luxurious residential complex consisted of two buildings, probably four stories high, at the center of a landscaped courtyard ringed by shops and other apartments. Four identical units occupied each floor of the central buildings. They followed the usual *medianum*-centered plan on a grand scale. Their reception rooms were two stories tall, with a double row of windows. Over the other rooms was a mezzanine that likely housed storage spaces and slave quarters. Including this level, a single apartment could easily have fifteen or twenty rooms.

Many *insulae* in Ostia were decorated with mosaics and frescoes. Although their windows were usually protected only by shutters, some had panes of glass or selenite. Apartments on upper stories might be provided with wooden balconies. In some cases, entire floors were jettied out to maximize space; the poet Martial claimed that apartment dwellers could shake hands across Rome's streets.[4]

The vast majority of apartments had no plumbing, forcing their inhabitants to draw water from public fountains or pay carriers to do it for them.* At least the lower floors of some *insulae* in Ostia, however, were connected by lead pipes to the local aqueduct. Likewise, though most apartment dwellers deposited human waste in chamber pots—emptied from the nearest convenient window†—a few Ostian units had private latrines, situated as far as possible from the main living area to minimize odors.[5]

Insulae were frequently built by wealthy speculators and leased to investors, who then sublet the individual units. The property was managed by a slave or freedman known as the *insularius*. Like a modern superintendent, the *insularius* was responsible for basic upkeep and repairs. He also collected the rent, which was due once a year, normally on July 1. We know from graffiti in Pompeii that apartments were advertised with painted inscriptions. Anyone interested in the "quality apartments" of the *Insula Arriana Polliana*, for example, could contact Primus, the slave of a prominent Pompeian aristocrat. Whatever the rents were in the *Insula Arriana*,‡ we can be sure that they were much more reasonable than those in Rome, where even modest apartments often cost two thousand sestertii a year—roughly double the average income of a laborer—and a senator was regarded as ludicrously thrifty for paying only six thousand. One of Cicero's clients paid thirty thousand sestertii for a third-floor apartment.[6]

---

* Rome's water carriers, like the milkmen of later centuries, were suspected of seducing women while their husbands were away.

† Being spattered by the contents of emptied chamber pots seems to have been a chronic hazard for Roman pedestrians. Sometimes the pots themselves slipped to the street, with potentially fatal consequences.

‡ The annual rent of an apartment in Pompeii was probably around five hundred sestertii, the amount that Caesar offered to pay as debt relief to those who lived outside Rome.

To judge from our literary sources, living conditions in most Roman *insulae* were less than opulent. Juvenal imagines an *insula* dweller cramped under the roof tiles with a tiny bed, a few knick-knacks, and a basket of mouse-eaten scrolls. Martial—who lived in a third-floor apartment on the Quirinal Hill—complained of the street noise that cascaded through his windows. So did Seneca, who had the misfortune of living directly over a bath. Noise was far from the only hazard. *Insulae* were often poorly maintained, and they had an unnerving habit of collapsing. Cicero, who seems to have been something of a slumlord, notes in a letter that one of his properties was falling into ruin and all the tenants had fled.[7]

The greatest danger was fire. Although their walls were usually masonry, the floors, partitions, and penthouses of *insulae* were made of wood.* A stray coal or dropped lamp could easily destroy an entire block. The problem was so pervasive that prudent investors hesitated before sinking money into the Roman real estate market. Less scrupulous investors were known to deliberately set their properties on fire for the insurance money. There was, finally, the risk of eviction. Anyone who failed to pay their rent on time was unceremoniously expelled. Martial describes watching a freshly evicted family trudge down the street, heading for one of the bridges that sheltered Rome's homeless.[8]

As Rome's population shrank in late antiquity, the *insulae* began to empty. At Ostia, aristocrats converted vacant apartment buildings into lavish summer homes. But soon even these were abandoned. Of the tens of thousands of *insulae* that lined Rome's streets in late antiquity, only one is visible today. It stands, half-excavated, on the slopes of the Capitoline Hill. Five of its stories are preserved—tenements over apartments, apartments over shops—looming above the invisible streets of the buried ancient city.

---

* The Roman terror of fire was so great that arson was made punishable by burning at the stake.

· 3 ·

What Were the Bars Like?

There were no fancy restaurants in ancient Rome. Wealthy Romans ate at home, attended by regiments of cooks and servers. The poor, by contrast, lived in apartments that usually lacked kitchens, fireplaces, or any other facilities for preparing meals. If they wanted hot food, they had to get it from a local bar.

Just as the English words *bar*, *tavern*, and *pub* have slightly different connotations, the Latin terms *taberna*, *popina*, *caupona*, and *thermopolium* were not quite synonymous. Some establishments served only food; others, only wine. Some had seats for customers; others, only service counters. Some doubled as hotels, brothels, or both. Without losing sight of those distinctions, I'll use *taberna* as a generic term for the places where most Romans drank their wine and ate hot meals.

The majority of what we know about Roman bars comes from the excavations at Ostia, Herculaneum, and—above all—Pompeii. Pompeii had more than 160 *tabernae*—roughly one for every 60 inhabitants. Almost all of Pompeii's *tabernae* were open to the street, with heavy wooden shutters that could be closed at night. Inside was a waist-high service counter, usually L- or U-shaped. For greater visibility, the front of the counter was often veneered with marble or coated with stucco. The counter of Pompeii's most recently excavated bar was painted with scenes ranging from a nereid riding a seahorse to a fierce-looking guard dog.*

---

* Over the image of the dog is a graffito reading, "Nicias is a shameless defecator." We don't know whether Nicias was the dog or the bar's owner.

The counter of a bar in Pompeii, with embedded food containers. *Author's photo*

The counter was sometimes complemented by the Roman equivalent of a pub sign, painted on a wall near the entrance. Next to the Caupona of Euxinus in Pompeii, for example, was a fresco of a phoenix—apparently the name of the bar—with the caption "The phoenix is happy, and you can be, too!"* Equally eye-catching were

---

* Another bar in Pompeii was named the Elephant. Sometimes menus were posted. An inscription outside a bar in Antibes encouraged passersby to come in and see the price list.

the elaborate lamps and windchimes hung over the counter, which often featured an apotropaic phallus or two.[1]

Although some Roman bars only served food to go, most had a seating area for customers who wanted to eat and drink on the premises. Usually, this was a small room adjacent to the service counter, provided with wooden stools and tables. A few bars had private rooms and gardens.* At the Praedia of Julia Felix in Pompeii, patrons could recline on masonry couches that imitated those in the *triclinia* of elite houses. The Caupona of Euxinus had a private vineyard, complete with shady alcoves that were probably reserved for guests.[2]

Wine came to *tabernae* in delivery carts wobbling with wine-skins. Stored in amphorae, it was poured into pitchers or cups.† The wine was usually cheap, local, and weak; bartenders were routinely accused of adding water to save money. Some establishments, however, served—or claimed to serve—more expensive vintages. A sign outside a Pompeiian bar advertised the famous Falernian variety, available for four times the cost of ordinary wine. At another bar in Pompeii, amphorae containing wines from every part of the empire were stacked along the walls, ready to be served to discerning patrons.[3]

Earthenware containers—*dolia*—filled with food were often embedded in the service counter. Although it used to be theorized that they held soups and stews, this idea seems unlikely; few containers were waterproofed with pitch. At Herculaneum, vestiges of carbonized grain, chickpeas, and beans were discovered in *dolia*. Analysis of the most recently excavated Pompeii bar found duck, fish, goat, and pig bones in a single container, along with a few snail shells. Unless these were the remains of an extremely unorthodox dish, they should probably be identified as scraps, tossed aside by the bar staff or customers. Another *dolium* in the same bar contained fava beans,

---

* Members of the middle classes may have eaten out in more upmarket settings. The exceptionally large garden in the House of Loreius Tiburtinus at Pompeii, overlooked by a dining room painted with scenes from the Trojan War, has led some archaeologists to speculate that house and garden functioned as a restaurant. The nearby House of the Moralist, with its frescoed advice about table manners (e.g., "Don't proposition other men's wives"), may have been a private dining club.

† Glass cups seem to have been the vessels of choice. A character in a Roman novel proclaims that he prefers glass, which never changes the flavor of wine.

which the Romans sometimes used to "purify" spoiled wines. A fresco in another Pompeiian bar shows sausages, cheeses, and dried fruit hanging from the rafters. Cooked foods were also on the menu: A Roman poet mentions pike being grilled outside a *taberna.* Heated or otherwise, the average quality of bar food does not seem to have been high. One poem describes it as "greasy"; another alludes casually to the cockroaches that flourished around service counters.[4]

Insalubrious though they may have been, Rome's bars seldom lacked customers. Some were open all night; a late antique urban prefect tried in vain to prohibit the sale of wine before midmorning. At any time of day, bars were places to gather, talk,* and relax over a cup of wine. A comic-strip-like fresco in Pompeii's Caupona of Salvius captures the atmosphere. Two men banter with a serving maid. Another pair, playing a game similar to backgammon, argue over the score. In the final panel, the squabbling players are thrown out by the bartender.[5]

Women who worked in bars were widely regarded as promiscuous. In an inscription set up by a pair of tavern keepers who jokingly called themselves Lucius Callidus Eroticus and Fannia Voluptas, the services of a girl are tallied on a customer's bill alongside bread and wine. To judge from the graffiti describing the bedroom prowess (and prices) of various barmaids in Pompeii, this sort of accounting was far from unusual.[6]

Literary depictions of Roman bars dwell on their seediness. Juvenal described a bar in Ostia as a place where thieves and fugitive slaves drank with eunuchs and undertakers. Centuries later, the historian Ammianus Marcellinus complained that Rome's lower classes spent half their lives in bars, gambling, arguing about chariot races, and—for some reason—snorting. Some of the bars in Rome's rougher areas were genuinely dangerous. A praetor was murdered in one by his political enemies, and at least two future emperors had their eyes blackened while slumming in *tabernae.*[7]

Bars owed much of their bad reputation, however, to elite snobbery. For wealthy Romans, the brawling, boisterous gathering places

---

* Bartenders were notorious rumormongers. It was taken as a truism that people who worked in bars knew all the local gossip.

of commoners always seemed unsavory, immoral, and more than a little threatening. It was a criminal offense to bring the young son of a respectable gentleman into a bar. A series of emperors, convinced that *tabernae* were hotbeds of conspiracy and unrest, limited the foods they could serve or closed them altogether.[8]

Ultimately, the bars of ancient Rome were nothing more or less than meeting places and refuges for the hundreds of thousands who had few other places to gather. When a well-known tavern keeper from Tivoli died, the highest compliment her heirs could think of was inscribed as her epitaph: "She drew visitors from far and wide to the haven of her bar."[9]

· 4 ·

Were There Garbage Dumps?

The streets of ancient Rome were filthy. Mud and manure caked the pavement. Packs of feral dogs roved the alleyways, living on scraps. Cockroaches infested damp places,* pigs rooted in piles of trash, and rodents scampered in cracks and corners, pursued by steadily agglomerating clowders of cats.[1]

The organic waste that littered the streets was likely scraped up on a semiregular basis and sold as manure to suburban farmers.† There may have been, as in some Greek cities, neighborhood cesspits into which inorganic garbage could be dumped. But there was no equivalent of the public trash-collection services most of us enjoy today. Property owners were responsible for hauling away their own refuse. Human nature being what it is, this meant that trash tended to accumulate everywhere.[2]

At Pompeii, alleys and many streets were carpeted with garbage, packed rock-hard by the wheels of passing chariots. Trash filled empty lots and was heaped in abandoned houses. Just outside the city walls were huge drifts of broken pots, smashed tiles, animal bones, and other waste. The rubbish heaps outside the Roman city

---

* The oriental cockroach (*Blatta orientalis*), native to the shores of the Black Sea, colonized Rome and provincial towns as distant as Londinium. From these advance posts, it scuttled to a city near you.

† Men known as *koprologoi* cleared manure from the streets of Greek cities. At Rome, the aediles were traditionally responsible for keeping the streets clean; they may have used public slaves or contractors for the purpose. The empress Messalina attempted to escape Rome in a dung-collection cart.

of Oxyrhynchus in Egypt were still up to thirty feet high when they were discovered by archaeologists.

The dumps that ringed Rome were on a scale still grander. Under the Republic, large public cesspits were dug outside the Esquiline Gate. When excavated in the nineteenth century, they were found to contain everything from household refuse to the bones of paupers. Dumping was prohibited within a certain distance of the walls, and stones were set up to mark the boundary. This rule, however, seems to have been honored in the breach. Garbage was routinely tipped into the Tiber, and hills of refuse built up on the Janiculum and elsewhere along the city's perimeter.[3]

The most monumental midden loomed over the warehouse district by the Tiber. As tall as the Pantheon, it consisted entirely of broken pottery—by one estimate, 53 million amphorae. Since the Middle Ages, it has been known as Monte Testaccio, the mountain of pots. Almost all the amphorae that make up Monte Testaccio held olive oil. Perhaps a tenth were imported from the rich olive groves of North Africa. The rest came from the province of Baetica, modern Andalusia. Spanish oil amphorae were huge, heavy vessels, capable of holding around 70 liters (18.5 gallons). Over the first three centuries CE, tens of thousands were shipped to Rome every year.

Let's imagine the journey of a shipload of amphorae at the end of the second century. The long civil war that made Septimius Severus master of the Roman world has finally ended. (Just a few years earlier, the emperor ceremoniously rode his horse over the naked corpse of his last remaining rival.) With peace has come renewed prosperity. Along Spain's Guadalquivir River,* the production of olive oil is booming as never before.[4]

Our story starts on one of the many estates that checkered the fertile valley between Seville and Cordoba. It belongs to a man of equestrian rank who prefers his comfortable townhouse to the villas

---

* The valley of the Guadalquivir (the ancient Baetis) was famously fertile. The only problem, according to the Greek geographer Strabo, was that it was overrun by crop-eating rabbits. The rabbits caused so much destruction in the Balearic Islands that the inhabitants once sent an embassy to Rome to beg for resettlement. Spanish farmers, however, learned to manage them with Libyan ferrets.

The author on Monte Testaccio. *Author's photo*

scattered across his rural properties. This particular estate, located among rolling hills a short distance from the river, is almost entirely planted with olive trees. The groves are worked by both free and slave laborers.* Although the slaves live in cramped quarters near the main villa and the tenant farmers have houses of their own, they do much the same work. Slave or free, they spend most of the year cutting down weeds and plowing the land between the trees to aerate the soil. The busiest months are November and December. This is the wettest time of the year, when rainstorms break over the hills and fill the river. But it is also the season when the olives ripen and fall.[5]

On a clear, cool morning, the olives are gathered, washed, and dumped into a trough, where a mule-driven millstone crushes them to paste. The paste is shoveled into buckets, which are stacked beneath a press—a heavy beam lowered with a winch. As the beam is brought down and wicker creaks and snaps, golden olive oil cascades

---

* This was a common arrangement. The Sabine farm owned by the poet Horace, for example, was worked by eight slaves and five tenant farmers. On large estates, free laborers were often hired to help with the harvest.

into the collection channel. Once the fluid has settled and separated, it is decanted into amphorae made at the local claypit, each stamped with the estate owner's name.

The amphorae are brought on muleback to storage depots near the banks of the river. In April or May, a merchant sails down from Cordoba with a purchase contract, and the amphorae are loaded into the hold, joining hundreds of others from estates upstream. So heavily laden that it scrapes every sandbar, the ship floats downstream to the sea. Throughout the voyage to Italy, it hugs the coast, close enough for the sailors to see the red roofs of port cities and smell the reek of garum factories.

Twenty-two days after leaving Spain, the ship sails into Portus. Over the past century, this artificial harbor has definitively displaced the older facilities at Puteoli and neighboring Ostia. The outer basin, with its smoking lighthouse, is crowded with ships. A colossal barge from the Egyptian grain fleet, painted with icons of Isis, looms over all the others. Our ship pauses to pick up a harbor pilot, who guides it into the hexagonal inner basin. Moments after it noses into a berth, customs officials descend on the decks, demanding to see the captain's contracts and inspect his cargo. After the usual rigmarole, members of the stevedores' guild begin to use pulleys and treadwheel cranes to lift the two thousand amphorae in the ship's hold onto wagons. These shuttle the amphorae into a vast concrete warehouse perfumed with oil.

The warehouse belongs to the emperor, as does everything inside. Olive oil is a staple of the Roman diet, a vital source of nutrients for the multitudes who live primarily on bread. In Rome, the price of olive oil, like that of grain, has been controlled by the emperors since the time of Augustus, and oil has occasionally been included in the grain dole. Recently, Septimius Severus decreed that all citizens eligible for a grain ration should also receive olive oil every month. The merchant who brought the amphorae from Spain is under contract with the imperial government to supply oil at a fixed rate. He has spent most of his career dealing with subordinates of the *praefectus annonae*, the official responsible for overseeing both the grain dole and the olive oil supply, and watches with a practiced eye as the amphorae are labeled* and weighed.[6]

The amphorae then begin the final leg of their journey. Sprawling though the warehouses at Portus are, they are meant only to shelter goods for a brief time, until they can be brought up the Tiber to the capital. Even when swollen with spring rain, the river is too shallow for a large seagoing vessel.[†] Most of the boats on the river are flat-bottomed barges, designed to skim over sandbars and rocks. The amphorae, their handles lashed together for security, are loaded onto a dozen barges. To cope with the current, which makes it difficult to row upstream, each barge is hitched to a team of oxen, who patiently tow it the twenty miles to Rome. It takes three days—partly because the teams have to be switched every few miles, but mostly because the river is so crowded.[7]

As the barges approach Rome, river traffic slows to a crawl. Tombs and villas crowd the banks. The metropolis finally comes into view as an incomprehensible accumulation of white and tan buildings, stained by the smoke of ten thousand charcoal fires. Where the current slows, just below the temples and tenements of the Aventine Hill, a tangle of piers marks the port of Rome. The barges are unloaded into one of the warehouses that hold oil, grain, marble, wood, and everything else consumed by the world city. After the stamps and inscriptions on each amphora have been recorded and checked, the seals are broken, and the oil is tipped into cavernous storage tanks.

In Rome, amphorae are often recycled as storage containers, repurposed as pipes or flowerpots, or shattered and mixed into concrete as aggregate. The bulbous shape and thick walls of Spanish oil amphorae, however, make them unsuitable for most secondary

---

* The labels were intended to discourage fraud. They indicated the weight of the amphora when empty, the weight of the oil it contained, the place from which the oil originated, the name of the export merchant, and the name of the inspector.

† Thousands of boats made their way up the Tiber to Rome each year. The maximum size seems to have been about 150 tons—roughly the average capacity of a Mediterranean merchant vessel in the Roman imperial era. The guild of divers, which had an office in Ostia, specialized in salvaging the cargoes of captains who misjudged the river's depth and ran aground.

applications. They are difficult to break into small fragments, and the oil that clings to their surfaces weakens any concrete made with them. Last but not least, they stink.

So once they have been drained, Spanish oil amphorae are tied in pairs over the backs of mules and sent to the state amphora dump—the future Monte Testaccio. The dump is already as tall as any of the Seven Hills, and it's growing every day. Although the lower slopes are covered with grass, most of the mound is the chalky red of broken pottery. Near the summit, rows of intact pots, weighted with shards, have been arranged into a terrace. Mule drivers roll the amphorae into the center of the terrace, where slaves with sledge-hammers smash them into hand-sized pieces. Other slaves rake the fragments into layers and sprinkle them with lime, binding them together and cutting the stench of rancid oil.

Unburdened, the mules descend the long path back down to the warehouses. In the distance, their drivers can make out the gilded roof of Jupiter's temple on the Capitoline and the bronze dome of the Pantheon. But the mules, heads down, see only bits of pottery, crunching to reddish dust beneath their hooves.

Dumping continued at Monte Testaccio until the late third century, when the Aurelian Wall cut the roads between the dump and the river.* During the Middle Ages, legends sprang up around the mountain of pots. Some claimed that it had been built with rubble from the great fire of Nero; others, that it was composed of pagan cinerary urns. The most prevalent explanation, however, was that the hill was made of vessels sent from the provinces as tribute. In a sense, this was correct.†

---

* The flow of oil amphorae continued long after Monte Testaccio was abandoned. During the fourth century, at least ten thousand amphorae were recycled into the concrete vaults of the Circus of Maxentius.

† In keeping with this theory, Monte Testaccio was sometimes called *Mons omnium terrarium*—"The mountain of all lands." At some point, it became customary to haul two carts filled with live pigs to the top of Monte Testaccio during carnival. The carts were then allowed to roll down the slope. When they inevitably crashed, spilling their squealing cargo, a crowd of revelers barbequed the pigs on the spot. More sober crowds ascended the hill on Good Friday, when Monte Testaccio was used to represent Golgotha. Until the beginning of the twentieth century, wine was stored in caves burrowed into the cool masses of ceramic.

Monte Testaccio is a microcosm of the Roman Empire. It reflects the reach of imperial power, which could draw millions of oil amphorae from distant parts of the Mediterranean. It attests to the productivity and complexity of the Roman economy, which could support long-distance trade on such a vast scale. It is evidence of consumerism on a level that would not be exceeded until the Industrial Revolution. And it bears witness, like all monuments of empire, to the inequities that made Rome's grandeur possible.

· 5 ·

Were There Bookstores?

$\mathcal{A}$ccording to the usual estimate, only around one in ten Romans could read. The literacy rate was lowest in rural areas, among slaves, and for nonelite women. Freeborn urban men, however, were reasonably likely to possess at least the basic literacy required to keep records and sign their names.* And the Roman elite—which associated itself with the production and consumption of literature—collected books on a scale unsurpassed before the invention of printing.

In Rome, public libraries were attached to Augustus's Temple of Apollo, Vespasian's Temple of Peace, the Forum of Trajan, and each of the great imperial baths.† The private libraries of the aristocracy were almost equally extensive. The sole example found intact—in the Villa of the Papyri at Herculaneum—was a room about ten feet to a side, with shelves along the walls and a double-sided case at the center. But even this modest space (almost certainly not the villa's primary library) contained upward of a thousand scrolls.[1]

Until late antiquity, virtually every book with literary pretensions was written on papyrus scrolls. A scroll was roughly the same height

---

* The graffiti of Pompeii are the most famous showcase of nonelite writing in the Roman world. Hundreds of Pompeiians—mostly male, with occupations ranging from architect to weaver—left their marks on every convenient wall. Although the grammar often strays from the Ciceronian standard, several writers quote lines of the *Aeneid*, presumably remembered from school.

† Ovid's poems on the art of love were banned from Rome's public libraries for being too risqué. Not long after, Tiberius's praetorian prefect Sejanus presided over the burning of a history that praised the assassins of Caesar. In late antiquity, Emperor Valens instituted a massive purge of magical and astrological texts, on the grounds that the owners of such books were trying to foretell or bring about his death.

Six carbonized scrolls, found fused together in the Villa of the Papyri, now in the Naples National Library. *Author's photo*

as a modern hardcover. The length ranged from ten to fifty feet, the equivalent of around twenty to one hundred pages of printed text. Longer works were divided; each of the 142 books in Livy's Roman history, for example, originally occupied a single scroll. The text was written as a continuous stream of letters, with no spaces and minimal punctuation. The codex—the book as we know it—appeared early in the imperial era for works of practical reference. Although Roman booksellers experimented with codex editions of Martial's poems at the end of the first century, it was only over the course of the third and fourth centuries, and thanks in large part to Christian preference, that scrolls were finally eclipsed.[2]

A small book market had existed in classical Athens and a more substantial one in Ptolemaic Alexandria. Rome, however, was the real birthplace of the book trade. The business was still in its infancy during the last days of the Republic, when Cicero relied on his friend Atticus—who had a staff of slaves trained as copyists—to stock his libraries.* But by the early imperial era, Rome had several

---

* On one occasion, Atticus sent two of his slaves to affix identifying tags to Cicero's books and build a set of bookcases.

well-established bookstores. One of these, owned by a man named Atrectus, stood in the high-rent district around Caesar's Forum; the titles of bestsellers were painted on the pillars that flanked its entrance. Like most of his competitors, Atrectus had likely been a slave copyist or librarian before gaining his freedom and entering the business of selling and publishing books.[3]

Most Roman authors—independently wealthy or attached to patrons—had no need to support themselves through their work. For some, publication consisted simply of reciting their works before an audience. Others gave copies to friends, with the understanding that these would be shared.* An extreme example of this strategy was adopted by a wealthy orator who distributed no fewer than a thousand copies of a speech commemorating his son.[4]

Authors with a keener interest in financial benefit used booksellers to publish their works. There was no equivalent of copyright or royalties. The bookseller paid a lump sum for the author's manuscript and kept all profits from sales of the copies he produced. Booksellers seem to have stocked a wide range of texts. One, for example, sold both Quintilian's weighty treatise on rhetorical education and the lighthearted epigrams of Martial.[5]

Some books were packaged for the luxury market. An edition of Martial bordered with expensive purple dye cost five denarii—more than most Romans made in a week. But shops also stocked cheap and reused scrolls, priced at only a few sestertii. By the second century, there were sellers who specialized in antique books. Aulus Gellius records browsing vintage works of fantastic fiction at a bookstall in Brundisium and finding—in a shop at Rome—a history that dated to the beginnings of Latin literature. One of Gellius's acquaintances discovered an antique manuscript of the *Aeneid*, supposedly in the hand of Virgil himself, for sale at a street fair.[6]

Educated Romans consumed a wide range of literature in both Greek and Latin. Besides the amateur productions of their friends—Pliny the Younger often subjected dinner guests to his own

---

* Cicero sometimes corrected works after initially distributing them, which resulted in the circulation of multiple editions.

poems—they read or listened to everything from edifying aphorisms to titillating Milesian tales.* Although works by popular authors like Martial sold thousands (and perhaps tens of thousands) of copies, they were eclipsed by the classics of the Augustan era. Of these, the most successful was Virgil's *Aeneid*. Like the *Iliad* in the Greek world† and the Bible in early modern Europe, the *Aeneid* was the book from which children were taught to read and the one book that any family with a library was sure to own. It was probably the only Roman book that existed, like modern bestsellers, in hundreds of thousands of copies.[7]

During late antiquity, bookstores declined in tandem with the old aristocracy. The copying of secular texts slowed and then ceased. The books in Roman libraries, public and private, crumbled on their shelves. Only a small contingent of survivors found their way into monasteries. Of the millions of books that existed in the final days of the Western Roman Empire, we have—leaving aside papyri—physical fragments of only a few hundred, the last vestiges of the ancient book trade.

---

* These erotic novels were wildly popular; after the defeat of Crassus at Carrhae, the Parthians found them in the baggage of captured Roman officers.

† Among Roman papyri from Egypt, fragments of the *Iliad* (and, to a lesser extent, the *Odyssey*) far outnumber those of any other literary work. After Homer, the most popular authors were lesser luminaries of the Greek literary canon—Demosthenes, Euripides, and Hesiod.

· 6 ·

How Was Free Bread Distributed?

$\mathcal{A}$t a time when the average city held only a few thousand inhabitants, Rome had a million. The population of the entire empire at its height may have been seventy million, which likely represented roughly a third of the global total. For centuries, in other words, something like one in seventy Romans, and one in two hundred human beings, lived in the city of Rome.

Rome was far too large to be fed by its hinterland or even by Italy.* From the Middle Republic to the final years of the Western Roman Empire, produce from every part of the Mediterranean Basin poured into the imperial city: olive oil, wine, fish sauce, and luxuries ranging from Indian pepper to hibernating land snails. By one estimate, annual imports of staple foods alone may have exceeded 400,000 metric tons. Of that figure, around half came in the form of grain.

The ancient Greeks had divided food into two categories: bread and things eaten with it. For the Romans, likewise, bread was part of virtually every meal. It has been estimated that the average Roman received three-quarters of his calories in the form of bread and consumed something like 450 pounds of grain each year. Ancient doctors noted that Roman children often developed bowed legs—a symptom of rickets, brought on by a diet that consisted of little but bread.[1]

---

* Not all of Rome's food was imported. A dense network of orchards, vineyards, and vegetable gardens encircled the city, producing crops to sell in the markets. Recently, during the construction of a new subway station, the remains of a suburban peach orchard were discovered, complete with an elaborate irrigation system, seedling planters, and some very venerable peach pits.

A distribution of free bread, as shown on a Pompeiian fresco now in the Naples Archaeological Museum. *Wikimedia Commons*

Whenever possible, the Romans ate bread made from wheat.* Although wheat was grown widely, only a few regions around the Mediterranean consistently produced surpluses large enough for export. Sicily, Sardinia, and North Africa—especially what are now Tunisia and eastern Algeria—all provided Rome with grain.† But the most vital breadbasket, responsible for the majority of the wheat that fed the capital, was Egypt.

---

* In classical Greece, most bread had been made from barley. Victors at the Eleusinian games received barley as a prize; at Sparta, helots grew barley for their masters' meals.

† Classical Athens had imported grain from Sicily, Egypt, Syria, and northern Italy. The most important source, however, was the Bosporan Kingdom, centered on the Crimean Peninsula. Much later, the Byzantine emperors periodically obtained grain from the same region.

Most of the provincial grain shipped to Rome was collected as a tax. In Cicero's time, for example, a fifth of the Sicilian grain harvest was claimed by the government. Under the emperors, wheat farmers in Egypt and North Africa paid their rents in kind, as did the tenants of many imperial estates. Tax wheat was delivered to state-owned granaries, from which it was forwarded to the coast for transport to Italy.

The barges that carried grain to Rome were the supertankers of the ancient world. At a time when the average freighter held roughly one hundred tons of cargo, a large grain barge could carry more than one thousand. During the second century, the author Lucian saw one of these behemoths docked at Athens. It was, he says, 180 feet long and more than 45 feet at the beam—around the size of a large ship of the line during the Napoleonic Wars. Although their cargoes were government property, grain barges were privately owned. To ensure a steady stream of deliveries, the emperors offered captains generous terms, especially if they were willing to sail in winter. St. Paul was on an Egyptian grain barge bound for Rome when an early winter gale shipwrecked him on Malta.[2]

Most of the Egyptian grain transports traveled together in a massive flotilla. Initially, this fleet docked at Puteoli. After the emperors developed the artificial harbor at Portus, wheat from Egypt and the other grain-exporting provinces was landed at the mouth of the Tiber. At Rome, the grain was stored in colossal warehouses.* One of these, the imperially owned Horrea Galbana, covered nearly 225,000 square feet. The Colosseum was only slightly larger.[3]

Much of the wheat kept in Rome's warehouses was dispensed through the famous grain dole. The dole had been introduced in the last years of the Republic, when the radical tribune Clodius made grain—already subsidized by the government—free for many of the Roman plebs. This policy was systematized and refined by Augustus and his successors. Under the emperors, roughly 200,000 people received free grain every month. Each recipient was given

---

* Pliny the Elder claimed that mixing olive lees into the mortar of grain warehouses discouraged insects.

five modii (around seventy pounds), enough to feed one adult. Eventually, portions of olive oil, pork, and wine were added. Far from being a sign of poverty, enrollment in the dole was seen as a status symbol; only Roman citizens who had long been resident in the capital were eligible.[4]

An official list was kept of those on the dole. Everyone on the list received a token—the *tessera frumentaria*—which they had to present in order to receive their allotment.* The grain was distributed at the Porticus Minucia on the Campus Martius. Dole recipients presented their token at one of forty-four windows on a designated day of the month. The epitaph of one Roman boy, for example, records that he received grain on the tenth day at window 39. Until the third century, those on the dole brought their grain to bakers to be milled and baked.† When the state assumed those tasks under Septimius Severus, water-powered grain mills were set up at strategic points in the aqueduct system, and daily distributions of bread replaced the monthly grain handouts.[5]

Although only around a fifth of Rome's inhabitants were enrolled in the dole, all benefited from government supervision of the grain market. In times of crisis, the emperors set maximum prices, limited the quantities that individuals could buy, and increased the amount dispensed by the dole. More generally, imperial officials tried to keep bread affordable by supervising the activities of shippers and bakers. They also released state grain onto the open market at subsidized prices.[6]

The government controlled the grain market because it had to. Any increase in the price of grain threatened the hundreds of thousands who were not on the dole with deprivation. Bread riots were a chronic problem. In 75 BCE, a hungry mob threatened to lynch the consuls. More than a century later, another mob pelted Claudius

---

* The *tesserae* were inscribed FRV (*frumentatio*). Though usually passed down through families, they could be bought and sold.

† The tomb of Marcus Vergilius Eurysaces, who grew rich turning state-supplied wheat into bread, can still be seen just outside the Porta Maggiore. Reliefs on the sides of the tomb show the process of baking, from the receipt of grain to delivery of the loaves. Above are a series of stylized cylinders, apparently meant to represent either grain measures or mechanical kneading devices.

with stale crusts. Besides preventing unrest in the capital, directing the surpluses of the whole Mediterranean world to a single city was a way of performing imperial power.* It was also a way of acknowledging Rome's special status in the empire. The goddess Annona, who personified the grain supply, appeared on imperial coins. Frequently, she was pictured with a ship's prow, signifying the emperors' role in importing grain from distant provinces.[7]

Despite its prodigious cost, the grain dole survived well into late antiquity. At Constantinople—where Constantine established a system modeled on Rome's—the dole persisted until the Persians conquered Egypt.† Rome's own dole, ended by the Vandal occupation of North Africa, was revived after the fall of the western empire by the Gothic king Theoderic, who understood that being a successor of the emperors meant feeding Rome.[8]

---

* Augustus epitomized this dynamic when, after being delighted by the singing of a slave choir, he gave each of its members a gift of grain.

† Justinian ceremoniously inspected the granaries at the end of each shipping season and then proclaimed to his subjects that the warehouses were full and all was well.

· 7 ·

How Bad Did It Smell?

The reek of ancient Rome would have struck a modern nose with the force of a gladiator's gauntlet. The one overwhelming smell was that of manure, human and animal, endlessly replenished by beasts of burden and emptied chamber pots. The Tiber, Rome's sewer, amplified the stench, especially during summer. At every corner and alleyway, the dusky undertones of ordure were paired with the piquant aroma of urine. Rome, in other words, smelled like dung. But it didn't *just* smell like dung.

Let's imagine a visit to the city in the early third century—more precisely, during the reign of Caracalla, though at a time when that murderous sociopath was off campaigning in the provinces. It is the first day of Floralia, the festival of flowers at the end of April.* You have joined the crowds flooding into the capital for the festivities.

Everywhere, the scent of roses: roses in the hedgerows, rose petals on the road, roses in the garlands of people passing by. Although the day is still in its first hour, the Appian Way is already crowded with suburban gentlemen in painstakingly pleated togas and farm families wearing rough-spun wool. Around you are the smells of the countryside: pine resin, fresh-cropped grass, and just a hint of cow manure. A courier gallops by on the bridle path, and the aroma of wet earth, kicked up by the horse's hooves, briefly fills the air.

---

* Floralia was one of the most beloved Roman festivals, not least because it bore more than a passing resemblance to Mardi Gras. Actresses in plays associated with the festivities were encouraged to shed their clothes onstage.

Tombs line both sides of the road, three and four rows deep. The grandest belong to families that vanished centuries ago. Grass grows from cracks in their walls, and trees sprout on their roofs. Other mausolea are new, their paint still bright, bronze statues shining in the sun. From a grove come the smells of a cremation: ashes, spent incense, and wine. There are shanty towns among the tombs, complete with ramshackle hotels and stables for the horses of travelers. Even from a distance, they reek of staleness and smoke.

As shanties give way to *insulae,* you cross the invisible limits of Rome. The smells of damp wool and bath oil are all around. Both men and women wear perfume: narcissus, lily, cinnamon, and scents unknown to you, mingling in the humid morning air.

There is no graceful way to walk in Rome. You have to creep like a sailor on a storm-tossed ship, stopping and starting, rushing forward and staggering back. You do your best to squeeze through, but the cross-traffic at the first big intersection stops you dead. As you ponder the best way forward, you hear the shouts that herald an approaching litter.

Litters are the menace of the Roman streets. Although the light ones hired at street corners are easy enough to evade, the huge private litters of the rich, with their tasseled awnings and hobnailed bearers, are lethal. This is an especially big one, carried by eight liveried slaves. You could press up against a wall with everyone else to avoid being crushed, but you opt for boldness. Navigating by the curses of battered pedestrians, and with just a bit of apologetic shoving, you emerge among the casualties in the litter's wake. Hurrying forward to the sweet spot just behind the bearers, you match your pace to theirs.

As the litter batters its way across the intersection, you smell attar of rose and exotic spices. Glancing up, you lock eyes with an aristocratic lady with piled curls and crimson silks. She favors you with a barely perceptible nod and then returns to reading a scroll as her litter turns down a side street.

For years, the emperor has been building an enormous bath just off the road. Even here, two hundred paces from the rising concrete domes, the air is acrid with lime. Ahead, at a turning of the Appian

Way, is the great fountain beneath the imperial palace.* You can already smell the moss and damp.

But you turn before reaching the fountain, skirting the gargantuan base of the Circus Maximus. The gates are closed—the games won't begin until later—but you imagine that you can smell the dust of the track, beaten flour-fine by countless races. The shops across from the circus are already open, and their wares are displayed along the street: a bookseller with heaps of musty papyrus, a spice merchant with cakes of incense, a baker with baskets of fresh bread. At the base of an apartment block slumped against the Aventine Hill, you follow the scent of fresh-cooked sausages to the service window of a tavern and order a cone of chickpeas.

Crunching on these, you find the way forward blocked again, this time by a festival procession. To bypass the traffic, you follow an alley up the Aventine. A century ago, this was a working-class neighborhood. But the rich, drawn by cheap rents, have colonized the hill. You pass the shuttered doors of their mansions as you climb. Stopping by a small fountain to finish your chickpeas, you smell roses again. You turn to see the neighborhood shrine, decked with garlands for the festival.†

From the placid Aventine, you descend into the chaos of the Forum Boarium. A sacrifice is taking place in front of one of the temples; you can smell the incense and roasting meat. The prevailing fragrance, however, is that of the river, reeking with sewage as always. You can see your destination now: the Theater of Marcellus, built by

---

* This is the Septizodium, a colossal ornamental fountain built against the side of the Palatine Hill facing the Appian Way. Roughly one hundred feet tall and perhaps five hundred feet long, it was decorated with marble columns from every corner of the empire. Statues of the seven planetary gods, haloed by the spray of fountains, stood in its first story. Early in the Middle Ages, the central part of the Septizodium collapsed. The surviving sections were fortified and eventually incorporated into a huge castle. During a thirteenth-century war, the larger of the surviving sections was destroyed. The smaller section, however, survived until 1588, when Pope Sixtus V ordered it demolished for building materials. The reused stone can still be seen in the base of the Column of Marcus Aurelius, the fountains of the Via Quattro Fontane, and the Sistine Chapel of Santa Maria Maggiore.

† Imperial Rome was divided into fourteen administrative *regiones*. These, in turn, were subdivided into 265 (later more than 300) neighborhood-sized districts known as *vici*. At a major intersection in every *vicus* stood an altar, where offerings were made to the emperors and the guardian deities of the district.

Augustus more than two hundred years ago. You make your way to an entrance, present your entry token, and climb the steps.

A light breeze—fortunately not from the direction of the river—wafts the smell of roasting chicken to your seat. You make a mental note to visit the theater's snack stalls after the show. A trumpet sounds, and an actress appears onstage. She draws a handful of flowers from an attendant's basket and scatters them into the crowd. Panels open in the roof of the stage building, and a gentle shower of rose petals descends. They float on the breeze, which blends the fragrance of the flowers with the scents of the city beyond: the perfume and the filth, incense, roses, roses.

II

WONDERS OF ENGINEERING

• 8 •

How Were Roman Baths Heated?

℮very day, millions of Romans exercised, socialized, swam, and lounged in the heated halls and pools of the baths.* The baths were places to meet friends, make connections, and perhaps even score a dinner invitation. They were places to buy a snack, have a massage, or face the dreaded tweezers of the hair remover. They were places to escape from a harsh and status-driven world. They were places to bask in the glory of the emperors. They were places to be Roman.[1]

Although Roman baths ranged in scale from cramped sheds to the vast imperial thermae, virtually all featured the same basic sequence of spaces: frigidarium (cold bathing room), tepidarium (warm room), and caldarium (hot bathing room).† These rooms often adjoined a palaestra, or exercise yard, and were sometimes complemented by a sudatorium (steam bath), laconicum (dry sauna), or natatio (swimming pool).[2]

The design of a bath depended on the ambitions of its builder and the nature of its site. Smaller baths usually had asymmetrical plans, centered on rows of barrel-vaulted rooms. In the Forum Baths at Pompeii, for example, two sequences of rooms—one for men, the

---

* The baths owed some of their popularity to the fact that admission was either free (in the case of establishments endowed by the emperors or a local benefactor) or quite inexpensive. For centuries, the usual charge was a quadrans, the smallest Roman coin. Women were sometimes charged slightly more; children were admitted free.

† The rooms could be visited in any order. The physician Galen, however, advised his patients to go from hot to cold. Although most people only spent hour or two in the baths, some sybarites were rumored to spend most of their time there, returning seven or eight times in a single day.

37

other for women—wrapped around a courtyard. On the more elaborate men's side, a short corridor led from the courtyard to the apodyterium, or changing room. From here, bathers could access both the frigidarium, centered on a single circular pool, and the tepidarium, where the air was heated by a brazier. From the tepidarium, bathers entered the caldarium, which had a raised marble basin on one end and a small heated pool on the other.

Large baths, by contrast, often had a symmetrical design inspired by Rome's thermae—vast entertainment complexes equipped with libraries, lecture halls, and galleries of statues.* In such baths, mirrored pairs of rooms were arranged around a central hall. Besides facilitating the circulation of crowds—the largest facilities could serve thousands of customers at once—a symmetrical plan allowed half of a bath to be closed for maintenance or economy.† The largest of all Roman thermae, the Baths of Diocletian, was a product of symmetrical planning on a colossal scale. At the center was a gargantuan vaulted frigidarium. On one side, the frigidarium opened onto an Olympic-sized natatio. On the other, it was connected via a domed tepidarium with the caldarium. Around this central axis were arranged identical sets of secondary rooms, each featuring a large palaestra. The precinct around the bathing block, planted with gardens and provided with every conceivable amenity, was larger than many provincial towns.³

Some Roman baths were built over natural springs. In the complex at Bath, England, spring water was collected in an oval reservoir before being channeled to the famous great pool, which was plated with some 190,000 pounds of lead. Although constructing a bath over springs removed the need for a remote water supply, the water often left mineral deposits that had to be cleaned from the pipes and pools. During the Middle Ages, thick deposits of travertine

---

* In late antiquity, baths sometimes became "museums" of mythological sculpture removed from temples and other public places. The statues assembled in the Baths of Zeuxippus at Constantinople were celebrated by poets. Although that collection has perished, two of the most famous masterpieces of classical art—the *Terme Ruler* and *Terme Boxer*—were discovered in the ruins of Rome's Baths of Constantine.

† Economizing was important; baths were ruinously expensive. The medium-sized Baths of Neptune at Ostia cost more than two million sestertii to build.

The church of Santa Maria degli Angeli, built into the frigidarium of the Baths of Diocletian. *Author's photo*

completely buried the spring-fed baths at Hierapolis—modern Pamukkale, Turkey—along with much of the surrounding city.

Many baths were supplied by wells or cisterns. At Castellum Tidditanorum (now Tiddis, Algeria), a city built on a steep slope, the baths were connected to a three-chambered cistern fed by channels cut into the rocky hillside above. The Mithraic Baths at Ostia were provided with a series of wells, from which water was raised to roof tanks by slave-operated compartment wheels. The Hadrianic Baths at Leptis Magna in Libya were equipped with wells, roof tanks for collecting rain, and a reservoir in the adjacent wadi that trapped seasonal floods.

The largest baths were fed by aqueducts. Across the empire, in fact, baths were probably the single most important factor motivating aqueduct construction. Even in Rome, the construction of an imperial bath complex usually involved either building a new aqueduct or supplementing the sources of existing conduits. The largest thermae were served by dedicated aqueduct lines that terminated in vast reservoirs, which could be filled at night and used to run the baths over the subsequent day.*

Aqueduct reservoirs were especially important in North Africa, where the water supply was subject to dramatic seasonal fluctuations. The Antonine Baths at Carthage, for example, were fed by the Zaghouan Aqueduct, which filled the cisterns of La Malga, a series of colossal vaults with a combined capacity of more than 1.8 million cubic feet. A supplementary set of cisterns stored around 700,000 cubic feet of water in the immediate vicinity of the baths.

Roman baths were warmed by furnaces, typically arranged in rows beneath or along the perimeter of the heated rooms. The furnaces were simple masonry structures, in which fires were kept stoked throughout the day. The usual fuel was wood,† harvested from local forests.[4]

The furnaces heated boilers, vessels of bronze or lead positioned directly above the flames. The best-preserved example—found in a private bath at Boscoreale, near Pompeii—is roughly six feet tall and two feet in diameter. It was connected to a cold-water tank by three lead pipes that could be opened or closed with valves to provide cool, warm, or hot water. The Stabian Baths at Pompeii, a relatively small public facility, had two boilers and a cold-water tank. The more substantial Legionary Baths at Lambaesis in Algeria featured four massive, aqueduct-fed boilers tied to the pools by a labyrinth of lead pipes and valves. A bronze half-cylinder known as a testudo was sometimes embedded in the wall of a hot pool. The outer face of the cylinder was in direct contact with the furnace; the inner face was open to the pool. Bathwater circulating through a testudo was warmed far more efficiently than it could have been through the thick masonry of the floor.

---

* Agrippa built the Aqua Virgo (which still feeds the Trevi Fountain) to supply his baths. Both Caracalla and Diocletian tapped new springs at the head of the Aqua Marcia to ensure that their thermae would have adequate water. The reservoir of the Baths of Caracalla featured thirty-two chambers, arranged in two stories. The Botte di Termini, which served the Baths of Diocletian, were almost equally expansive.

† The most efficient way to produce fuel from a hardwood grove is coppicing—that is, cutting trees back to stumps that sprout dozens of sapling-sized shoots. Around Rome, entire forests were likely managed in this way. Emperor Severus Alexander reportedly assigned tracts of woodland near the city to individual baths.

The furnaces also heated the air of the baths. The hot fumes they produced were channeled into the hypocaust,* a raised floor supported by brick or stone piers. As the fumes filled the space between the piers, they warmed the floor above, which was usually composed of large tiles covered by a layer of mortar. Fumes escaped from the hypocaust via wall flues designed to further warm the rooms. The walls of some baths were covered in *tegulae mammatae*—literally, "nipple tiles"—whose namesake projections created gaps through which hot air could flow. From the first century onward, these were replaced by tubuli, rows of box tiles that distributed heat more evenly. Some wall flues were left open at roof level, creating a draft† that kept the furnaces burning.[5]

The radiant warmth of the floor and walls was often supplemented by solar heat.‡ Wherever possible, baths were built with their hot rooms facing south or west to maximize exposure to the sun. Glass windows became increasingly common over the course of the imperial era. The exterior wall of the caldarium in the Baths of Caracalla consisted almost entirely of windows, and the light streaming through was amplified by glass mosaic and a ceiling of reflective bronze.[6]

However balmy their rooms, baths were not especially clean. In republican Rome, water was funneled through public troughs before reaching the baths, and the water was almost always muddy after a heavy rain. Even the clearest pools were contaminated by mass bathing; Marcus Aurelius described bathwater as a repulsive blend of "oil, sweat, and filth." Although they had no germ theory, the Romans were aware that the baths could be unhealthy. In his medical encyclopedia, Celsus warned that bathing with an open wound was a cause

---

* Pliny the Elder claimed that hypocausts were invented by an entrepreneurial Equestrian named Sergius Orata to heat oyster ponds near the Bay of Naples. Eventually, Orata began installing hypocausts in villas and flipping them for a handsome profit.

† The flues sometimes failed to funnel efficiently, allowing smoke to well up through the floor. Some baths deliberately heaped smoke-producing darnel grass into their furnaces to clear the rooms at the end of the day.

‡ In a characteristic fit of moral dudgeon, Seneca sniffed that the Roman bathers insisted on walls of windows so that they could tan as they luxuriated in the pools. The great Scipio Africanus, by contrast, had been content with a windowless chamber and muddy water.

of gangrene. That such warnings were disregarded, however, is clear from another medical treatise, which advised readers to use wound plasters that wouldn't fall off in the baths. The water may have been made especially insalubrious by the well-meaning policy, attributed to Hadrian, of allowing the sick* to bathe before the general public.[7]

In an era before pool chemicals, the only way to clean a bath was to drain and refill it. We have no idea how often this was done. In all likelihood, the water was changed only when it became so cloudy that it repelled bathers.† Conditions may have been at least slightly more salubrious in larger baths, where the pools were often fed by a continuous flow of aqueduct water and the outflow was used to flush public latrines. The wastewater from the Baths of Caracalla was so copious that it powered a subterranean grain mill—another instance of the technological ingenuity that made the Roman baths possible.[8]

---

* A late antique bishop of Scythopolis opened a bath reserved for lepers.

† The work of cleaning baths—and especially their hypocaust systems—was so unpleasant that it was reserved for condemned criminals. The rooms around the pools were equally unsanitary; cockroaches seem to have been a chronic problem.

· 9 ·

How Were Greek Temples Built?

$\mathcal{A}$ Greek temple was nothing more or less than the dwelling place of a god. It sheltered the god's statue.* It protected votives and offerings given to the god. And it provided a spectacular backdrop for the sacrifices, hymns, and communal meals that made up the public part of ancient Greek religion.

The first Greek temples were simple mud-brick structures with thatched roofs. Only in the seventh century BCE, probably inspired by contact with Egypt, did the Greeks begin to build in stone. Almost immediately, temples assumed the form they would have for the next thousand years. Their most distinctive feature was a peristyle—a colonnaded portico surrounding the cella, the chamber that housed the god.†

Two sets of architectural conventions developed. The Doric order, used on the Greek mainland and in the colonies of Sicily and Italy, was less ornamental, with thick columns and plain capitals. Ionic, native to the Aegean islands and Asia Minor, was a sprightlier

---

* The cult statue, the physical embodiment of the god, might be a timeworn wooden figurine or unshaped stone. Usually, however, it was a magnificent colossal sculpture, sometimes fashioned—like the Athena in the Parthenon and the Zeus at Olympia—of gold and ivory.

† From the beginning, the new model temples had gabled roofs with terra-cotta tiles. The invention of these tiles represented a definitive step in the transition from mud-brick, determining the rectangular shape of the buildings, the low pitch of their roofs, and perhaps even the use of stone columns.

The so-called Temple of Concordia in Agrigento, Sicily. This Doric temple owes its excellent preservation to the fact that it became a church in late antiquity. *Author's photo*

style, characterized by graceful scroll capitals.* The elaborate Corinthian order rose to prominence only under the Romans.

Greek temples were almost always built by the corporate community of a polis. The process of construction was supervised by one or more civic committees. An architect was chosen at the outset. Contracts were then let out to master builders and artisans, who would be assisted by both free and slave laborers.

The pace of construction was set by several factors. Especially in the Archaic period, the most ambitious projects tended to be undertaken by tyrants, eager to legitimize their rule and willing to mobilize every available resource. As long as he remained in power, a tyrant could build more quickly than any democracy or oligarchy. If

---

* Geology influenced the distribution of the orders. Most of the Greek mainland and Magna Graecia were underpinned by friable limestone, which was well suited to Doric's massive proportions. Many of the cities that built Ionic temples, by contrast, had access to marble, dense and durable enough to be carved into thinner and more elaborate architectural elements.

he was dethroned, however, the regime that replaced him was seldom motivated to complete his vanity projects.

A related variable was the size of the temple. As column drums and architrave blocks grew, so did the complexity of construction. Even with all the resources of the Athenian Empire, cutting, shaping, and lifting the fifty thousand cubic feet of marble used in the Parthenon—a large but not colossal temple—took nine years.

Technology was a final contributing factor. Cranes, compound pulleys supported by wooden frames, appeared around the end of the sixth century BCE. Because the loads they could carry were limited, their use reduced the average size of blocks and drums. They accelerated the work, however, by allowing relatively small teams of professional builders to lift stones into place.

In all periods, and whatever the scale of the project, construction began with choosing a site. Temples were most often built in a prominent place near the center of a city. Sometimes the location had sacred significance; the Erechtheion at Athens was built over a fissure supposedly made by Poseidon's trident. Temples were frequently designed to face east, so that morning sunlight could pour through the doors during sacrifices.

Because overland transport was difficult and expensive, stone was sourced as close as possible to the construction site. Blocks were carved out with iron picks and detached from their beds with metal or wooden wedges. Though not finished in the quarry, they were shaped to reduce their weight. Quarrying usually took place in the summer months, when the roads were hardest and oxen for the stone carts* could be hired from local farmers.[1]

The colonnade was usually built first. Greek columns were typically made up of drums, pinned together with dowel rods. In the earliest stone temples, column drums were hauled up dirt ramps.†

---

* Heavy carts, capable of hauling multiple two- or three-ton blocks, were the standard means of transporting stone. If blocks were too heavy for wheeled transport, sledges or rollers were used. An Ephesian architect devised wooden frames that allowed twenty-five-ton blocks to be pulled along like colossal rollers.

† During the construction of the Archaic Temple of Artemis at Ephesus, ramps filled the temple to the tops of the columns. The architrave blocks were positioned on sandbags and eased onto the capitals by releasing the sand.

After cranes came into use, blocks were lifted with ropes looped around projecting bosses or carved channels. A simple derrick sufficed for small stones. The largest blocks required two massive hoists working in unison.[2]

Greek masons never used mortar. Initially, stones were held in place by their own weight. Later, they were bonded with dowels and clamps—usually bronze or iron, sometimes cypress wood—sealed in place with lead. Greece has few large trees, so obtaining beams to support a temple's roof was often a problem. Timber for the trusses of the Temple of Asclepius at Epidaurus, for example, had to be imported all the way from Crete. Partly because wood was in such short supply, the largest temples were often left partially uncovered, the cella open to the sky.[3]

Once all the blocks and columns were in place, the wall faces were smoothened and the columns fluted with fine-toothed chisels. Marble was polished; limestone was coated with stucco.* The rooflines of Ionic temples often featured a continuous band of reliefs. Doric temples were ornamented with the relief panels known as metopes, and they sometimes sprouted free-standing statues in their pediments. All this sculpture, like everything else above the tops of the columns, was splashed with color. Red, blue, and black seem to have been especially prevalent.

Funding often ran out before a temple was completed. At a time when a family could live comfortably for a year on 200 drachmas, fluting a single column in the Temple of Apollo at Didyma cost around 4,500. Building even a small temple required twenty or thirty talents,† roughly the scale of the largest private fortunes in classical Athens. The Parthenon probably cost around five hundred talents—nearly as much as the annual income of the Athenian

---

* Temples were sometimes given optical refinements, apparently to make them look more symmetrical from a distance. Columns were carved to swell slightly in the middle and tilted inward toward the cella. Corner columns were thickened, and whole facades were given a convex curve. The refinements were most subtle and most effective in the case of the Parthenon. They became increasingly rare after the classical period.

† An Attic talent of silver (around fifty-seven pounds) was equivalent to six thousand drachmas.

Empire—and the statue of Athena inside was worth more than the entire building.*

Athens paid for the Parthenon with the contributions of her subject allies. Most Greek cities, however, were forced to rely on their own resources. Public money might be supplemented by subscriptions or with donations from wealthy citizens. During the Hellenistic era, kings sometimes intervened; Alexander the Great provided funds to finish the Temple of Athena at Priene. Even with such assistance, construction tended to proceed in fits and starts. But when it was done—if it was done—a temple was a work of art, fit for the immortal gods.

---

* The chryselephantine statue of Athena Parthenos, sculpted by Phidias, probably cost about seven hundred talents. Much of the expense came from the heavy gold plates—removable in a time of crisis—attached to the statue's sides. Early in the third century BCE, the tyrant Lachares melted the gold plates to pay his troops. A few of the coins minted from the metal are still extant.

· *10* ·

How Was the Pantheon Built?

𝒯he Pantheon, the best-preserved monument of imperial Rome, was built in the marshy plain known as the Campus Martius. In the last years of the Republic, Pompey built a large theater there.* A generation later, Augustus and his alter ego Agrippa constructed a series of spectacular public buildings on the Campus. Among these was the Pantheon, a temple that honored all the gods alongside the imperial family.

The Augustan Pantheon, destroyed by fire, was replaced by the current structure during the reigns of Trajan and Hadrian. The Pantheon we see today consists of a rotunda—a huge domed room—fronted by a colonnaded porch, with a transitional block between. The symmetry of the rotunda, whose interior diameter and interior height are both exactly 150 Roman feet, has impressed architects since the Renaissance. But the impression made by that space, where the golden seal of the oculus plays over walls and floor beneath the spiraling coffers of the dome, is beyond purely mathematical analysis.

---

* After the end of antiquity, most of Rome's remaining inhabitants moved to the Campus Martius, conveniently close both to the Vatican and to the fountains of the last reliable aqueduct. The vaults beneath the seats of Pompey's theater were colonized; then, as the ground level rose, houses were built over the seats themselves. By the Renaissance, the theater was completely covered. Its outline, however, survives, mirrored in the buildings constructed on top of it. A few of the spaces beneath the seating vaults have been converted into restaurants.

The rotunda of the Pantheon, illuminated by the oculus. *Author's photo*

Understanding how the Pantheon was constructed begins with the building material that made it possible. Rome stands on thick deposits of tuff, a soft igneous rock laid down by prehistoric eruptions.* Although Roman tuff is easily carved (as the excavators of the catacombs discovered), it is too soft and porous to serve as a good building stone. It carries, however, the seeds of an antidote. The tuff deposits around Rome contain pockets of the reddish, gravelly volcanic sand known as pozzolana. By trial and error, Roman masons discovered that pozzolana made exceptionally strong mortar when

---

* The last eruptions in the Alban Hills may have taken place as recently as the Bronze Age. The tuff beneath Rome (traditionally and incorrectly referred to as tufa) was laid down by the same kinds of pyroclastic flows that buried Herculaneum. Other terroirs of tuff made better building stone. The variety known as peperino, believed to be heat resistant, was used in the huge wall that protected the Forum of Augustus from Rome's frequent fires. The most prestigious building stone in central Italy, however, was travertine from Tivoli, employed to clad both the Colosseum and St. Peter's Basilica. Marble began to be imported from Greece during the second century BCE. The quarries at Luna (later famous as Carrara) were opened in the age of Augustus.

combined with water and lime.* They began to experiment with a new way of building walls, combining pozzolana mortar with chunks of rubble—and so Roman concrete was born.

Over the following centuries, Roman concrete developed into an increasingly sophisticated building material. Unlike modern concrete, which is typically poured into forms, Roman concrete was troweled in thin layers over beds of aggregate. The aggregate could be varied to modify the strength and weight of the mixture. Foundations were stiffened with chips of heavy basalt; vaults and domes were lightened with bits of ceramic, tuff, or pumice.† Because Roman concrete was not reinforced, it tended to crack and fail under tension. But its compressive strength—its capacity to carry loads—is equal to that of good modern concrete made with Portland Cement. And thanks to its distinctive chemistry, Roman concrete is far more durable than its modern counterpart. The maritime variety compares favorably with even the most resilient building stones.

By the reign of Trajan, when the new Pantheon was begun, Roman builders were using concrete in everything from foundations to domes. Besides limitless supplies of pozzolana, lime, and graded aggregates, they had access to bricks of standard sizes, churned out on a semi-industrial scale in Rome's suburbs. They could also rely on precut columns and shaped blocks of exotic marble shipped to Rome from quarries owned by the emperors.

Apollodorus of Damascus, the designer of Trajan's Forum, may have been responsible for the Pantheon.‡ Whoever he was, the

---

* The Romans recognized two types of pozzolana: *harena fossicia* ("pit sand" from the vicinity of Rome) and *pulvis puteolanus* ("powder" from the Bay of Naples). These were geologically similar and produced comparable concrete. It was eventually discovered that concrete could also be made by using crushed terra-cotta in place of pozzolana; the dome of Hagia Sophia consists of bricks suspended in a matrix of terra-cotta-infused mortar. Those who could, however, used pozzolana. Herod the Great imported vast quantities from the Bay of Naples to construct the harbor of Caesarea Maritima.

† The concrete walls of the Palace of Domitian used fragments of exotic marble, damaged by fire, as an aggregate. During the Renaissance, ancient marble statues were sometimes burned for lime and combined with pozzolana to make an especially fine stucco.

‡ Originally a military engineer—he wrote a treatise on siege engines and was responsible for the first permanent bridge over the Danube—Apollodorus seems to have designed all of Trajan's major building projects. He was less friendly with Hadrian, who reportedly had him executed for unwisely candid comments about the emperor's own architectural pretensions.

architect must have worked with one of Rome's leading contractors. Contractors had a core staff of master craftsmen, often slaves or freedmen, who directed a shifting cast of free day laborers and seasonal workers over the course of a project. At any given time, there were perhaps two or three hundred men at work on the Pantheon—a considerable number, but a far cry from the thousands involved in building the Colosseum or the Baths of Caracalla. With the usual breaks for winter weather and allowing time for all that concrete to cure, the Pantheon could have been finished in six or seven years.[1]

The Pantheon's foundations were made of concrete. Beneath the rotunda, they formed a ring about twenty-four feet wide and more than twenty feet deep (no sounding has ever reached the footings). On this mighty base, the walls of the rotunda rose, faced with brick. Most of the bricks used in the Pantheon were *bipedales* or *sesquipedales*—that is, two feet or one and a half feet square. These were often cut in half to make triangles, keyed into the concrete behind. The concrete fill was set down in the usual way, layer by layer over fist-sized chunks of travertine. At intervals of around four feet, bonding courses of *bipedales* were laid across the wall.

The walls of the rotunda were twenty feet thick, but only a few sections were solid all the way through. A series of eight deep recesses—the entrance and seven niches, alternately rectangular and semicircular—indented the interior at floor level, and chambers punctuated the fill above. These had the practical purpose of admitting air into the mass of concrete and dissipating some of the heat produced by the curing process. Relieving arches—the parabolas of brick visible on the rotunda's exterior—helped to direct the gargantuan weight of the rotunda toward the masonry "piers" between the recesses. And because the arches, made almost entirely of brick, set more quickly than the concrete fill in which they were embedded, they stiffened the structure as it rose.

Despite these innovations, the Pantheon's rotunda settled during construction. The effects are visible in the floor, which is almost two feet lower around the edges than it is at the center. As the concrete set, huge cracks appeared in the walls, some several inches wide. It was likely in response to these that a buttress was built from the

The brick relieving arches built into the walls of the Pantheon. *Author's photo*

neighboring Basilica of Neptune to brace the structure before the builders started the dome.

As far as we know, the Romans had never attempted to build a dome remotely approaching the Pantheon's in scale. They understood, however, that the dome of the Pantheon was subject to both downward and horizontal thrust—that, in other words, it would tend to fall in and push out. The architect of the Pantheon managed horizontal thrust (prevented the dome from spreading) by making the walls of the rotunda extremely thick and embedding the lower third of the dome in their mass. Rings of concrete were laid on top of the dome to further counteract hoop stress. Downward thrust was minimized by tapering the dome's thickness as it rose. The concrete was mixed with progressively lighter aggregates, with only volcanic scoria—porous and light enough to float on water—used around the oculus.* The oculus itself strengthened the dome, both by obviating

---

* The best scoria came from the vicinity of Vesuvius. It became difficult to acquire after the eruption of 79, which buried many of the deposits.

the need for a structurally dangerous crown and through its masonry rim, which functioned like the keystone of an arch.

Some scholars believe that at least the lower reaches of the dome could have been built with relatively light centering. It seems more likely, however, that a dense forest of scaffolding, which must have filled most of the interior, was needed to support the dome as it rose. We should probably imagine a wooden structure with trusses like those used in Roman bridges and roofs.*

Once the rotunda was completed, it was time to construct the porch. This was a traditional colonnaded structure, of a type that the Greeks and Romans had been building for centuries. It was octastyle—had eight columns across the front—with another eight columns behind. As in most Roman temples, the capitals were Corinthian. Unlike the Greeks, the Romans preferred monolithic columns. The Pantheon's are made of Egyptian granite, shipped down the Nile from the quarries of Aswan and Mons Claudianus. Though impressive enough from the ground, these columns—forty Roman feet tall—seem too short for the building. This fact, along with the existence of a secondary cornice line above the portico roof, has led some scholars to speculate that the Pantheon was designed for columns fifty Roman feet tall, which were either lost in transit or diverted to another building project.†

Once cranes had raised the columns and the pediment blocks, the process of decoration began. The portico was roofed with trusses of cast bronze, from which a vaulted bronze ceiling was suspended. Gilded tiles were laid over the dome.‡ A bronze eagle,

---

* The roof of Old St. Peter's was supported by its original Roman trusses until the demolition of the church. The main beams were three feet thick, nearly eighty feet long, and honeycombed (we are told) with the nests of thousands of rats. The porch of the Pantheon featured intricate bronze trusses that were, infamously, melted down by Pope Urban VIII; the recovered metal weighed about 152 metric tons. The pope presented seven rivets from the dismembered trusses to distinguished guests. One—now in Berlin—still survives.

† At the same time that he was finishing the Pantheon, Hadrian was also working on the Temple of the Deified Trajan. As a monument to his adoptive father, the Temple of Trajan was far more politically significant than the Pantheon. The fifty-foot columns intended for the Pantheon may have been diverted to that project. Another candidate is Hadrian's colossal Temple of Venus and Rome.

‡ Both the gilded roof tiles and the bronze ceiling of the portico were melted down by the cash-strapped Byzantine emperor Constans II.

carrying a wreath, seems to have been emblazoned on the pediment. The exterior of the rotunda was covered with white marble and stucco, and the interior was encrusted with a dazzling array of exotic stones, their rich colors and variety proclaiming the wealth and vastness of the empire.

Colossal statues of Augustus and Agrippa were probably displayed in the niches on either side of the entrance. Statues of gods and emperors must have stood in the alcoves and aediculae of the interior. The inner face of the dome was patterned with twenty-eight vertical rows of coffers—an Archimedean perfect number. The coffers' brick faces were coated in plaster and decorated with rosettes, stars for the artificial heaven of the dome.

Over the past nineteen centuries, the Pantheon has been despoiled, neglected, redecorated, and occasionally even repaired. But alone among the great buildings of the imperial capital, it remains substantially intact, the most compelling extant witness to the building technology of ancient Rome.

· *11* ·

How Much Weight Could a Roman Bridge Carry?

$\mathcal{T}$he first Roman bridge, the Pons Sublicius, was made entirely of wood.* In later centuries, there would be wooden bridges throughout the provinces, especially in northwestern Europe.† Most Roman bridges, however, were stone.[1]

The techniques used to construct a stone bridge were broadly standardized. If it had more than a single span, the first task was laying the foundations of its piers. Around the Mediterranean, where rivers are often dry in the hot months, builders waited for summer. Otherwise, cofferdams were necessary. A double row of logs or planks was driven around the site of each pier and made watertight with compacted clay. After the space within had been drained with screw pumps or water wheels, the exposed riverbed was cleared down to bedrock or hard clay. Where these were too deep to reach, the ground was stiffened with pilings.[2]

The piers of a Roman bridge usually consisted of huge stone blocks clamped together with iron. The thicker the pier, the greater its stability. To avoid restricting the river, however, Roman builders tended to make piers only around a third the width of the arches they

---

* No metal was used in its construction. The taboo may have stemmed from the fact that the bridge was built before nails were used widely in Rome. (A prohibition of similar origins excluded iron tools from the grove of Dea Dia.) Alternatively, nails may have been banned to make the bridge easier to disassemble for defensive purposes. The famous story of Horatius, who single-handedly held back an Etruscan army as the bridge was demolished behind him, lends credence to this theory.

† The original London Bridge was made of wood. The beams of a Roman bridge that crossed the Rhone at Geneva were so solid that they lasted until the sixteenth century.

supported. The arches were usually semicircular, which often had the effect of raising the bridge deck high above the roads at either end. A few builders experimented with flatter segmental arches. Whatever their arc, the arches were made of heavy blocks laid over a falsework frame. From the first century onward, stone was supplemented and sometimes replaced by brick-faced concrete.

The most spectacular Roman bridges date to the early imperial era. During the reign of Augustus, the Via Flaminia was carried over the river Nera on four soaring arches. The largest, rising more than 100 feet above the water, was 105 feet wide. The Pont Saint-Martin, still perfectly preserved, has a single span of 120 feet. The Roman bridge at Mérida, Spain, has no fewer than sixty-two arches and extends a half-mile over the floodplain of a meandering river. Even this structure was dwarfed by Trajan's bridge over the Danube, whose twenty towering piers supported a deck 3,700 feet long.*

Ancient pedestrians and vehicles were comparatively light; by far the heaviest load a Roman bridge carried was its own weight. Lacking any scientific method of modeling stresses, the Romans made most of their bridges far stronger than they needed to be.† A remarkable number of Roman bridges carry modern traffic. As of 2019, the famous bridge at Alcántara, Spain, built during the reign of Trajan, was crossed by a quarter-million vehicles every year. It shows no signs of failing. Nor does the Pont des Marchands in Narbonne, which has supported a neighborhood of multistory shops and houses since the Middle Ages.

The blocks that made up the arches of a Roman bridge—the voussoirs—were locked together in compression, transferring the force of their own weight and the loads placed on them to the abutments on either side. The load-bearing capacity of a bridge thus depended both on the solidity of its abutments and on the strength (shearing point) of its voussoirs.

---

* The most remote Roman bridge was the Band-e Kaisar, in what is now southwestern Iran. Built for the Sassanids by Roman prisoners of war, it was also a dam designed to irrigate the surrounding region. It remained in use through the nineteenth century.

† Roman bridges typically collapsed only when their piers were undermined by floods. This was the fate of Augustus's bridge over the Nera and the Pons Aemilius ("Ponte Rotto") over the Tiber.

The Roman bridge at Mérida. *Author's photo*

The six arches of the bridge at Alcántara, for example, are made of tough local granite laid without mortar. Besides pockets of gravel packed between the arches and the roadway, the rest of the bridge consists of the same material. The structure, braced against the high banks on either side, is impressively solid. By one estimate, its largest span is still capable of supporting fifty-seven US tons. The Alcántara bridge, in other words, could handle even the heaviest trucks on American highways, which have a maximum weight of forty tons.*

There were few complexities in the design of Roman bridges. They were supported by the pressure of stone on stone and anchored in place by their own weight. But despite this simplicity, and despite the corrosive action of frost and floods, many still carry the roads that led to Rome.

---

* It would probably buckle under a freight train. On American railroads, a single loaded car can weigh more than 140 tons, and a locomotive might be almost twice as heavy. The basic methods used by Roman engineers, however, were replicated in hundreds of nineteenth- and early twentieth-century railroad bridges. One of the most impressive is the Rockville Bridge, which crosses the Susquehanna River near Harrisburg, Pennsylvania. At 3,820 feet, it's almost exactly the length of Trajan's bridge over the Danube. Each of its forty-eight spans is made of stone shaped by skilled masons who had—in many cases— immigrated from Italy.

· *12* ·

What Did Roman Military Engineers Design?

The architecti of the Roman army were the ancient world's only professional engineers. Exempt from the normal duties of soldiers, they were trained to design a dazzling array of structures and machines. On campaign, they supervised the construction of everything from catapults to siege works. In times of peace, they were responsible for frontier defenses, highways, aqueducts, and much more, all while serving as consultants for civilian projects in nearby cities.

Perhaps the most familiar product of Roman military engineering is the marching camp—the temporary fortification that campaigning armies built every night to protect their tents and supplies. Marching camps were laid out by surveyors traveling ahead of the troops. When they found a level and defensible site, they marked out a rectangular grid of streets and designated places for the general headquarters, stables, kitchens, tents, and latrines. As the soldiers arrived, they began to construct the defenses. Using the pickaxes that were part of their standard kit, they dug a trench around the camp, normally around five feet wide and three deep. Along the inner face of the ditch, a turf rampart six feet high was erected, topped by a palisade of sharpened stakes.* The whole process, from surveying to completion, took only two or three hours.[1]

---

* An inscription found at a legionary base in what is now Algeria records how, during a visit from Hadrian, the soldiers rapidly constructed a marching camp. This seems to have been a routine exercise. Archaeologists have discovered similar "practice" camps at several places along the northern frontier.

Between camps, the engineers were responsible for overcoming every obstacle in an advancing army's path. They became especially proficient at building bridges. On the banks of a large river, the flatboats carried in the baggage train of every legion were launched, anchored in a row, and connected with planks to form a pontoon bridge. On one occasion, when no boats or planks were handy, some enterprising engineers fashioned a bridge from wine barrels. The longest pontoon bridge on record—built on a whim by Caligula— extended three miles from Baiae to Puteoli.[2]

If the current was exceptionally strong, a more substantial structure was needed. In 55 BCE, Julius Caesar ordered his army to bridge the Rhine near modern Koblenz, where the river is roughly a quarter-mile wide and up to twenty-five feet deep. The engineers drove pairs of pilings, angled to deflect the force of the water, into the riverbed. Crossed braces were fastened between the pilings, form- ing trusses—buttressed against the current by an additional row of inclined timbers—that were then connected with beams to form a roadway. The entire bridge, from the felling of the first tree to the laying of the last beam, was completed in ten days.[3]

Although Roman military engineers made few advances on the siege techniques of the Hellenistic era, they excelled at apply- ing those techniques on a grand scale. At Alesia, Caesar's engineers famously built two lines of siege works, one encircling the Gallic fort, the other protecting the Roman camps. With their towers, trenches, moats, and ramparts, these lines totaled some twenty-five miles in length. More than a century later, legionary engineers constructed a siege ramp nearly two thousand feet long and two hundred feet high to reach the mountaintop stronghold of Masada.[4]

Military engineers also designed the permanent forts that housed the troops, which ranged from tiny emplacements with room for a dozen men to mighty legionary bases sized for six thousand. The largest forts were self-contained cities, provided with every- thing from hospitals to baths and protected by up to three rings of walls and ditches.

Through the late first century, Roman forts were built of turf and wood. Legionary bases required whole forests of mature timber:

By one estimate, around four hundred acres of woodland were cut to construct the fortress at Caerleon. Nearly a million nails, buried to prevent local tribes from using their iron, were discovered in the half-finished legionary fort at Inchtuthil. From the second century onward, forts were ringed with massive masonry walls. More than sixty thousand tons of stone were used in the second-century reconstruction of Caerleon's enceinte.

Roman military engineers were also responsible for the vast network of highways that connected Italy with the far-flung frontiers. Despite their benefits for trade, Roman roads were designed, first and foremost, to enable the rapid transit of troops in all seasons and all terrains. Amid the marshes of the Rhine Delta, the swamp mud was mounded into causeways, stiffened with tens of thousands of pilings. Through the Iron Gates of the Danube, a highway was built along sheer cliffs, alternately cut into and cantilevered from the rock face. Other roads were slashed through desert sands or chiseled from mountain ice.

More extensive even than the road network was the chain of forts, watchtowers, and walls that protected the empire's northern frontiers. The system evolved gradually, achieving its mature form over the course of the second century. Although most segments—like the Limes along the Upper Rhine—consisted of a trench and wooden palisade punctuated by watchtowers, some were nearly as impressive as the Great Wall of China.

The most monumental section was Hadrian's Wall, which ran seventy-three miles along Britain's northern frontier. Around fifteen feet tall and as much as ten feet thick, it was studded with turrets and milecastles, guarded by a string of forts, and supported by a massive system of trenches and roads. The whole complex was built by detachments from the three legions stationed in Britain, with short sections assigned to individual centuries.* Later in

---

* Hadrian's successor, Antoninus Pius, moved the British frontier one hundred miles north. The turf-and-timber barrier that defended this frontier—the Antonine Wall—is less famous than its southern cousin, largely because its remains are poorly preserved. The timber palisades that defended the German Limes, likewise, have rotted away, leaving only the impression of the ditch along their outer face.

A section of Hadrian's Wall near Once Brewed, with the remains of Milecastle 39 in the foreground. *Author's photo*

Roman history, military engineers designed border forts as spectacular as any medieval castle. On the Syrian frontier, for example, Justinian built the great fortress of Zenobia, large enough to contain an entire planned town—with a forum, bath complex, and two churches—and protected by a circuit of walls so massive that they remain almost intact today.*

Ambitious governors sometimes ordered the engineers in legions under their command to construct massive public works. During the reign of Claudius, the governor of Lower Germania built a twenty-three-mile canal connecting the mouths of the Rhine and Meuse Rivers. A few decades later, under Vespasian, soldiers from three legions and twenty auxiliary units were involved in the construction of a three-mile canal (complete with bridges) near Antioch. Vespasian's engineers were also responsible for the spectacular

---

* Several of Britain's late Roman "Saxon Shore" forts were solid enough to be reactivated during the Middle Ages. One, at Portchester, served as a prison during the Napoleonic Wars. The castle at Pevensey was garrisoned during World War II.

tunnels that diverted flash floods around Antioch's harbor at Seleucia Pieria. The Car Dyke in England—a Roman canal nearly sixty miles long—is thought to have been dug with legionary labor, apparently for the dual purpose of draining marshland and supplying the local troops with grain.[5]

Thanks to their wide-ranging expertise, military engineers were often requested as technical advisors for civilian building projects. Pliny the Younger, a provincial governor during the reign of Trajan, was sent a legionary surveyor to determine the feasibility of a planned canal. On another occasion, he requested the services of a military engineer to help salvage a collapsing aqueduct. Experienced engineers were moved from legion to legion as their skills were required and often were called back to service after the end of their enlistment.[6]

One such man was Nonius Datus, a legionary engineer based in what is now Algeria. Around the middle of the second century, his assistance was requested by the city of Saldae, which was planning a new aqueduct. The most difficult part of the project would be a quarter-mile tunnel through a mountain. Datus traveled to Saldae, surveyed the aqueduct's course, and marked the place where the tunnel would be dug. Then, having instructed the local authorities to set teams of men working from both ends, he returned to his camp.[7]

Years later, Datus received a desperate letter. The aqueduct was still unfinished, and excavation of the tunnel had stalled after the workmen became disoriented and began digging in opposite directions. An engineer was needed again—and so Datus, now a reservist, returned to Saldae. Along the way, he was waylaid by thieves, who beat him and stole his equipment. Undeterred, he proceeded to the jobsite, where he again surveyed the line of the tunnel, reorganized the work teams, and ensured that the aqueduct would be completed on schedule. When the aqueduct was finally done, Datus set up a monument in the legionary base at Lambaesis. The inscription detailed his work on the project and reproduced letters of praise from local authorities. Above the text were personifications of Hope, Efficiency, and Perseverance. A Roman military engineer needed all three.

• 13 •

Did the Colosseum Cost More than St. Peter's Basilica?

*T*he Colosseum and St. Peter's Basilica are the two attractions that every tourist visits in Rome. Each encapsulates, in its way, the grandeur of the Eternal City. On first approaching the bleached bones of the Colosseum or being enveloped by the marble immensity of St. Peter's, the universal reaction is awe. But sooner or later, as wonder subsides to manageable levels, the thought arises: How much did all this cost?

Let's start with St. Peter's. By almost every measure, St. Peter's Basilica is the biggest church ever built. It contains 778 columns, 395 statues, and 44 altars. Before electric lighting, 4,400 lanterns were needed to illuminate the exterior. The interior has standing room for 60,000 worshippers. It took 120 years to build. Although the pace of construction varied, as many as 2,500 laborers were involved in some periods; Pope Sixtus V kept relays of 800 men working 24 hours a day to finish the dome.

From the start, and despite such cost-cutting measures as limiting the use of travertine and scavenging marble columns from ancient ruins, the project was extremely expensive.* The costs were counted in the gold coins known as ducats and scudi. Ducats, modeled on the Florentine florin, contained 3.5 grams of gold. Scudi,

---

* Famously, the Protestant Reformation was sparked by a papal scheme to finance construction by selling indulgences. Martin Luther objected to such things (and had little good to say about Rome in general).

which replaced ducats in the Papal States in 1531, were slightly smaller and contained less pure gold.*

Although the records are incomplete, some of the expenses associated with the building of St. Peter's are known. In the first year of construction—1506—the project cost 13,500 scudi. The bill was 30,000 scudi in 1507 and around 15,000 each year from 1508 to 1510. For moving the 330-ton Vatican obelisk to its current position in St. Peter's Square—a delicate operation that involved 900 men, 75 horses, and 44 colossal winches—Domenico Fontana was awarded 70,000 scudi. The dome of St. Peter's—whose scaffolding required 500,000 pounds of rope—cost 200,000 scudi from base to crown. The Baldacchino over the high altar also cost about 200,000 scudi. Building the colonnade around St. Peter's square required 850,000 scudi. Paving the piazza took an additional 88,000.

In 1694, at the pope's request, architect Carlo Fontana esti-mated the total costs of building St. Peter's Basilica. The project, he calculated, had used slightly more than 111 million cubic Roman palms of stone.† After deciding, for reasons never explained, that the average cost to move, shape, and place a cubic palm of stone was 32.5 baiocchi (that is, around a third of a scudo), and after compiling the additional costs of the marble columns and decorative finishes, Fon-tana concluded that St. Peter's Basilica had cost 46,800,498 scudi.

Leaving aside the accuracy of this estimate, let's try to put it in context. In the mid-sixteenth century, one scudo could buy 28 chickens, 110 pounds of flour, or a month's rent in a cheap Roman apartment. During the same period, a master builder earned roughly 5 scudi a month, and the architect of St. Peter's was paid 50 scudi a month. The great composer Palestrina received 8 scudi a month as choirmaster of St. Peter's, which was about as much as a junior pro-fessor at the University of Rome.

Caravaggio was paid between 150 and 400 scudi for most of his paintings. A century earlier, Raphael received 1,200 scudi for each of the frescoes in the Vatican Stanze, and Michelangelo earned the equivalent of roughly 3,300 scudi for painting the ceiling of the

---

* For the sake of consistency, I've given all the costs associated with St. Peter's in scudi. Costs associated with the Colosseum are in sestertii.

† A Roman palm is equivalent to 0.73 feet (0.22 meters).

Sistine Chapel. When he died in 1564, Michelangelo's life savings were found to consist of 8,400 scudi. The famous poetess and courtesan Tullia d'Aragona, by contrast, died with little more than her prized pearl necklace, which was auctioned off for 40 scudi.

In 1536, King Henry VIII reportedly promised 50,000 scudi to any assassin who managed to kill Cardinal Reginald Pole (five men tried; none succeeded). At that time, 50,000 scudi was equivalent to the annual income of Rome's wealthiest merchants and cardinals. The annual income of the Papal States was roughly 2.5 million scudi.

To judge from these numbers, the construction of St. Peter's cost roughly as much as 19 years of the Papal States' annual income, 936 high-profile assassinations, 15,600 Sistine Chapel ceilings, or 3.9 million years of rent in a cheap Roman apartment.

I'll convert the cost of St. Peter's into modern dollars later. First, however, let's compare the Colosseum. Because no literary source or inscription provides any figures, we have to approximate the labor and material costs. Using an approach pioneered by architectural historian Janet DeLaine, I made the following estimates[1]:

Task	Cost in Sestertii
Excavating foundations	500,000*
Laying foundations	10,000,000†
Perimeter wall	50,000,000‡

---

* I used a nineteenth-century construction manual to estimate the labor required to clear the Colosseum's foundation trench with hand tools. If I did the math correctly, something like 70,000 man-days of labor would have been required to excavate and haul away 170,000 cubic meters of rocky soil—but this does not account for the fact that the workmen had to cut into bedrock on the north side of the foundation trench and contended throughout with a high water table. So let's say, conservatively, that 125,000 man-days of labor were required. I'll assume that the workmen earned an average of 4 sestertii a day, the going rate for a laborer in first-century Rome.

† By my best estimate, the foundations of the Colosseum required around 250,000 cubic meters of concrete. DeLaine suggests that a cubic meter of concrete cost the equivalent of ten days' wages for a laborer to install.

‡ The Colosseum consumed around 100,000 cubic meters of travertine—roughly one-fiftieth, incidentally, of all the travertine ever quarried by the Romans. The stone, cut into blocks with an average weight of four tons, was lifted into place by treadwheel cranes. Travertine is a hard and heavy stone, difficult to work and transport. It was correspondingly expensive. Each cubic meter, by DeLaine's estimate, cost the equivalent of one hundred days' wages for a laborer. The basic cost would have been amplified by the fact that each block had to be lifted by muscle power. Iron was also much more expensive than it is now.

Task	Cost in Sestertii
Substructures and vaults	20,000,000*
Seats	3,000,000[†]
Decoration	2,500,000[‡]

Adding up these figures brings us to 86 million sestertii. This number, I suspect, is too low because it fails to account for the many challenges of construction on a grand scale. So I think it's reasonable to assume that the Colosseum cost something on the order of 100 million sestertii.

At the time the Colosseum was built, one sestertius could buy four cups of wine. A tunic cost around fifteen sestertii, and the annual rent for a decent apartment was probably around five hundred sestertii (except in central Rome, where it was three or four times that amount). Relatively speaking, in short, the Colosseum cost a lot.[§] Translating its cost into modern dollars, however, is difficult.

Attempts to convert premodern currencies usually take one of two approaches. One method compares ancient and modern currencies by bullion value—that is, in terms of their gold or silver content. When the Colosseum was built, the highest-value Roman coin, the

---

* Although the key structural elements of the Colosseum were travertine, the vaults and substructures under the seats used roughly 100,000 cubic meters of tuff and concrete. Tuff—a soft volcanic stone—was considerably less expensive than travertine. Concrete was cheaper still. The relative economy of the materials, however, was offset by the complexity of constructing so many vaults, ramps, and passageways.

† Except for the uppermost tier, which had wooden benches, the seats of the Colosseum were made of Carrara marble. Although this was one of the least expensive varieties of marble, it still cost far more than travertine, perhaps the equivalent of 150 man-days per cubic meter. I've never seen any estimate for the amount of marble used in the Colosseum. The lowest tier of seats, the Senatorial Podium, was built entirely of marble; the seats above had brick substructures faced with marble slabs. On that basis, I assume that around five thousand cubic meters of marble were used throughout the building.

‡ The corridors of the Colosseum were plastered, painted, and equipped with lead pipes for water fountains. More than 150 life-size statues stood in the arches of the upper stories, and bronze quadrigas crowned the main entrances. The statues alone, to judge from attested prices, would have collectively cost well over a million sestertii.

§ But if my estimate is anything like correct, the Colosseum was far from the most expensive building project in Rome. Simply finishing Nero's Golden House cost 50 million sestertii; the total cost was many times that. Domitian reportedly spent nearly 300 million sestertii gilding the roof and doors of the vast Temple of Jupiter on the Capitoline Hill, and the Aqua Claudia and Aqua Anio Novus, the two greatest aqueducts of the imperial city, cost 350 million sestertii to complete. Even these were dwarfed by the Forum of Trajan, whose cost may have approached one billion sestertii.

aureus, contained 7.3 grams of gold. There were one hundred sestertii in an aureus, making a sestertius equivalent to .073 grams of gold. Multiplying that figure by the current price of gold will give you the bullion equivalent of a sestertius. This calculation made some sense in the era of the international gold standard, when the value of the dollar and other major currencies was, like the Roman currency, tethered to the value of precious metal. But today the values of gold and silver fluctuate independently of each other and of the dollar. A generation ago, gold was only three hundred dollars an ounce; as I write this (in 2025), the price is more than ten times that.

An alternative approach compares the ancient and modern values of equivalent goods. A loaf of bread, for example, cost roughly half a sestertius when the Colosseum was built. Multiplying the cost of an average modern loaf by two would thus give you an equivalent to the value of the sestertius in dollars. But if we try the same equation with wheat or any other good, the ratio will be different. The average price of a modius of wheat in early imperial Italy was around eight sestertii; comparing this amount to a modern peck of grain gives a dramatically lower dollar equivalent for the sestertius. The problem is that we aren't really comparing equivalent goods. To return to the first example, the bread produced by the preindustrial, shortage-prone Roman Empire, where food consumed the greater part of most families' budgets, was fundamentally different from the cheap and abundant bread of a wealthy industrialized nation integrated into a global market.

The economies and societies of the ancient and modern worlds, in short, are so dissimilar that any attempt to convert their currencies is an exercise in futility. We can, however, use wages and purchasing power to determine *relative* values. Reasoning, in other words, that an unskilled laborer in ancient Rome was the equivalent of an unskilled laborer in modern America, we can equate 1,000 sestertii (a Roman laborer's estimated annual income) with the $35,000 that the average unskilled construction worker receives today. On that basis, an early imperial sestertius would be the effective equivalent of about $35, giving the Colosseum a cost equivalent to something like $3.5 billion.

We can apply the same method to St. Peter's Basilica. In late sixteenth-century Florence, an unskilled construction worker earned around 33 scudi a year. Wages were slightly higher in Rome, where the annual income of an unskilled laborer seems to have averaged around 40 or 50 scudi. If we take $35,000 as the equivalent of 50 scudi, we get a value of $700 for one scudo. At $700 a scudo, the construction of St. Peter's Basilica cost the equivalent of $32,760,348,600—nearly ten times my estimate for the Colosseum.

• *14* •

Could the Romans Have Built
the Egyptian Pyramids?

$\mathscr{T}$he Great Pyramid of Giza, built by the pharaoh Khufu in the twenty-sixth century BCE, consists of an estimated 2.3 million stone blocks with an average weight of more than two tons. For nearly four thousand years, until it was overtopped by the tower of a medieval cathedral, it was the tallest structure ever built by humans. The oldest of the Seven Wonders of the Ancient World, it is the only one that survives today.

Although Pliny the Elder dismissed the pyramids as megalomaniacal, every Roman who toured Egypt stopped to see them. A few were so impressed that they built pyramid tombs of their own. No Roman emperor, however, was buried in a pyramid,* for the excellent reason that it would have been seen as a hallmark of tyranny and an utter rejection of Roman principles.[1]

But let's imagine that an emperor decided to build a monument in Egypt on the model of the Great Pyramid. Let's imagine, further, that this Roman pyramid would be built not at Alexandria—the provincial capital—but near its model at Giza.

A Roman emperor would have to contend with the same basic problems that Khufu had faced two and a half millennia before. Most immediately, he would have to assemble and feed a vast workforce. The pharaohs of the Old Kingdom built their pyramids during the

---

* A different Egyptian tomb—the Soma of Alexander the Great—may have at least partly inspired the Mausoleum of Augustus in Rome, an imposing circular structure crowned by a landscaped garden.

flood season, when the fields were underwater and most agricultural workers were unemployed. An emperor would doubtless have followed suit. Many craftsmen could have been recruited from Memphis, still a substantial city in the Roman period. Laborers would also have been readily available. Farmers in Roman Egypt were obligated to spend several days each year repairing dikes, canals, and other public works.* The corvée system could have been extended to pyramid building. Construction might also have been facilitated by the guild-like associations into which the craftsmen of Roman Egypt were organized. The government often called on these organizations to produce goods for the military; their services could just as easily have been deployed in a state-sponsored construction project.

Even if the Romans had set out to imitate the Great Pyramid, they would never have created an exact replica. Khufu's pyramid reflected an essentially Egyptian (and specifically Old Kingdom) conception of divine kingship. It was designed to perpetuate the pharaoh's role as a living god and guardian of his people. Roman architects, unaware of or indifferent to this fact, almost certainly would have simplified the design. Some of the changes they likely would have made are suggested by the Pyramid of Cestius, built at Rome during the reign of Augustus. That structure is 100 Roman feet square and 125 Roman feet tall. Although the casing is white Italian marble, the bulk of the pyramid consists of Roman concrete.†
The tomb chamber is crowned by a barrel vault.

To judge from this example, a Roman replica of the Great Pyramid would likely have featured arches and vaults of brick-faced concrete in place of the huge granite slabs that supported the ceilings of chambers and passageways in Khufu's pyramid. I doubt, however, that a Roman replica of the Great Pyramid would have had a concrete core. Although it would have been easier to lay than millions of limestone blocks, Roman concrete dried slowly and deformed under great weight. Masonry was more reliable.

---

* Egypt's corvée system was not abolished until 1889.

† An even larger pyramid, the so-called Tomb of Romulus, was located near the Vatican. When it was demolished during the Renaissance, the concrete core resisted conventional tools and had to be smashed with a giant trip hammer. The ruins of yet another pyramidal tomb can still be seen along the Via Appia.

The Pyramid of Cestius. *Author's photo*

Khufu's workmen quarried limestone with wooden mallets and copper chisels, which had to be sharpened frequently.* The Romans, using iron tools, would have cut and shaped stone much more efficiently. They would also have produced more regular blocks, which would have been easier to lay than the often roughly cut backing stones of Old Kingdom pyramids. I'll assume that our Roman pyramid, like Khufu's, would have been built primarily of limestone from the immediate vicinity. The casing stones, however, would have had to be shipped down the Nile by a process unchanged since the time of the pharaohs. Blocks would have been hauled to the river on wooden sledges over tracks of compacted stone chips.† The barges

---

* Because copper chisels were too soft to cut them, the Egyptians shaped granite blocks with dolerite poundstones. With enough workmen, this arm- and mind-numbing process could be remarkably efficient: Hatshepsut managed to quarry, transport, and erect two large granite obelisks in the space of only seven months.

† During the pharaonic era, the Egyptians usually mounted large blocks and monoliths on sleds, pulled by teams of men over smooth trackways. A relief from the tomb of a Middle Kingdom official named Djehutihotep shows an approximately sixty-ton statue on a sled being hauled by 172 men. A worker balanced on the statue's toes pours water or oil onto the track, apparently to reduce friction.

that carried them would have landed as close as possible to the building site—perhaps, as in the case of the Great Pyramid, via an artificial basin that filled during the annual flood.

Greek and Roman authors speculated about how the stones of the pyramids were lifted into place.* Herodotus believed that the blocks were heaved heavenward with levers; Diodorus, that they were hauled up over mounds of earth. Pliny the Elder speculated that the pyramids were surrounded with ramps of natural salt, which dissolved when touched by floodwater. A Roman emperor would have done well to disregard these armchair theories and rely on local expertise. Thanks to ongoing temple construction, the builders of Roman Egypt were familiar with the techniques of monumental masonry. Unlike their Old Kingdom predecessors, they were also familiar with the use of cranes, which likely would have been used to place the casing stones of a Roman pyramid. The construction of the Great Pyramid is believed to have taken at least two decades.† With their cranes, iron tools, and imperial resources, the Romans could have built a structure on the same scale more quickly. The Pyramid of Cestius was completed in only 330 days.[2]

Had he escaped assassination, Julius Caesar might have settled in Alexandria. Mark Antony certainly would have, had he been victorious at Actium. Avidius Cassius, the general who tried to raise the eastern provinces against Marcus Aurelius, orchestrated his rebellion from Egypt. Vaballathus, son of the rebel queen Zenobia, could have made Alexandria the center of a new, Eastern Roman Empire.

---

* This question is still a matter of controversy, especially in the case of the Great Pyramid. Although the blocks were undoubtedly brought up ramps on sledges, it is unclear how many ramps there were and how they were arranged. The uppermost courses may have been levered into place. We do know at least how the Egyptians built ramps: One still in place against the first pylon of the Temple of Amun at Karnak consists of a series of mud-brick walls with earth packed between them.

† Within the constraints of Bronze Age technology, only the exceptional fertility of the Nile Valley and the pharaoh's absolute power made the Great Pyramid possible. After the Fourth Dynasty, royal pyramids were smaller and more cheaply built, with cores of rubble or mud-brick. This development suggests that—even for the pharaohs—Khufu's pyramid lay at the limits of possibility.

Yet even if the Roman Empire had come to be centered in Egypt, it's difficult to imagine an emperor being buried in a pyramid. Leaving aside the political and practical considerations mentioned earlier and the fact that any motivated ruler could simply have reused an existing tomb,* it wouldn't have made cultural sense. Although they ruled Egypt, the Roman emperors were not of Egypt. They stood outside the sacred bond between pharaoh and subjects that had given meaning to the pyramids and justified the effort of creating them. Lacking that, a pyramid was just a pile of stones.

---

* Most of the pyramids were reused for burials, sometimes multiple times. No fewer than eighty-seven Roman-era skeletons were found packed into the mortuary temple of Menkaure's Pyramid. The bones of a bull, apparently also from the Roman period, were discovered in Khafre's sarcophagus.

· 15 ·

What Happened to the Wonders of the Ancient World?

$\mathcal{A}$ccording to a list standard since the Renaissance, the Seven Wonders of the Ancient World were the Great Pyramid of Giza, the Hanging Gardens of Babylon, the Statue of Zeus at Olympia, the Temple of Artemis at Ephesus, the Mausoleum at Halicarnassus, the Colossus of Rhodes, and the Lighthouse of Alexandria.*

Of these, the Great Pyramid is the only survivor. If the Hanging Gardens existed, their site has not been located. The Colossus, felled by an earthquake less than a century after its completion, was sold for scrap in late antiquity. The Statue of Zeus was brought to Constantinople and there destroyed by fire. The other three wonders have also perished. Their afterlives, however, are worth describing in detail.

The Mausoleum at Halicarnassus was built in the mid-fourth century BCE, a generation before Alexander's conquests. At the time of its construction, Halicarnassus and the rest of Asia Minor were part of the Persian Empire, which extended from the Aegean to India. The Persian governor of Halicarnassus and the surrounding region was Mausolus, a local dynast married to his sister Artemisia.

---

* The oldest known list of the Seven Wonders—a Greek poem dating to the second century BCE—is identical, save for replacing the Lighthouse of Alexandria with the Walls of Babylon. The same seven appear in the only extant ancient work on the wonders. The familiar list, however, was never definitive, and a number of Greek and Roman authors proposed additions or alternatives, including the Egyptian Labyrinth, the Temple of Zeus at Cyzicus, and the Colosseum.

The site of the Mausoleum at Halicarnassus. *Author's photo*

After Mausolus died, Artemisia—so distraught, it was said, that she stirred his ashes into her wine—presided over the construction of her brother-husband's tomb.

A massive rectangular structure, the tomb rose in tiers to a colonnade and pyramidal roof. Four famous Greek sculptors worked on the project, each decorating one side. A rank of colossal statues lined the base, and hundreds of life-size sculptures crowded the cornice of the first tier. Above were an elaborate frieze and the colonnade, garnished with portraits of Mausolus, Artemisia, and their predecessors. Lions guarded the colossal quadriga atop the roof.[1]

The mausoleum was instantly and lastingly famous. Both the Trophy of Augustus at La Turbie, France, and the Trophy of Trajan at Adamclisi, Romania, are thought to have been inspired by it. Another replica—a second-century tomb in Milas, Turkey, known as Gümüşkesen, the "silver purse"—still features a colonnade and pyramidal roof.

The mausoleum's own roof and colonnade were shattered by medieval earthquakes. By the twelfth century, when Eustathius of Thessalonica described it as "still marvelous," the tomb was probably a shapeless mass of rubble carpeted with vegetation. Its remains were destroyed between 1494 and 1522 by the Knights of St. John, a military religious order that had established a stronghold at Halicarnassus. Thousands of green lava blocks from the tomb were built into the walls of the knights' castle. Most of the marble statues and reliefs were burned for lime. Only a few slabs showing battles against Amazons and centaurs were preserved, along with a scattering of monumental lions.

While dismantling the mausoleum's foundations, the knights discovered a marble staircase. As they dug all around it, prying up courses of heavy stone blocks, an opening appeared. A few men squeezed through. They found themselves in a room decorated with a beautiful frieze that depicted a mythical battle. Beyond was a chamber containing an alabaster sarcophagus. The evening retreat was sounded before the knights could open it. When they returned the following day, the sarcophagus was empty. The only traces of treasure were golden spangles, fallen from an ancient burial shroud.*

The knights were driven from their castle soon afterward, and Halicarnassus became the sleepy Turkish village of Bodrum. In 1856, an employee of the British Museum named Charles Newton set out to rediscover the mausoleum's site. In a neighborhood where almost every house had marble fragments built into its walls, he started digging. Almost at once, he struck the foundations of the mausoleum: a platform of large greenish blocks, many still clamped together with iron. Newton spent several months tunneling along the foundations, trying to determine which of the properties above he would have to buy. Then, after lengthy negotiations with local homeowners, work started in earnest.

At first, only a few stray artifacts came to light.† When Newton turned to the area just north of the tomb, however, he found

---

* The knights supposed that thieves had come in the night and robbed the tomb. The mausoleum had actually been pilfered long before. In late antiquity, thieves with hammers and chisels attacked the huge stone that blocked the entrance to the tomb. Unable to break through, they tunneled around it, digging deep into the tomb's superstructure. After some trial and error, they broke into the burial chamber.

† The most remarkable of these was an alabaster jar—apparently a gift from the Persian court to one of Mausolus's ancestors—inscribed with the name of Xerxes I in several languages. A century later, a Danish team clearing the site stumbled on a ritual deposit of food made during Mausolus's funeral. It included the butchered carcasses of twenty-one sheep, five cattle, and fourteen chickens.

more than twenty sculptures, toppled from the upper reaches of the mausoleum by a medieval earthquake. Buried by sediment washing down from a nearby hill, they had escaped the depredations of the knights. Alongside what he enthusiastically identified as portraits of Mausolus and Artemisia, Newton recovered several lions and parts of the quadriga that had crowned the roof. His finds fill a room in the British Museum, where visitors can wander among the fragments of the ancient world's greatest tomb.

Like all Greek deities, Artemis had many forms. Though most often worshipped as a youthful huntress, the guardian of wild places, she was also identified with Selene, whose crown was the moon's crescent, and with Hecate, queen of ghosts. At Ephesus, where she was assimilated to an Anatolian mother-goddess, Artemis's cult image stood rigid as a column, the serene face framed by cascades of earrings, the torso bulging with protuberances variously interpreted as breasts, bull testicles, and bags of offerings.

The site of the Temple of Artemis at Ephesus. *Author's photo*

After the first Temple of Artemis at Ephesus was destroyed by a flood, a colossal new structure (financed in part by the fabulously wealthy King Croesus) rose in its place. The first temple in the Greek world to be built entirely of marble, it was surrounded by a forest of forty-foot columns. The bases of the columns were carved with painted reliefs, which shimmered through the clouds of smoke and incense drifting from the great altar.

For more than two hundred years, the temple built by Croesus drew crowds of pilgrims and visitors. But in 356 BCE—on the very day, it was later said, that Alexander the Great was born in Macedon—it was burned to the ground by a madman named Herostratus, who wanted to be remembered forever. Or so the Ephesians claimed. Marble buildings are not easy to burn, and some scholars suspect that the priests set the fire themselves, aware that the temple's foundations had settled beyond repair.

The site was cleared, and another temple was begun, even more magnificent than its predecessor.* Work continued for more than a century. The new Temple of Artemis was raised above its flood-prone site on a platform with thirteen steps. It was nearly four times the size of the Parthenon and more than twice as tall. Each of 127 columns was 60 feet high. The gleaming marble pediment was centered on a tall window, where images of the goddess were displayed.

The temple stood, honored by emperors and kings, until it was devastated by marauding Goths in the third century. Not long after, as Ephesus became a predominantly Christian city, the temple began to be plundered for building material. A later legend claimed that some of its columns were incorporated into Justinian's Hagia Sophia. The stones that were not pilfered vanished beneath mud laid down during floods of the local river. By the time western travelers began visiting Ephesus in the early modern period, the site of the temple had been lost.†

In 1863, a British railroad engineer with the eminently Victorian name of John Turtle Wood set out to rediscover the Temple

---

* Construction was well underway by the time Alexander the Great added Ephesus to his expanding empire. The conqueror offered to pay for the temple's completion if the Ephesians would inscribe his name on the pediment. The offer was politely declined.

† The most prominent ruins near the ancient harbor—which actually belonged to a Roman bath complex—were often mistaken for those of the temple.

of Artemis. Wood began with no clear ideas about where to look. Ancient descriptions stated only that the temple had been built on low ground near a river, a short distance outside the city center. At first, Wood dug almost randomly, sinking a series of test pits at various points around the city. He found inscriptions and tombs, but nothing that pointed the way to the temple. Pit by pit, year after year, despite frequent bouts of malaria and setbacks ranging from a broken collarbone to murderous bandits, Wood soldiered on. He began to excavate in the city theater, hoping for a clue to the temple's whereabouts. Incredibly, he found one.

On one of the theater's walls was a long inscription from the reign of Trajan, describing a procession to the Temple of Artemis. The processional route had been circular, exiting from one of the main city gates and entering through the other. If he dug from these gates, Wood reasoned, he would eventually reach the temple. He concentrated on the road from the Magnesian Gate, which was lined with thousands of tombs. Just as the last of his funding ran out, his workmen found a wall of massive blocks, which an inscription identified as the precinct of the Temple of Artemis. On the final day of December 1869, six years after the search began, they struck the stones of the temple itself.

Wood's excavation continued for another four years. Even by nineteenth-century standards, it was not a model of painstaking archaeology. At one point, gunpowder was used to blow up the remains of a Byzantine church. When not assisted by dynamite, progress was slow; the sand and mud that covered the temple were waterlogged. Trench walls repeatedly collapsed, killing one workman and injuring others. There were many other setbacks. A subterranean spring flooded the excavations. Mice ate the inscription squeezes. A ship filled with finds sank. But in the end, Wood managed to clear the site of the temple, having moved—by his calculation—132,221 cubic yards of sediment and debris. His prize finds, including a column base sculpted with reliefs of Alcestis and Thanatos, were sent to the British Museum.*

---

* It took fifteen men fifteen full days to clear the eleven-ton drum. In London, twenty draft horses were needed to haul it from the Thames to the British Museum.

A generation after Wood concluded his excavations, the British Museum sent David George Hogarth to clarify the history of the Temple of Artemis. Finding Wood's hole filled to the brim, Hogarth used a steam pump lent by the Ottoman Railway Company to remove 100,000 cubic meters of water. Even after the pool had been drained, his workmen had to spend every morning pumping the previous night's seepage so that they could dig, thigh-deep in mud, during the afternoon. Beneath the muck, Hogarth discovered the foundation deposit of the Archaic temple. Almost as soon as the first finds surfaced, however, the winter rains set in, and the nights turned cold enough to freeze the pools in which the workmen toiled. Hogarth had to wait until spring to recover the rest of the treasure: fistfuls of electrum coins, earrings and scarabs of precious metal, and upward of a thousand gemstones.

Since 1965, the Austrian Archaeological Institute has resumed work, revealing—among much else—the original temple of the eighth century BCE. The Austrians have also erected a single truncated column, pieced together from dozens of fragments, to stand sentry over the puddles and broken stones that mark the site of the Temple of Artemis.

Between the two harbors of Alexandria, the Greek world's greatest city, a causeway led to a low limestone island. On that island stood the tallest structure ever built by the Greeks or Romans, visible for thirty miles along the level Egyptian shore: the Pharos,* the Lighthouse of Alexandria.

The appearance of the lighthouse is known from a series of smaller replicas—most notably the Roman lighthouse at A Coruña, Spain, and a Hellenistic tomb in Taposiris Magna, Egypt—as well as from literally thousands of artistic representations, ranging from

---

* *Pharos*, originally the name of the island on which the lighthouse stood, served as a metonym for the lighthouse itself. Like *mausoleum*, it eventually became an improper noun. The French and Italian words for *lighthouse*, *phare* and *faro*, are derived from it. Incidentally, *minaret*, now used for the tower of a mosque, originated from an Arabic word that meant, among other things, *lighthouse*—quite possibly a reference to the Lighthouse of Alexandria.

A colossal statue of a Ptolemaic queen in the guise of Isis, recovered from the site of the Lighthouse of Alexandria. *Author's photo*

Roman coins issued at Alexandria to a painted glass found at Bagram, Afghanistan. It seems clear that the Pharos had three tiers: a square base, an octagonal middle section, and a cylindrical tower. A ramp or staircase spiraled through the structure's center, leading up past storage rooms and dormitories to the beacon at its top.*

The lighthouse survived the civil wars and conflagrations that obliterated the Tomb of Alexander and destroyed every book in the great library. It outlasted the catastrophic tsunami of 365. It endured as the Roman Empire crumbled and Alexandria dwindled into a shadow of its former self.

An earthquake in 956 brought about the collapse of the highest, cylindrical stage. More damage occurred during the earthquakes of 1261 and 1303. By 1329, when Ibn Battuta visited Alexandria for the

---

* The nature of the beacon is unclear. It may have been an open flame built on the roof of the tower. Or perhaps it was sheltered by the colonnaded belfry that appears on some Roman coins, surmounted by a colossal statue of Zeus Soter. The light of the flames may have been amplified by burnished bronze mirrors or replaced by mirrors during the day.

first time, only the square base survived. When he returned seventeen years later, even this section had become too dangerous to enter. In the fifteenth century, the Mameluke Sultan Qaitbay demolished the ruins of the Pharos to construct the fort that still guards Alexandria's harbor. Stones from the lighthouse—most visibly the huge granite blocks that frame the citadel's main door and the entrance of its mosque—were built into the fort.

Qaitbay's workmen, however, never touched the parts of the lighthouse that had collapsed into the harbor during medieval earthquakes.* In 1961, the Egyptian navy raised a colossal statue from the seabed near the fort. No further work was done until 1994, when French archaeologist Jean-Yves Empereur began to dive in the harbor. All around Qaitbay, Empereur found a debris field that covered more than five acres of seabed. Here, up to thirty feet below the surface, were around five thousand of the limestone blocks that had formed the walls of the lighthouse. Among them were more than two dozen sphinxes and granite monoliths, weighing up to seventy-five tons, that had served as lintels and doorjambs. Perhaps the most remarkable finds were colossal statues, each around forty feet tall, of a Ptolemaic king in the guise of a pharaoh and a Ptolemaic queen as Isis.

Recently, twenty-two blocks were hauled up from the harbor to help researchers create a digital twin of the lighthouse. If this project succeeds, the Lighthouse of Alexandria will, after seven centuries, rise again above the waves.

---

* Alexandria's harbor has changed dramatically since antiquity. Thanks to strong westerly currents and modern infilling, the causeway that joined Pharos to the mainland has grown into a broad peninsula. Other parts of the harbor district have subsided up to fifteen feet, apparently due to liquefaction of the soil caused by earthquakes and tsunamis.

III

SOLDIERS AND GLADIATORS

· *16* ·

How Did the Romans
Arm Their Soldiers?

The imperial Roman army consisted of legionaries—citizens who served as heavy, close-order infantry—and auxiliaries, noncitizens typically deployed as light infantry or cavalry.* Legionaries often wore segmented plate armor, which protected their shoulders better than mail. Their shields were usually rectangular and always curved. Their helmets had neck guards and hinged cheek pieces. Besides his dagger, each legionary carried a pilum—a javelin designed to punch through armor at close range—and a gladius, a brutally effective short sword. Although auxiliaries could be equipped as anything from slingers to heavy infantry, they often wore mail shirts† and carried flat, oval shields. Their most characteristic weapons were a stabbing spear and the long slashing sword known as the spatha.‡

---

* When not training or campaigning, soldiers wore a knee-length tunic, complemented in cooler climates by breeches or trousers. Over their tunics, they donned wool cloaks, sometimes hooded, to ward off the weather. Off-duty soldiers were distinguished from civilians—who also wore tunics and cloaks—by their military belts. Initially, they wore separate belts for their dagger and sword, crossed gunslinger-style. Later, these were replaced by a single broad belt, often studded with metal plates and ornaments. (In battle, some men wore an apron of heavy leather strips that dangled from their belts; although this garment may have had a protective function, it was probably more decorative than practical.) Soldiers were also closely associated with caligae, hobnailed high-laced sandals worn with socks in cold weather. Caligula's nickname came from his childhood habit of wearing miniature military sandals.

† Although mail may have been cheaper than plate, it was not easy to make. On the basis of a mail shirt found at the South Shields fort on Hadrian's Wall, it has been estimated that a shirt could require more than fifty thousand rings, and it would have taken a single craftsman upward of two hundred days to complete.

‡ The distinctions between the arms of auxiliaries and legionaries were never absolute. Legionaries sometimes wore mail and gradually adopted longer swords and oval shields.

85

Auxiliaries provided almost all the Roman army's cavalry. Some units—like Numidian skirmishers—wore only a short tunic into battle. Others, such as Sarmatian cataphracts, were armored from head to toe. In general, however, cavalrymen were equipped with mail shirts and oval shields. Although a few heavy units wielded long, two-handed lances, most carried a stabbing spear and several short javelins.

Soldiers of the imperial era were normally given their armor and weapons on recruitment. The cost of the equipment was then deducted from their pay in installments.* When a man left the army, he could sell his arms. Many pieces of armor have been discovered with multiple names, apparently of successive owners, inscribed on them. A helmet found in the Thames had the initials of no fewer than seven soldiers punched into its neck guard. During public exercises, auxiliary cavalry wore parade armor, which included elaborate helmets with hinged masks and leather headpieces for their horses. Other units simply cleaned and polished their battle gear for special occasions.[1]

Infantry and cavalry alike modified their arms freely. Faced with the fearsome sickle-shaped swords of the Dacians, for example, some legionaries took to wearing vambraces. Helmets are often found with reinforcing bars riveted to the bowls. When they had the money, soldiers decorated every available surface of their armor.† The elaborate dagger sheaths and ornamental plates often discovered around military camps attest to customized armor shops run by civilians or veterans.[2]

Supplying hundreds of thousands of soldiers with weapons and armor was a formidable logistical challenge. Only the simplest weapons—like lead slingshot bullets—could be manufactured in the field.‡ Making a composite bow, for example, took more than a year,

---

* In late antiquity, officers received part of their salary in the form of silver or gilded armor.

† Such customization could be very expensive. Pliny the Younger gave a young centurion forty thousand sestertii—equivalent to the annual salary of thirty-three legionaries—to purchase equipment. Regular enlisted men were not immune to the lure of glitz. No fewer than eighty-eight gemstones, fallen from rings, were found in the bath drains of the legionary camp at Caerleon.

‡ Soldiers sometimes made slingshot bullets by pressing their fingers into mud and pouring molten lead into the impressions. Usually, however, bullets were cast in clay molds that were sometimes etched with slogans. When Octavian was besieging Perugia, for example, a soldier in the city produced a batch labeled "Destination: Octavian's arsehole."

the components being glued together as the wood seasoned. The best spears, likewise, had to be cut from groves of specially coppiced ash and hazel trees.[3]

Under the Republic, arms had been produced by civilian contractors based in cities. Enemy craftsmen were sometimes pressed into service. After Scipio took Carthago Nova, he immediately put two thousand Carthaginian artisans to work making weapons for the Romans. The professional army of the imperial era continued to rely on urban workshops in the eastern provinces. Italian cities, likewise, produced weapons for newly raised legions, especially during civil wars. But along the northern frontier, where large settlements were few and far between, arms were made in military camps.[4]

Many camps had dedicated workshops. Excavation of a fort near Hofheim, Germany, revealed the remains of a forge, complete with tools, iron bars, and a slag-heaped hearth.* At other military sites, troves of scrap metal have been found, apparently collected for melting and reuse. Soldiers who were trained craftsmen—swordsmiths, shield makers, fletchers—were exempted from other duties. They could be impressively efficient. Over the course of two days, a military workshop in Roman Egypt produced cart nails, leather straps, two varieties of shield, bows, catapult frames, and ten swords.[5]

Around the end of the third century, in tandem with the reforms of Diocletian, arms began to be mass-produced in the factories known as *fabricae*. There were fifteen in the eastern provinces, twenty in the west. Some made both shields and weapons; others specialized in breastplates, arrows, horse armor, or ballistae. All were designed primarily to equip the field armies, whose mobility limited in-camp manufacture. Workers in the *fabricae* were enlisted as soldiers and received the rations and brands of recruits.[†]

Although a few *fabricae* were connected with legionary fortresses, most were located in cities, and they seem to have been staffed by civilian craftsmen. They were overseen by minor bureaucrats, who

---

* The same fort produced evidence for a tannery. This must have been a busy workshop, as a single tent (housing eight men) required around seventy goat hides.

† The factories that produced military clothing, by contrast, were staffed by state-owned slaves.

enforced a relentless production schedule. A worker could be expected to produce a fully gilded helmet, complete with cheek guards, every five days.* Punishments for shoddy workmanship were draconian: A manager who presented an underweight breastplate to the emperor was summarily executed. In the Roman military-industrial complex, casualties were never limited to the battlefield.[6]

---

* During the civil wars of the late Republic—an earlier episode of mass production—some helmets were so poorly made that soldiers had to cover them with wicker to ward off sling bullets.

• 17 •

Why Didn't the Romans Conquer Parthia?

The Parthian Empire was smaller and less populous than the Roman Empire. It lacked a professional army. Its kings were constantly embroiled in conflicts with their siblings and subordinates.* In their many wars with the Parthians, the Romans usually had the upper hand. Legions twice burned the Parthian capital, and Trajan briefly captured Mesopotamia. No emperor, however, managed to lastingly conquer any substantial part of their eastern rivals' territory.

Almost everywhere except the border facing the Parthians, Rome's frontiers mapped fairly neatly onto ecological limits.† But Mesopotamia, the Parthian territory closest to Rome, was populous, fertile, and studded with cities. There was no cultural barrier between it and Roman Syria. In Mesopotamia, as in Syria, the lingua franca

---

* As enthusiastic polygamists, Parthian kings tended to produce many sons. Unlike the Ottoman sultans—who customarily murdered their brothers the moment they assumed power (or, later, imprisoned them in the gilded cage of the harem)—Parthian potentates often suffered their siblings to live. The siblings weren't always properly appreciative.

† More specifically, the Roman frontier tended to follow the limits of reliable wheat and barley cultivation. This fact was most obvious in Africa and the Near East, where the provinces terminated at the Sahara and Syrian Deserts. In continental Europe, the frontier was shaped largely by the courses of the Rhine and Danube, which facilitated the transport of men and supplies. But where the soil was especially fertile, as in the valley of the Upper Rhine, the Romans pushed their military cordon beyond the rivers. Augustus briefly advanced the German frontier to the Elbe; Marcus Aurelius considered establishing tiers of provinces north of the Danube. In each case, however, the primary motivation seems to have been the establishment of a buffer between the barbarians and the more valuable—and vulnerable—provinces to the south.

was Aramaic, and Greek was widely spoken.* The cross-frontier cultural links strengthened in late antiquity, when both regions became hotbeds of Christianity.[1]

Rome's inability or unwillingness to expand eastward is partially explicable in military terms. In stark contrast to the legions, Parthian armies consisted largely of cavalry. Noblemen galloped into battle on huge Nisaean warhorses,† mailed like medieval knights. Their lances, it was said, could transfix two men without shattering. Equally dangerous were the light cavalry, armed with bows that had superior range to anything in the Roman arsenal. At the Battle of Carrhae, Crassus and his seven legions were encircled by Parthian horsemen, who showered them with arrows. When Crassus detached a force to engage with the enemy, the Parthians withdrew, lured the detachment forward, and destroyed it. They subjected the Romans to another withering barrage the following day, forcing Crassus to surrender. The disaster at Carrhae, however, was remembered because it was exceptional. More often than not, Roman armies defeated their Parthian counterparts.‡ In the light of that fact, it seems unlikely that purely tactical concerns prevented the Romans from conquering more of their rivals' territory.[2]

Logistics raised more fundamental problems. For most of its nine-hundred-mile length, the eastern frontier of the Roman Empire ran through inaccessible mountains and deserts. The only sections suitable for large-scale campaigning were Armenia and Upper Mesopotamia. Both were problematic. Lucullus's legions were caught by the snowstorms of the Armenian mountains. So, a generation later, were those of Mark Antony. During Nero's Parthian war, many

---

* Parthian aristocrats were as likely to know Greek as their Roman counterparts. After the Roman defeat at Carrhae, the Parthian king enjoyed watching the head of Crassus being used as a prop in a production of Euripides's *Bacchae*.

† These huge, swift horses, originally bred in Media, were famous as far away as China. Taller and heavier than Roman warhorses, they were strong enough to wear barding and carry an armored rider.

‡ Arrian, who governed Cappadocia under Hadrian, described in detail how he arranged his forces to deal with the Parthian-style heavy cavalry of the Alans. Eventually—imitation being the sincerest form of flattery—the Romans equipped cataphracts of their own. By the time Justinian sent Belisarius to reconquer Italy, heavy cavalry equipped with bows were the dominant striking arm of the Roman army.

soldiers lost fingers and toes to frostbite. It was comparatively easy for an army to march through Mesopotamia, as long as it paralleled the Tigris or Euphrates. But away from the rivers' irrigated flood-plains, much of the region was waterless and barren. Crassus and his legions struggled over endless hills of sand. A century and a half later, scarcity of water and fodder forced Trajan to raise his siege of Hatra.[3]

Both mountains and deserts, however, could be crossed by well-provisioned Roman armies. Nero's commanders set up a supply line that began at Trapezus on the Black Sea, crossed the Pontic Alps, and followed the Araxes River into Armenia—a distance of well over three hundred miles. During the same war, Domitius Corbulo led a 275-mile forced march over a desolate plateau. Trajan brought about eighty thousand men—an army twice the size of Alexander's—through Mesopotamia without suffering significant casualties.[4]

That most of Mesopotamia remained in Parthian hands was a historical accident, in the sense that the Romans would probably have kept the region if Trajan had lived longer. But it also reflected the calculation, made by a series of emperors, that the conquest of Mesopotamia—let alone the Parthians' eastern provinces—was undesirable. In their wars with the Parthians, the emperors sought quick victory, ideally seasoned with a goodly leaven of loot. Both sides seem to have expected that war would leave the balance of power basically unaltered, with only a few border cities changing hands. Even Trajan envisioned a limited conquest that would leave everything east of Mesopotamia under the control of a Parthian king allied to Rome.[5]

The Parthian Empire was simply too big to conquer. Alexander himself had struggled to subdue the vast and rugged Iranian Plateau. And beyond the plateau stretched the steppes of Central Asia, open to the lightning raids of nomads. The Romans, like the Ottomans a millennium and a half later, could have pushed their eastern frontier to the foothills of the Zagros Mountains. Any campaign beyond would have involved them in a world they were ill equipped to attack, let alone rule. The emperors seem to have understood that it would have been foolhardy, even in a time of peace, to strip the European frontiers and empty the treasury in pursuit of Alexander's dream. Fantasies of eastern conquest, in short, faded before geopoliti-cal realities. The existence of two empires in the Middle East—the "two eyes of the world," as a Persian diplomat put it—came to seem embedded in the natural order of things. Until the final, cataclysmic war that brought about the end of antiquity, it was taken for granted that the Roman Empire would always have an eastern neighbor.[6]

What Did Gladiators Do After They Retired?

$\mathcal{T}$he average gladiator did not survive to retirement. Sooner or later, whether an untried tyro or a battle-scarred champion, he fell to the bloody sands of the arena and was dragged away through the funeral goddess's gate. Although the odds of any given match ending in death were relatively low—during the first century, perhaps one in five—most of those who lived by the sword also died by it.

Some gladiators, however, were allowed to retire after completing the term—perhaps three or five years—stipulated by their sentence or contract. A very skilled fighter might be released in the arena by the sponsor of the games and publicly awarded a *rudis*, the wooden sword that symbolized his freedom.* Once, after watching an epic struggle between two well-matched gladiators, the emperor Titus freed both combatants.[1]

Regardless of whether they won or lost, gladiators were paid every time they fought. They received additional prizes when they were victorious; the emperor Claudius liked to toss gold coins to men who had performed bravely. After being granted the *rudis*, a gladiator named Spiculus received a mansion and estate from Nero. Few gladiators, however, could support themselves for the rest of

---

* Although it may have appeared so, the award of a *rudis* was never spontaneous. A sponsor did not own the gladiators who fought in his games and had the right to free them only if the gesture was arranged in advance. Receiving the *rudis*, moreover, only automatically liberated a gladiator if he had been a free man before entering the gladiatorial school. If he had been a slave, he remained one—albeit one who was no longer obligated to fight in the arena.

their lives on their winnings. Many had families; Claudius freed one gladiator after receiving a petition from his four sons. And some ex-gladiators lived on for many decades after retirement. The tombstone of a *paegniarius* (mock fighter) named Secundus records that he died at the age of ninety-nine.[2]

The career options of retired gladiators were limited by their low social status. Whether freeborn, former slaves, or prisoners of war, they were *infames*, disgraced. This meant that—like executioners, undertakers, and actors—they were unable to hold office, appear in court, or even (in the case of former slaves) make their own wills. Some gladiators continued to fight after their release, especially if they were famous enough to be invited back to the arena for exhibition matches. A prominent *rudiarius*—freed gladiator—would receive top billing before the games and be handsomely compensated after. Tiberius paid some stars 100,000 sestertii for a single appearance.[3]

Alternatively, an ex-gladiator could become a referee. Each gladiatorial match was supervised by a head referee, the *summa rudis*, and his assistant, the *secunda rudis*. These men intervened with shouts and wooden switches when a fighter broke the rules or was incapacitated. (The tombstone of a gladiator named Diodorus laments that he was killed after a referee allowed his defeated opponent to get back on his feet.) To judge from the tombstone of a *summa rudis* who lived to the age of sixty, some referees had long careers. In addition to or instead of serving as a referee, a retired gladiator might train new fighters at a gladiatorial school.[4]

Outside the ambit of the arena, many gladiators became bodyguards. During the turbulent last years of the Republic, the rival politicians Clodius and Milo recruited whole gladiatorial troops. Gladiators shadowed Nero and his drinking companions whenever they went carousing in dive bars and brothels. Aristocratic ladies sometimes hired former gladiators to protect them on journeys. Wealthy landowners might recruit private armies captained by gladiators to patrol their estates.[5]

Because of their low status, gladiators were normally excluded from service in the legions. Amid the civil wars of the Late Republic, however, a consul briefly formed Julius Caesar's gladiators into a cavalry unit. During the chaotic Year of the Four Emperors, Otho enrolled two thousand gladiators as legionaries. A century later, Marcus Aurelius formed a cohort of gladiators optimistically named the *obsequentes*, "obedient ones." Caligula made Thracian gladiators captains of his personal bodyguard.[6]

Not all former gladiators dedicated their lives to violence. A few became farmers; the Roman poet Horace, retiring to his estate, compared himself to a gladiator who had given up his weapons and moved to the countryside. Other gladiators may have become black-cloaked priests of the war goddess Bellona or dueled in the Sacred Grove of Aricia for the crown of the priest-king of Nemi.[7]

Especially in the eastern provinces, where athletes had long been honored, a few former gladiators achieved respectability. One, later a referee, became an honorary citizen of no fewer than seven cities. Another gladiator was included in an embassy to the emperor. Vitellius made a freedman whom he had rescued from a gladiatorial school a member of the Equestrian order. According to the *Historia Augusta*, when Marcus Aurelius once reprimanded a former gladiator for trying to become a Roman official, he was told that many other ex-gladiators already held government posts. There is no reason to doubt that—as Juvenal claimed—the sons of gladiators could be found in the Equestrian seats of Rome's theaters; the social and legal restrictions that hindered former gladiators did not apply to their children. The *Historia Augusta*'s suggestion that Emperor Macrinus was a former gladiator is less believable.[8]

Gladiators unburdened by political ambition might exploit their sex appeal.* Rumor alleged that the wives of Roman senators took gladiators as lovers. Empress Messalina reportedly had an affair with an ex-gladiator named Sabinus, and it was whispered that the real father of Commodus, son of Marcus Aurelius, was a gladiator. (According to an alternate version, Empress Faustina confessed her attraction to Marcus, who—after consulting with some astrologers— had the gladiator killed so that Faustina could bathe in his blood.)[9]

---

* Two graffiti from Pompeii call the gladiator Celadus "heartthrob of all the girls." Since they were probably written by Celadus himself, this may have been wishful thinking.

For more than a half-millennium, gladiators were at the center of Roman society. They were applauded by slaves and emperors. They were figured in mosaics, modeled by figurines, stamped on lamps. Their blood was said to cure impotence, and the very sand on which they fought was gathered for spells. But the gladiators themselves remain elusive—distant marionettes playing out the fantasies of a civilization.

Were Spectators Ever Harmed in the Colosseum?

$\mathscr{I}$n 55 BCE, Pompey the Great staged an elephant hunt in the Circus Maximus. Twenty elephants were released onto the racetrack, pursued by spearmen from North Africa. The elephants defended themselves, tearing away the hunters' shields with their trunks. But as more and more javelins struck home, the huge animals attempted to escape, hurling themselves against the iron fences that protected the spectators. The barriers bent and shook. Only the swift response of the hunters, who surrounded the elephants and brought them down, prevented disaster.[1]

The Roman games must have been unnerving to watch. Beast hunts routinely featured big cats—lions, leopards, and tigers—that could leap over high walls, as well as elephants and rhinos tremendous enough to crash through almost any obstacle. The hunters threw spears and shot arrows in every direction. So did the gladiators—many of whom were condemned criminals with nothing to lose. Amid all those leaping lions and scattershot spears, one imagines, at least a few spectators at the Colosseum must have ended up closer to the action than they would have liked.

By most estimates, the Colosseum could hold around fifty thousand spectators. The worst seats were at the top, where slaves and women stood on rickety benches. Below were the nonelite sections of the *maenianum*, the general admission section, where spectators crowded onto narrow stone benches. The lowest part of the *maenianum*, separated by a walkway from the rows above, was reserved for members of the Equestrian order. These benches were wider and made of marble—signs of the social standing* of the men who occupied them. But the really luxurious seating was in the podium, closest to the arena, where the imperial family, vestal virgins, and members of the senate sat with their attendants on cushioned chairs.

The podium and its elite occupants were protected by several lines of defense. A high travertine wall ringed the arena, crowned by a protective barrier. This likely resembled the fence around the arena in the amphitheater of Nero,† where projecting elephant tusks supported a net of gilded wire studded with lumps of amber. At the net's base were rows of ivory rollers, designed to prevent big cats from crawling up the wall. In the Colosseum, armed guards likely patrolled the walkway between the barrier and the first tier of the podium. Sharpshooters armed with bows seem to have also been stationed nearby, ready to react if an animal or gladiator tried to reach the spectators.[2]

As far as we know, no animal ever managed to make it over the barrier of the Colosseum. Nor are we aware of any fatalities in the stands caused by the arrows and javelins of the beast hunters. There were, however, other risks to spectators at the Roman games. Heatstroke was a problem in the lower rows; Caligula allowed senators to wear sun hats during the games. There was also a risk of tumbling down the stairs, especially after the emperor had free wine distributed to the spectators.[3]

Disasters occurred in amphitheaters outside Rome. During the reign of Tiberius, a temporary wooden amphitheater in the city of Fidenae collapsed, killing twenty thousand spectators. In the reign of Nero, a brawl broke out in the stands of Pompeii's amphitheater that left dozens dead. Wary of future unrest, the senate banned Pompeii from hosting gladiatorial games for the next ten years.[4]

Gladiators normally posed little danger to spectators. Their weapons were designed for close combat, and no gladiator who

---

* Or, rather, social sitting.

† Though a temporary structure, Nero's amphitheater was famous for its opulence. It was decorated with so much amber that an expedition had to be sent into what is now Poland to collect more.

A fresco from Pompeii, now in the Naples Archaeological Museum, showing the riot in the amphitheater. *Author's photo*

hoped for freedom was likely to risk his future on a throw wild enough to end up in the stands. Yet gladiators did occasionally cause spectator fatalities. According to Valerius Maximus, writing in the reign of Tiberius, an equestrian named Rufus dreamed one night that he would be killed by a gladiator. The next day, at the theater of Syracuse, Rufus was shocked to recognize the gladiator from his dream. Persuaded by his friends that he was being ridiculous, Rufus took his seat and watched the gladiator beat his opponent to the ground. As the gladiator prepared to deal the final blow, he raised his sword high—and skewered Rufus, seated in the front row, through the heart.[5]

Although we have no way of knowing whether this anecdote has basis in truth, its setting in the theater of Syracuse lends it some plausibility. Greek theaters were not designed for gladiatorial combats or beast hunts. Only a low wall, if anything, separated their stages and orchestras from the seats. Unless temporary barriers or nets were set up, the first rows were uncomfortably vulnerable.

Spectators in the Colosseum may have been effectively protected from gladiators, but they were still exposed to the whims of the emperors. During the reign of Domitian, a man sitting near the imperial box complained that the emperor had rigged the games so that his favorite gladiators always won. Furious, Domitian sent guards to drag the man from his seat and feed him to wild dogs in the arena.* A century later, it was rumored that Commodus planned to shoot random spectators at the Colosseum in imitation of Hercules's slaughter of the Stymphalian birds.[6]

We don't know how many spectators were injured or killed over the centuries in the Colosseum. Our sources mention such accidents only if they happened to involve an emperor or famous figure. But to judge from what we do know, a day at the Colosseum was never free from danger, even for those in the stands.

---

* On another occasion, Domitian forced a senator to fight a lion at his Alban villa.

Was There a Secret Tunnel into the Colosseum? Were Naval Battles Staged in the Arena?

*D*awn at the Colosseum. Through the December haze, the rising sun flickers on the assembled statues of the amphitheater and burns streaks through the frost on the Colossus of Nero. Groups of men, cloaked against the chill, are gathering in the plaza below. The emperor is giving games today, and anyone who can beg, borrow, or steal an entry token wants to see the show. The attendants are already at their stations, checking tokens and waving the first patrons through the bronze-gated public entrances. The seats inside are still mostly empty, the white stone dotted here and there by dark-cloaked ushers. The carefully raked arena is quiet.

But beneath the sand, chaos reigns. The service passages—always dark, always hot, always reeking of sweat and manure—are especially unpleasant this morning, as slaves maneuver some very reluctant lions into position. The roars of the big cats mingle with the groan of overloaded ropes and the squeak of pulleys. One corner of the Colosseum's underworld, however, stands apart from the mayhem. Only a few paces from the snarling and shouting, a tunnel extends into the distance. The walls and floor are marble; the ceiling is figured stucco. Oil lamps burn expectantly in niches.

The marble and oil lamps were stripped away fifteen centuries ago. But the tunnel, half-filled with debris, is still there, connecting the Colosseum with an unknown destination. Its purpose remains one of Rome's most enduring archaeological mysteries.

The hypogeum of the Colosseum. *Author's photo*

The arena of the Colosseum was underpinned by the hypogeum, a bilevel network of subterranean passages, cages, and lifts. Although stairways tied this underworld to the rest of the amphitheater, the main entrances were four tunnels. The one on the eastern side connected the hypogeum with the Ludus Magnus, the largest of the four gladiatorial schools associated with the Colosseum.* Little is known about the tunnel on the opposite, western end, which was cut during the construction of Rome's metro in the 1940s. The tunnels on the north and south sides have not been explored. Both were likely used to bring animals and scenery into the hypogeum, and the northern tunnel may have been linked in some way with the storehouse for equipment used in the games.

All four primary tunnels were laid out during the construction of the Colosseum. Shortly after the amphitheater was completed, however, a fifth tunnel was chiseled through the concrete

---

* The other three were the Dacian, Gallic, and Morning Schools. The Dacian and Gallic Schools were named after the nationalities of the slaves initially trained in them; the Morning School was for beast hunters, who usually performed before noon.

foundations. Unlike the others, this tunnel was richly decorated. The walls were lined with marble slabs, later replaced by painted plaster. Satyrs and maenads danced among vines in the stuccowork of the ceiling. The marble floor basked in the suffused glow of skylights.

Around the beginning of the sixth century, the tunnel was stripped of all reusable decorative materials and filled with rubble. When the hypogeum was excavated in the nineteenth century, the archaeologists cleared only enough of the tunnel to confirm that it turned sharply in the direction of the Caelian Hill. It may have been connected in some way with the passage to the Ludus Magnus, but it probably terminated somewhere on the Caelian, near the temple built to honor the deified emperor Claudius.

The tunnel—often called the Passage or Cryptoporticus of Commodus—is widely believed to have been the emperor's private passageway, connecting the palace with the imperial box in the Colosseum. This assumption has been challenged by Nathan Elkins, who suggests that the tunnel was made for the gods.[1]

The best seats in the Colosseum were two platforms on the short axis of the arena. One platform was the imperial box, where the emperor sat with his family, attendants, and guards. The other was likely the *pulvinar*, where images and attributes of the gods and deified emperors were displayed on elaborate thrones. It's often claimed that the imperial box was located on the south side of the arena. Elkins, however, uses numismatic evidence to place the imperial box on the north side. Instead of serving as a special entrance for the emperors, he suggests, the so-called Cryptoporticus of Commodus was a means of conveying the thrones of the gods to and from the *pulvinar* and of carrying the images themselves away after the games.

Many other features of the Colosseum are difficult to explain. Take the ring of bollards—stone pillars—that stood around the perimeter of the Colosseum at a distance of sixty feet from the entrance gates. Five are still intact on the east side; originally, there were probably eighty. It has been suggested that the bollards were anchors for the velaria—awnings—that protected spectators from the sun. Those awnings were suspended from tall wooden posts that

The bollards around the Colosseum. *Author's photo*

socketed into corbels along the arena's attic. By a method still unclear to scholars, the 240 posts supported a lattice of ropes, over which marines from the imperial navy spread sheets of sail-like canvas. Some scholars believe that the bollards were components of a system that kept the ropes of the velaria in tension. The posts, however, are not deeply embedded enough to resist serious pressure. And during the games, all those long ropes would have seriously disrupted the flow of spectators in and out of the arena. It seems more likely that the bollards were nothing more or less than crowd-control barriers, supporting ropes or chains that funneled people toward the public entrances.

We aren't even sure why the Colosseum is called the Colosseum. To the Romans, it was simply Amphitheatrum—"the amphitheater." It's often said that the original Colosseum was the gigantic statue of Nero (later rebranded as the sun god) beside the arena. According to this theory, the name was transferred to the amphitheater only around the tenth century, after the statue had vanished. But all this is conjecture. It's possible that the Colosseum has always been the Colosseum.

We also have no clear idea how many spectators the Colosseum could hold. The only ancient source to give a number—a fourth-century survey of the marvels of Rome—claims that the Colosseum had 87,000 *loca*. Although *loca* normally means *seats*, it's hard to believe that there was room for so many in the Colosseum. Depending on the height of each row, the Colosseum had between forty-five and fifty rows of stone seats, with additional wooden tiers in the *maenianum summum*. Some scholars believe that the total length of the amphitheater's seating was roughly 65,000 feet. Assuming that each spectator received around eighteen inches of space, that gives a total capacity of 40,000–45,000. Other estimates, positing shorter rows and a steeper *maenianum summum*, suggest that as many as 70,000 spectators could have crowded in.*

We don't know, finally, whether the arena of the Colosseum was flooded for naval battles. A naumachia—mock naval battle—was the most expensive and most brutal of all Roman spectacles. One staged by emperor Claudius on the Fucine Lake involved one hundred ships and nineteen thousand combatants, all criminals and prisoners of war who were expected to fight to the death. In Rome, Augustus constructed a huge basin for naumachiae and sponsored a fight with thirty large ships and three thousand fully armed marines. Most later emperors used this basin for their naumachiae, though Nero staged two in his wooden amphitheater.[2]

Both Titus and Domitian, the emperors who completed the Colosseum, are said to have shown naumachiae there. In one of his epigrams on the Colosseum's inaugural games, the poet Martial marveled at the "waves of the sea, where there was dry land moments before." Cassius Dio, apparently describing the same event, notes that the naumachia reenacted a naval battle of the Peloponnesian War and that it was preceded by a display of swimming horses and bulls.[3]

Many scholars, however, are dubious that a naumachia could have been staged in the Colosseum. Unless they were the size

---

* Every one of the Colosseum's seats was torn out during the Middle Ages. The small section of seating visible today is an inaccurate twentieth-century restoration. Scholars who want to reconcile modern estimates with the number of *loca* given by our sole ancient source posit that 87,000 was the measurement of the seating area in Roman feet. Though not impossible, this theory is unprovable.

of rowboats, only a few ships could have maneuvered within the restricted space of the arena. The lead pipes that fed the Colosseum's water fountains seem inadequate to the task of rapidly filling an artificial lake. And the chambers and passageways under the arena would have been difficult to drain. It is sometimes suggested that our sources are mistaken or misinterpreted.* Titus is known to have staged aquatic events in the artificial lake of Augustus, and Domitian built a temporary lake of his own nearby; perhaps these were conflated with the Colosseum.[4]

Scholars who prefer to trust the testimony of our sources have suggested an alternative solution. The Colosseum's hypogeum was completed years after the rest of the building. Originally, it is argued, there was a simpler system of tunnels beneath the arena, covered by beams and a wooden floor that could have been removed before a naumachia. The fact that the hypogeum was lined with waterproof mortar may suggest that the builders of the Colosseum anticipated the space being submerged. But the four sewers that drained it were apparently designed to carry away rainwater, not the millions of gallons needed to flood the amphitheater.† Even if the arena were filled only to the depth of a few feet, it would have taken hours to drain.

Unless new evidence comes to light, we will never know for certain whether naval battles were staged in the Colosseum—and this, as we have seen, is just one of the mysteries surrounding Rome's most iconic ancient building.

---

* We have reason to doubt each of the authors who mentions naumachiae in the Colosseum. Suetonius's account of Domitian's games is brief and confused, Cassius Dio wrote a century and a half after the events he describes, and Martial never explicitly states that the aquatic spectacles he admired took place at the arena.

† There was a large drain beneath each axis of the Colosseum. These connected with an annular channel twenty-five feet below the pavement, which was tied in turn to a sewer that flowed to the Tiber. The west sewer was still operational when it was cut by the subway tunnel in the 1940s.

IV

DAILY LIFE

• *21* •

Was There a Middle Class?

*A*ncient Rome had nothing like the large middle classes of modern capitalist societies. Outside the elite, most people lived close to the subsistence level. But a small segment of the population, poised between affluence and poverty, exhibited some of the traits and aspirations that we associate with the middle class.

Formally, the Roman elite consisted of three social orders: senators, equestrians, and decurions. At a time when most Romans earned less than one thousand sestertii a year, senators were required to have fortunes of at least a million.* Equestrians had to be worth a half-million. The minimum for decurions, who sat on the councils of provincial cities, was often 100,000 sestertii, though less would suffice in a small settlement. Although the three aristocratic orders made up only around 1 percent of the population, they controlled—according to a recent estimate—almost a quarter of the empire's wealth.[1]

Perhaps 10 percent of those outside the elite could be defined as moderately prosperous. This Roman equivalent of the middle class did not have a collective identity or consciousness. From the perspective of the elite, however, its members shared a lack of respectability. Roman aristocrats liked to believe that wealth was only part of their preeminence. They set great stock in their lineage.

---

* Most were far wealthier. Cicero, with properties worth around 13 million sestertii, was probably about average. The fortunes of the senators Crassus (200 million) and Seneca (300 million) were among the largest in Roman history.

They attended the finest rhetorical schools.* They had, they assured themselves, good taste.[2]

Politics was a suitable career for a Roman gentleman. So was advocacy in the courts. A gentleman might discreetly invest in mercantile and industrial enterprises, but he could be denied a place in the Senate if it was known that his wealth derived from such sordid means. The only really respectable source of income was the sale of produce from landed estates. Virtually every other occupation was unbecoming. The vulgar professions, according to Cicero, included paid labor (which was akin to slavery), buying and selling (inherently deceitful), the crafts (it was unseemly to work with one's hands), and the production of anything that appeased the base appetites. Actors and dancers were beneath contempt. Architects, doctors, and teachers, by contrast, were respectable—but such careers were suitable only for freedmen.[3]

Some jobs casually dismissed by Cicero paid well. Skilled craftsmen could become prosperous, especially if they worked with gold, silver, or jewels.† So could merchants who dealt with commodities like garum. The atrium of Umbricius Scaurus, who owned one of the finest mansions in Pompeii, was splashed with advertisements for his "top-grade mackerel sauce."[4]

Ultimately, nothing but fine gradations of snobbery separated the lower reaches of the aristocracy from the more prosperous members of the subelite. The upper middle and upper classes are difficult to disentangle in the archaeological record. At Pompeii, both modest private houses and relatively spacious apartments have been described, rightly or wrongly, as "middle class." Whether these labels were accurate remains unclear. Artifacts like Arretine ware— glazed pottery that imitated gold and silver vessels—have also been

---

* Some upwardly mobile middle-class parents tried to give their sons an elite education. Horace's father—a freedman tax collector—sent him to the finest schools in Rome. Another freedman's son, Quintus Sulpicius Maximus, was a noted Greek poet by his death at age twelve. Other parents were skeptical about the benefits of such learning; in Petronius's *Satyricon*, a freedman explains that he is having his son learn a bit of law, which is much more lucrative than literature.

† Some of the most prosperous silversmiths in late antique Constantinople became bankers (*argentarii*). Although they handled very substantial sums, they were prone to bankruptcy.

associated with moderate prosperity. No aspect of material culture, however, can be automatically linked with a middle class. We can say only that, at Pompeii and many other sites, evidence exists for a substantial group of subelite consumers with disposable income.

In the city of Rome,* the middle class seems to have consisted largely of freedmen. Although our impression of their prominence may be skewed by the fact that freedmen—eager to commemorate their achievements and legitimize their families—were exceptionally likely to build monumental tombs, the prosperity they achieved was real. Many elite families set up slaves as shopkeepers and skilled craftsmen. Once these slaves had bought or been granted their freedom, they maintained close ties—and sometimes business partnerships—with their former owners, giving them an advantage over freeborn competitors.[5]

The wealthy freedman was a stock character in Roman literature. Juvenal describes one who owned five shops in Rome and earned 400,000 sestertii a year. In Petronius's *Satyricon*, the freedman Trimalchio claims to be worth thirty million and says that the size of his fortune will be inscribed on his tomb. This was barely satire. The epitaph of a real freedman in Rome, a former dealer of goat skins, enumerated the fruits of his wealth: a house of marble, alms for the poor, and a mausoleum set aside in perpetuity for the descendants of his own former slaves. The tomb of another freedman, trained as a doctor and surgeon, carefully listed the sums he had paid for his liberty, for membership on a civic board, and for benefactions to his adopted city. Many freedmen advertised their occupations on their tombs. Marcus Vergilius Eurysaces, who made bread for recipients of the grain dole, had reliefs of baking carved on his mausoleum. The gravestone of Gaius Julius Helius, a cobbler, was graced with shoes.[6]

---

* Although most members of the Roman elite owned at least one country estate, their natural habitat was the city. The Roman middle class, likewise, was predominantly urban. A few prosperous farmers, however, belonged to the same milieu. One decurion in the North African city of Mactaris set up an inscription commemorating his rise from agricultural laborer to magistrate. Another African inscription praised a man as both a good farmer and a skilled public speaker.

The gravestone of Gaius Julius Helius, now in Rome's Centrale
Montemartini Museum. *Author's photo*

Although freedmen were prominent in many places outside Rome,* the middle classes of cities close to the frontier tended to be dominated by veterans. Legionaries earned around as much as skilled craftsmen and received a discharge bonus equivalent to a decade's pay in either cash or land. Their officers, paid up to fifty times more than regular soldiers, left the army wealthy men. Some veterans made themselves merchants, selling swords or pottery near their former camps. Many more became farmers, often on a substantial scale. A papyrus from Oxyrhynchus in Egypt mentions a veteran who owned lands with more than a dozen tenants. Another Egyptian veteran had properties in several villages and routinely sent gifts to local officials.[7]

Some veterans rose to the rank of town councilors.† One retired *primipilus* (first centurion) became a decurion of several cities in Pannonia. Another former officer became such a fixture of local government that his adopted city honored him with a gilded statue. The epitaph of Lucius Gavius Fronto, who had served as a *primipilus* and camp prefect, records that his son was an important imperial official and that his grandson had been made a Roman senator.[8]

For a few families, being middle class was a one- or two-generation prelude to joining the elite. But hundreds of thousands never made the leap. They continued to work as craftsmen or farmers, living comfortably and buying modest luxuries. Or they settled back, after a brief taste of prosperity, into the anonymous multitudes of the poor.

---

* At Herculaneum, to judge from an inscribed list of male citizens, freedmen and their descendants made up a majority of the population.

† Like freedmen, successful veterans often advertised their prosperity with impressive tombs. The temple-mausoleum of Lucius Poblicius, decked with sphinxes and Corinthian columns, still dominates the Romano-Germanic Museum of Cologne.

• 22 •

How Did the Rich
Spend Their Money?

*W*ealth was regarded with suspicion in classical Athens. Although aristocratic families remained prominent in public life, the city's democratic ethos discouraged the open display of luxuries. In contemporary Sparta, likewise, citizens were supposed to maintain an ostentatious equality in their clothing and meals. Only on the fringes of the Greek world, at rich colonies like Syracuse and Sybaris,* could riches be flaunted.[1]

In the more oligarchic atmosphere of late republican and imperial Rome, by contrast, few limits† were set on conspicuous consumption. The wealthiest Romans discovered a dizzying array of ways to disburse, dissipate, and outright squander their fortunes. Some of the most spectacular involved feasting. A single four-pound red mullet (a small but delectable fish) could cost 1,200 sestertii—more, in other words, than most Romans made in a year. During the reign of Tiberius, three large mullets sold for 30,000 sestertii. Those with even more expensive tastes could serve songbirds to their guests. A small bird might retail for 6,000 sestertii; a full course would cost 100,000 or more.[2]

---

* *Sybaritic* was already a byword for sensuous luxury in classical Greece. One wealthy Sybarite reportedly traveled to Athens with a retinue of a thousand slaves, including fishermen, fowlers, and cooks trained to prepare his favorite meals.

† The Romans passed a series of sumptuary laws intended to limit excessive spending on luxuries. A famous example, proposed during the war with Hannibal, forbade women to wear more than a small amount of gold or clothing dyed more than one color. It was repealed two decades later, thanks in large part to lobbying by the matrons of Rome. Like most Roman sumptuary laws, however, it had always been honored in the breach.

Such sums were almost routine for the most extravagant members of the Roman aristocracy. The mansion of the epicure Lucullus, for example, contained a dining room where no meal was served that cost less than 200,000 sestertii. One of Nero's companions burned through four million sestertii gathering enough roses to decorate a banquet hall in the dead of winter. Another profligate—possibly inspired by Cleopatra—dissolved a pearl worth one million sestertii in vinegar, drank it, and so enjoyed the taste that he took to serving a round of liquified pearl to his dinner guests. The famous gourmand Apicius reportedly spent 100 million sestertii in his quest for the perfect dinner.[3]

The silverware at a Roman banquet matched the opulence of the food. During the reign of Claudius, one rich freedman owned a silver platter that weighed five hundred pounds. The metal alone was worth nearly 200,000 sestertii. The aristocratic commander of a legion in Germany carried silver dishes weighing twelve thousand pounds wherever he went. Impressive though all this polished plate was, it paled beside Chinese silk, which was literally worth its weight in gold. Vast amounts were paid for Scythian emeralds and diamonds from India. One senator owned a ring with an opal valued at two million sestertii; an envious Mark Antony condemned the man to death and confiscated his ring. Julius Caesar once spent six million sestertii on a lustrous pearl for his mistress.[4]

The Roman elite showed a similar lack of restraint when furnishing their houses. A candelabrum from Greece might cost 50,000 sestertii; an agate vase, 300,000 or more. Nero owned a crystal cup worth one million.* The same emperor's embroidered couch covers, imported from Parthia, cost four million. Cicero paid 500,000 sestertii for a sideboard of African citrus wood, and tables of the same material sold for up to three times as much. Although the most valuable paintings and sculptures of the Greek masters were monopolized by the emperors, many expensive antiques were privately owned. Some Romans collected memorabilia of famous

---

* One aristocrat spent 70,000 sestertii on a fluorspar cup and liked to nibble the rim whenever he drank. Another broke his precious fluorspar dipper, worth 300,000 sestertii, to prevent Nero from confiscating it.

A Greek antique: This bronze krater (mixing bowl) belonged to King Mithridates VI of Pontus. It was later displayed at Nero's villa at Antium and is now in the Capitoline Museums. *Author's photo*

philosophers; a lamp owned by the Stoic master Epictetus was sold for 12,000 sestertii, and a staff of the Cynic Peregrinus Proteus—otherwise notable for immolating himself at the Olympic games—went for 24,000.[5]

The houses in which the Roman elite admired their antiques and staged their decadent dinners were among the most elaborate and expensive ever built. In one mansion on the Palatine, the garden alone—shaded by six towering lotus trees—was valued at three million sestertii. By the reign of Tiberius, any mansion that covered less than four acres was considered small.* The Villa of the Gordians, just outside Rome, reportedly had a peristyle with two hundred columns, each a monolith of rare and beautiful stone. The walls of the reception rooms were plated with silver and gilded bronze.[6]

Wealthy Romans usually owned several houses. The most visible would be a townhouse in a fashionable hilltop neighborhood; Martial mocked a man for keeping mansions on three of Rome's hills. In spring, the Roman elite retreated to seaside villas by the Bay of Naples. The fourth-century senator Symmachus had no fewer than five villas by the bay, each a few miles from the next. In summer, the jet set decamped to airy villas in the countryside. Though only moderately wealthy for a senator, Cicero owned eight villas, along with a few lodges on the roads between his properties so that he would never be forced to stay at a public inn.[7]

Villas were usually surrounded by carefully landscaped grounds.† The orator Hortensius created an expansive wooded park around his favorite villa and filled it with animals trained to gather at the sound of a horn. Another villa, built on the shore of a lake, featured artificial grottoes and a purpose-built river teeming with fish. The villas of Lucullus on the Bay of Naples were famous for their elaborate fishponds connected to the sea by sluices and tunnels. The fish alone—sold separately after Lucullus's death—were worth four million sestertii. A small addition to a villa, such as a renovated bath, might cost nearly one million sestertii.‡ The houses and grounds were worth far more. Marius's villa at Misenum, for example, went for 10 million, and Pompey sold a few of his estates

---

* Hadrian's villa at Tivoli, with its gardens and pools, covered 200 acres. The walls of Pompeii, a city with more than ten thousand inhabitants, enclosed only 160 acres.

† The gardens of Domitian's great Alban villa (now beneath the papal summer palace at Castel Gandolfo) descended a steep ridge via terraces that supported cisterns, a theater, and a lakeside nymphaeum. Tiberius's villa at Sperlonga incorporated a natural sea cave, used as a dining room. It was decorated with a sculptural group representing the blinding of the cyclops Polyphemus by Odysseus.

‡ If we can believe the satirist Juvenal, a private bath might cost 600,000 sestertii—and still be less expensive than a new colonnaded drive.

for 70 million sestertii.* Especially in the heart of Rome, the land over which these mansions sprawled was extremely valuable. Caesar reportedly spent 100 million sestertii simply buying the property on which his forum was constructed.[8]

During the late republican era, a political career could be costlier than any estate.† When Julius Caesar was aedile, he provided at personal expense games that featured 320 pairs of gladiators. One of his contemporaries constructed two wooden theaters that could pivot to join together, forming an amphitheater. Most extravagant of all was Marcus Aemilius Scaurus, who imported 360 marble columns from Greece to decorate a temporary theater. Such gestures drove ambitious politicians deeply into debt: At one point, Caesar reportedly owed more than 30 million sestertii to his creditors.[9]

A final way the Roman elite frittered away their fortunes was on their own funerals. When cremation was in vogue, they had their pyres loaded with precious incense. The funeral procession of Sulla included a life-size figure of the late dictator made from compressed incense and cinnamon. Nero reportedly burned more than a full year's crop of Arabian incense at the funeral of his wife Poppaea.‡ One wealthy freedman stipulated in his will that his heirs were to spend no less than 1.1 million sestertii on his funeral.[10]

With their surrounding gardens, tomb complexes might cover an acre or more. The funerary plot of a rich man in Gaul, which included a pond and orchard, had a permanent staff of four groundskeepers. The largest tombs, like the Pyramid of Cestius or the Mausoleum of Caecilia Metella, were almost pharaonic in scale—fitting monuments to a life of excess.[11]

---

* It was dangerous to own a suburban estate that was too opulent. Claudius ordered the last private owner of the Gardens of Lucullus to take his own life; the body was cremated in the gardens, on a pyre positioned so that its flames would not damage any of the ornamental trees. A century and a half later, Commodus executed the fabulously wealthy Quintili brothers because he coveted their villa on the Via Appia.

† Politics were still expensive in imperial Rome. Under the less scrupulous emperors, offices could be bought—at, of course, an extortionate price. Holders of the major priesthoods were obligated to host inaugural banquets that often cost more than a million sestertii.

‡ Elite funerals were often accompanied by gladiatorial matches and other entertainments. During the reign of Tiberius, the people of one Italian town refused to allow a man to bury his wealthy father until he had promised funerary games.

How Expensive Was Purple Clothing?

$\mathcal{T}$he terms *Tyrian* and *royal purple* were used to describe the whole range of hues, from crimson to cobalt, that ancient dyers produced from murex shellfish. But the most iconic color was deepest violet, almost black, with the iridescent shimmer of dried blood.* Unlike most ancient vegetable dyes, royal purple was virtually immune to washing and weathering. When Alexander the Great captured the Persian treasury at Susa, he found stores of purple dye, still fresh, that had been taken from Greece 190 years before.[1]

True royal purple could be produced only from three related species of sea snails, collectively known as murex. (This had been discovered, according to myth, when Hercules was walking with his dog on a beach near Tyre. The dog gobbled up a snail, and Hercules saw that its mouth was stained purple.) Picked by hand or caught in traps, the snails† were kept alive until the time came to punch through their shells and extract the "flower of purple"—the hypobranchial gland, which secretes milky mucus.[2]

---

* Not all our evidence is literary. Examples of ancient royal purple cloth have been discovered in Athens's Kerameikos Cemetery, the (supposed) tomb of Philip II at Vergina, a royal Bronze Age burial at Qatna, and other funerary contexts from Egypt to the Crimea. Royal purple vestments dating to the Early Middle Ages are preserved in a number of European cathedral treasuries, notably those of Trier, Aachen, and Maastricht. The paintings found on the walls of Pompeiian houses and Macedonian tombs provide glimpses of royal purple garments, as do the mosaics of San Vitale in Ravenna.

† The flesh of murex snails was sometimes eaten to strengthen the stomach. If incinerated—which would have improved the smell, if nothing else—it was thought to relieve toothache and blisters.

The process by which reeking heaps of glands were trans-
muted into precious dye has been lost. According to Pliny the Elder,
the glands were placed in vats, salted, and heated in water for an
extended period. Modern attempts to replicate these steps, however,
have been only partially successful. Although dyeworks peppered the
Mediterranean coast from Spain to Syria, the most famous center of
production was Tyre, notorious for the density and pungency of its
facilities. In late antiquity, Tyre was chosen as the site of an imperially owned "purple factory,"* complete with a textile mill and a fleet
of snail-collecting boats.[3]

Because thousands of snails[†] were required to manufacture a
gram of dye, purple cloth was always a luxury. Aristocratic mummies
in New Kingdom Egypt were sometimes wrapped with purple ban-
dages. Homer's immortal nymphs wove sea-purple robes. Clytem-
nestra spread a purple carpet for Agamemnon. In Rome, members
of the Equestrian order wore tunics with narrow purple stripes; a
broader stripe marked the tunics of senators. The toga praetexta,
donned by high officials, had a purple hem. The toga picta of a
triumphing general was purple with gold embroidery. Tragic actors
wore mock-purple cloaks. So, in grim parody, did criminals condemned to the arena. Fashionable dinner guests sported purple robes.
Luxury editions of books were bound with purple covers. Sacrificial
sheep were sometimes splashed with purple dye.[4]

Persian monarchs wore purple cloaks, and Alexander imitated
them. Purple draped the dining couches of the Ptolemies. When Jesus
was being mocked as "King of the Jews," a tattered purple mantle was
flung over his shoulders. Roman emperors wore an all-purple toga[‡]
and even signed their names with purple ink. They were buried in
sarcophagi made of porphyry, the stone closest in color to royal purple.
Caligula executed a king of Mauretania because he envied his purple
cloak. Nero, who made it illegal for anyone besides himself to wear the

---

* Quality control was remorseless. By imperial decree, any employee found to have
colored cloth with substandard dye was to be executed.

† A dump discovered near a late antique dyeing facility on the south coast of Turkey is
believed to contain the shells of some sixty million snails.

‡ Marcus Aurelius tried to balance the budget by selling purple robes and other
treasures from the palace storehouses. A century later, the king of Persia sent Aurelian a
pallium dyed an especially brilliant shade of purple. A series of later emperors tried unsuc-
cessfully to replicate the color.

finest shades of purple, sent undercover agents into Rome's markets to catch sellers of contraband dye. A series of late antique emperors likewise forbade any private citizen to sport the imperial color.* Eventually, even outfitting a ship to fish for murex snails was prohibited.[5]

In classical Athens, a purple cloak cost three minas—300 drachmas—when a family of four could live comfortably for a year on 200. The finest purple cloth was worth its weight in silver, and an especially rich garment could cost two talents—12,000 drachmas. During the reign of Augustus, a pound of Tyrian purple dyestuff cost more than four thousand sestertii. A cloak of second-rate purple might sell for ten thousand and a finer garment for ten times that. Early imperial legionaries, for comparison, earned nine hundred sestertii a year.[6]

According to Diocletian's price edict—which listed the maximum prices that could legally be charged for some 1,500 goods and services—purple slippers could cost no more than 80 denarii.† Prices for garments were far higher: up to 15,000 denarii for a wool cloak with purple bands, 40,000 for a purple-striped silk undershirt, and 48,000 for a hooded dalmatic. A pound of purple wool was worth 50,000 denarii; a pound of purple silk, 150,000.[7]

To contextualize those numbers, an egg—according to the price edict—was worth 1 denarius; a pint of Egyptian beer, 2; a bundle of asparagus, 6; a pound of pork, 12; and a sow's udder, 20. A chicken cost 30 denarii; a fattened pheasant, 250; and a peacock, 300. A pound of soap was 24 denarii; a pound of ivory, 150; a pound of Arabian saffron, 2,000. Up to 400 could be charged for a sheep; 7,000 for a pack donkey; 25,000 for a Bactrian camel. An attorney might ask 1,000 denarii for pleading a case; a mature male slave could be sold for no more than 30,000.

A pound of purple silk, in other words, was worth as much as 75,000 pints of beer; 7,500 succulent sow udders; 600 fattened pheasants; 150 lawsuits; 6 Bactrian camels; or a single first-class male lion.‡

---

* This law was clearly honored in the breach. Employees of the imperial factory at Tyre confessed to making a sleeveless purple tunic for an ambitious deacon. An imperial investigation revealed that the same factory had used at least three hundred pounds of purple silk for illegal private commissions.

† The denarius of the early imperial era had been debased into oblivion over the course of the third century. The price edict's denarius was a unit of account; 72,000 were equivalent in value to a pound of gold.

‡ The maximum price for a lioness (or a second-class lion) was 125,000 denarii. A leopard was worth up to 75,000; a first-class bear, 25,000; and an ostrich, 5,000.

· 24 ·

How Did Elections Work?

$\mathcal{T}$here was no concept in the classical world more mistrusted or despised than democracy. Most city-states were oligarchies. Kings and chieftains ruled the rest. Democracy, in the opinion of nearly all ancient intellectuals, was fundamentally flawed—a system dominated by the poor and their demagogues.[1]

This prejudice was shaped by the experiences of classical Athens, the most iconic ancient democracy. At Athens, the *ekklesia* (the assembly of all citizens) met forty times a year, enacting laws, issuing taxes, and declaring war. Every citizen was expected to attend and vote, and those over thirty were eligible for selection as officials. There were more than a thousand officials, all serving one-year terms on boards and committees. Most, including the five hundred city councilors, were chosen by lot. Around a hundred officials, however, were elected by the *ekklesia*. Of these, the most important were the ten strategoi, the generals.*

Generals were expected to have professional expertise in how to wage and win wars. As a result, they were exempt from the usual limitations on office holding and could be elected year after year. Chosen every spring, they held office from that summer to the next. At least one general accompanied every military expedition. Those who remained in Athens supervised the conscription of citizens and

---

* Important officials in other Greek cities were also elected. In Sparta, for example, the twenty-eight members of the Gerousia (literally, Council of Old Men) were elected. So were the five strategoi of Cyrene.

maintenance of the fleet. If the *ekklesia* decided that a general was not performing adequately, he could be deposed, tried, and punished. After the Battle of Arginusae in the Peloponnesian War, the assembly voted to execute all eight commanding generals for failing to rescue the crews of disabled triremes.[2]

Despite that precedent, there seems to have never been a shortage of candidates for general. Men were not expected to put themselves forward for the post; they were nominated by friends and allies. Nor were they permitted to campaign. They were simply proposed to the *ekklesia* and chosen by a show of hands.*

In the less egalitarian atmosphere of the Roman Republic, by contrast, all the tricks of modern electioneering were tested and refined. The Republic was an oligarchy with suppressed democratic tendencies.† Candidates for office were inevitably rich and usually members of well-established families. But every year, these proud magnates subjected themselves to the choice of the people.[3]

Besides the consuls, the chief officials of the Republic, the Romans elected praetors, quaestors, and aediles—responsible, respectively, for administering justice, supervising state finances, and maintaining the city. By the Late Republic, these were the steps of the cursus honorum, the sequence of offices that culminated in the consulship.‡ On a parallel path to power were the tribunes of the plebs, whose far-reaching authority was potentially opposed to that of the other magistrates.

---

* Spartan elections went to the candidate who received the loudest applause.

† The Greek historian Polybius described the Roman constitution as a blend of monarchic, oligarchic, and democratic elements. By his account, the two consuls had the kingly authority of leading armies and proposing legislation. The senate, the all-powerful advisory council, provided aristocratic supervision over the affairs of state. The Roman people voted on laws and elected officials. Modern historians have traditionally interpreted the Republic as an oligarchic power-sharing arrangement, designed to allow members of prominent families to compete among themselves. The fact that every office from the consulship down was held with colleagues and limited to one-year terms made it difficult for any individual to dominate the entire political system and ensured ambitious aristocrats access to offices that gave them authority and prestige. Over the past few decades, the democratic elements of the Roman constitution have received more recognition.

‡ Sulla mandated a minimum age for each step in the cursus: twenty-nine for quaestor, thirty-nine for praetor, forty-two for consul. Among the most ambitious candidates, there was fierce competition to win each office in the first year of eligibility. Only the consulship could be held multiple times, normally after an interval of at least ten years.

Roman officials were elected by popular assemblies. Consuls and praetors were chosen by the *comitia centuriata*, which was organized into 193 voting groups known as centuries. Early in Roman history, the centuries had been military units levied in order of wealth.* To the end of the Republic, they continued to be convened by property class and called in order from richest to poorest. Each century had a single vote, determined by the majority of its members' ballots. The wealthiest Romans were allocated dozens of centuries. The multitudes of the landless poor, by contrast, were permitted only one. The system was thus weighted in favor of the rich, whose votes effectively determined every election.

The other important voting assembly was the *comitia tributa*, responsible for choosing quaestors and aediles. The same body, convened without the few Patrician clans, appears to have selected the tribunes of the plebs. Here, Romans voted by tribe, a historical division based on the city region or rural district where they lived or from which they had emigrated. There were thirty-five tribes, four urban and the rest rural. In theory, this arrangement gave outlying areas outsize influence. A steady influx of rural-registered immigrants into Rome, however, seems to have corrected the imbalance. Although the tribal assembly was not intrinsically biased toward the rich, only wealthy citizens were likely to travel into Rome from the rural districts to vote.

Roman voters were presented with a choice between politicians, not—normally—between dramatically different policies. During the Late Republic, some men were described as *optimates* or *populares*, upholders of tradition or supporters of reform. These groupings, however, never approximated political parties or even clearly defined positions. They were nothing more or less than labels, indiscriminately applied.

---

* In keeping with their military origins, the centuries of the *comitia centuriata* were divided into officers, enlisted men, and "others" (i.e., those too poor to afford weapons). Most of the centuries (170 of the 193) belonged to the enlisted class. These were divided into eighty-five centuries of "younger soldiers" (men aged seventeen to forty-six) and eighty-five centuries of "older soldiers" (men between forty-six and sixty).

Elections were held in summer or early autumn. The date was announced by the presiding magistrate, traditionally three market days—three eight-day weeks—in advance. By then, most candidates had been campaigning for months. A letter supposedly written by Quintus Cicero, brother of the famous orator, offers advice on the process. The candidate (our word comes from the shining *toga candida* worn by Roman office seekers) should spend time in the Forum with a crowd of clients and supporters.* He should greet citizens and shake hands. He should avoid talking about divisive issues. Whenever possible, he should smile.[4]

Some Romans were better at campaigning than others. When the haughty Publius Scipio Nasica was canvassing in the Forum, for example, he shook the calloused paw of a farmer and joked that the man must walk around on his hands. Bystanders, interpreting this comment as an insult, spread the word that Scipio had no respect for working men, and he lost the election. A senator lost an election for praetor after it was remembered that he had presided over a public banquet at which the seats were covered with rank goat skins and food was served in coarse clay pots. Though technically illegal, bribery of the electorate was rampant. One senator, accused of bribery in a consular election, secured his acquittal by bribing the prosecution. Then, as consul, he strengthened the penalties of the antibribery law.[5]

As the election approached, political graffiti went up all over Rome,† painted at intersections and along important streets. To judge from examples preserved at Pompeii, they usually proclaimed a prominent individual or organization's support for a candidate. This might be accompanied by a slogan—"An honest young man," "Worthy of public office"—or by a call to action: "Get up and vote!" More elaborate notices outlined campaign promises and even praised

---

* Candidates were often accompanied by a nomenclator, a slave trained to memorize the names of potential allies and supporters.

† Sometimes, a sign painter included his own name by way of advertising. At Pompeii, a certain Aemilius Celer was especially prolific. He seems to have been rather protective of his work; to the end of one sign, he added, "If any jealous person destroys this, may he fall ill." A notice on a tomb in Rome voiced the hope that any candidate who scribbled graffiti on it would lose his election.

candidates in verse. Parodies appeared alongside the official signs, in which such groups as "runaway slaves" and "midnight drinkers" advertised their endorsements.[6]

On the day designated for the election, the Roman people assembled to vote. Originally, the process was public. Citizens stated the name of the candidate they supported to a polling officer, who tallied the vote with a dot on a writing tablet. Later, the secret ballot was introduced. Each citizen received a wax tablet at the base of a narrow wooden platform known as the voting bridge. Once he had marked the initials of his preferred candidate, he walked up the bridge and deposited his ballot in a vase or basket, which was elevated to discourage tampering.[7]

Election interference, a time-honored Roman tradition, worsened amid the chaos of the Late Republic. Unscrupulous candidates hired thugs to stand along the bridges and threaten voters. In extreme cases, gangs blockaded the voting enclosure or hurled rocks at the assembled citizens. Some elections were ended when mobs tore down the bridges and destroyed the ballot boxes. Others were invalidated by vote tampering; in one instance, Cato the Younger noticed that many ballots had the same handwriting.[8]

A Roman denarius depicting an election. One man is receiving a tablet from an attendant; the other is placing his ballot in a receptacle. *Public domain*

By the end of Cato's career, however, elections no longer mattered. Once he became dictator, Julius Caesar simply appointed his supporters to the offices they desired; Cicero joked that it had become harder to win a seat on the city council of Pompeii than to join the Roman senate. Although Augustus campaigned in the traditional manner on behalf of his friends, it was an open secret that the careers of Rome's politicians were determined by his whim. Tiberius finally transferred elections to the senate, ending the tumultuous half-millennium history of popular voting in ancient Rome.[9]

• 25 •

How Did They Pay Taxes?

𝒯he citizens of a Greek polis typically had few financial obliga-
tions. Spartans, for example, were required only to supply the public
mess halls. Lower- and middle-income Athenians, likewise, paid
no taxes. Wealthy citizens, however, were responsible for the public
programs known as liturgies, which ranged from training theatrical
choruses to outfitting triremes. The rich also paid a special tax to
support the troops in times of war.

At first, the Roman system was even simpler. The Early Republic periodically levied a property tax on citizens to pay military
expenses. Otherwise, it derived most of its revenue from the sale and
rent of public lands and from such indirect taxes as the 5 percent duty
on freed slaves. The vast influx of wealth brought by the conquest of
the Hellenistic kingdoms allowed the Republic to end direct taxation
of Roman citizens throughout Italy. In the newly conquered provinces, however, land and poll taxes were instituted. These were often
collected by the private contractors known as *publicani*,* who tended
to maximize their profits at the provincials' expense.[1]

To stem such abuses and support his new standing army,
Augustus reformed the tax system. The *publicani* were restricted
to customs duties, and the elites of provincial cities were made
responsible for collecting the taxes of their fellow citizens. A duty

---

* In the Gospels, publicans are equated with sinners; Jesus urges them not to extort
money or take more than their due. In Roman Egypt, tax collectors arrived with retinues
of hired thugs who beat anyone reluctant to pay.

of 4 percent was imposed on the sale of slaves, and another of 5 percent, on inheritances.* Recurring censuses were established to keep the tax rolls updated.[2]

Because the Romans tended to keep existing systems in place when they annexed a territory, taxes differed from province to province and even from city to city.† To complicate matters further, provincial cities collected taxes of their own, primarily in the form of customs duties. Rates on interprovincial trade were usually between 2 and 5 percent. Tariffs on goods from outside the empire, by contrast, were as high as 25 percent. Taxes could be paid in cash, in kind, or both, depending on local custom. Cyrene paid in silphium, a plant prized as an aphrodisiac; the Frisians paid in oxhides. According to one ancient author, land taxes ranged from one-seventh to one-fifth of the crop and could be tariffed by property type, with fertile farmland charged most and pasture, least.[3]

The most relentlessly taxed province was Egypt. Between the ages of fourteen and sixty, all male Egyptians had to pay a poll tax. Even the dead were charged for the year of their demise. Farmers had to surrender a portion of their grain and were taxed separately for all other crops and every animal. Tradesmen were taxed on their wares. Additional duties were levied to maintain canals and dikes, to entertain officials, and to supply temples. During the reign of Marcus Aurelius, more than forty different taxes, rents, and fees were collected in the modest Egyptian town of Karanis.

In the wake of the financial crises of the third century, Diocletian overhauled the Roman tax system. The land and poll taxes were now assessed by standard units of area and population, on a rate determined by the annual needs of the state. The practice of taking censuses was revived to keep assessments updated. To circumvent the persistent problem of inflation, most taxes were levied in kind.

---

* After the Jewish Revolt, every Jew in the Roman Empire was forced to pay a punitive tax of two drachmas per person to the treasury of the Temple of Jupiter Capitolinus. The tax remained in effect through the third century.

† In return for exceptional loyalty or services, some communities were granted freedom from taxation. The citizens of Aphrodisias, a "free" city in what is now Turkey, proudly inscribed every document that confirmed their immunity on a wall of their theater, including a decree exempting them from the much-resented nail tax.

Both before and after these changes, the Roman tax rate was something like 5 percent of the empire's GDP—a level comparable to that of eighteenth-century France. Virtually all modern states derive a much higher percentage of their revenue from taxes and levy taxes at rates that would have horrified the Romans. The Romans, however, had a much harder time paying their taxes than we do.[4]

Most Romans were farmers, living close to the subsistence level. In a good year, they produced enough to feed their families and a small surplus for taxes and other expenses. In a bad year, there would be a smaller surplus or none at all. Although tax systems in some parts of the empire—notably Egypt—took account of droughts and floods, and emperors occasionally remitted the taxes of areas affected by natural disasters, tax collectors were never known for their compassion.

Even at the best of times, the tax burden was regressive. The same rates were applied to rich and poor, falling with crushing weight on those with the least to spare. Tax collectors and financial officials were almost always corrupt, demanding bribes or inflated payments. The poor, lacking the allies or resources to resist these demands, had no choice but to pay*—unless, like desperate families in Egypt, they abandoned their lands and fled.[5]

The taxes paid by the rich, by contrast, were modest in relation to their means. During the Pax Romana, elites across the empire became wealthier than ever before. In many places, spurred by a combination of political savvy and noblesse oblige, they poured their wealth into public buildings. The monumental cityscapes they created are the most durable legacy of the inequitable tax system of the Roman Empire.

---

* Alternatively, they could try to commit tax fraud. A recently published papyrus from the Judaean Desert records a trial for forgery and tax evasion in the reign of Hadrian. The main defendant appears to have concocted a scheme that involved the fictive sale of slaves, either to avoid paying taxes on those transactions or to reduce his apparent wealth (and tax liability).

How Did They Cope
with Natural Disasters?

*U*sually, the Mediterranean world was a good place to live. The climate was temperate. Most regions received enough rain to grow wheat or barley. Droughts, though common, were localized; short-distance trade, facilitated by numerous natural harbors, relieved most food shortages. But in Rome—the ancient Mediterranean city we know best—the weather was often less than clement. Rain rushing down deforested hills filled the Tiber, sometimes submerging half the city.* Winter could bring bitter cold and heavy snow: One blizzard blocked streets with seven-foot drifts. With summer came blistering heat and terrifying fires. On at least three occasions, tornadoes struck the city.† Earthquakes leveled whole districts without warning.¹

Most Greeks and Romans attributed natural disasters to the gods. Zeus was the source of all weather, and the thunderbolt

---

* During the great flood of 1598, the water around the Pantheon was twenty-one feet deep, and boats could row as far as the base of the Spanish Steps.

† In 156 BCE, a storm—apparently a small tornado—roared through the center of Rome, destroying a portico near the Circus Flaminius, damaging many houses in the vicinity, and obliterating the riverside mansion of the Pontifex Maximus. A century later, another tornado appeared with a sudden thunderstorm, tearing up trees and flattening a bridge. Finally, just before the assassination of Julius Caesar, what appears to have been yet another tornado touched down in the heart of Rome, overturning a statue of Cicero, breaking the doors of a temple, and destroying buildings and trees. We have much more detail for the early modern period. On the evening of June 11, 1749, a tornado formed over the Tyrrhenian Sea and tore a twenty-mile path along the Tiber. Entering the southeast corner of Rome, it left a trail of devastation roughly two hundred feet wide, stripping roofs from buildings and even cobbles from the streets, before leaping the walls and heading toward Tivoli.

was his weapon. Poseidon was the earth shaker,* worshipped as "restrainer of the earth" and the "stabilizer" in hopes of staying his wrath. Early Christians also ascribed disasters to divine wrath. The liturgy of the Greek Orthodox Church still marks the anniversaries of seven ancient earthquakes.[2]

Philosophers proposed rationalist theories. Thales, for example, connected changes in the weather with the motions of the heavens and conjectured that the earth floated in a universal sea, whose motions were felt as tremors. His student Anaximander hypothesized that thunderstorms were produced by currents of wind agitating clouds and that variations in the wetness of the soil produced subterranean cracks and convulsions. The first truly systematic discussion was Aristotle's *Meteorology*. Aristotle conjectured that the sun's heat draws warm, dry air from the land and cool, damp air from the sea. The interactions of these air currents produce the weather. Wind, according to Aristotle, is generated when warm air—which tends to rise—meets the rotating sphere of the heavens. Earthquakes are the counterparts of windstorms, produced by air currents moving through hollows in the earth.[3]

Reactions to natural disasters tended to combine reverence and practicality. Once, for example, an earthquake struck just after a Spartan army marched into the territory of a neighboring city. Some of the soldiers, regarding the quake as a sign of divine disapproval, wanted to retreat. But the Spartan king, reasoning that an earthquake was as likely to be a sign of approbation, simply sacrificed to Poseidon and continued forward.[4]

Although earthquakes rattled every period of classical history, we know most about those that took place in the Roman imperial era.† Perhaps the most destructive occurred in 365, when a tremor

---

* It was believed that Poseidon had used an earthquake to tear open the Vale of Tempe, the gorge between Olympus and Mount Ossa.

† Earthquake damage is still visible at some archaeological sites. At Scythopolis—Beit She'an in modern Israel—visitors can see the broken columns of the arcades along the main street, lying where a late antique earthquake felled them. At the center of Selinus— modern Selinunte in western Sicily—the earthquake-shattered columns of a colossal temple form a heap three stories high. At Pompeii, traces of the earthquake that rattled the city seventeen years before the eruption of Vesuvius are everywhere. The Temple of Jupiter overlooking the city's forum was still under restoration when it was buried by the volcano.

Mount Silpius, the ancient citadel of Antioch, looming over the rubble of the 2023 earthquake. *Author's photo*

centered near Crete—where parts of the coast were uplifted by thirty feet—sent tsunamis roaring across the Mediterranean.* The harbor of Alexandria was destroyed, and ships were deposited miles inland.[5]

In the winter of 115, Antioch was leveled by an earthquake with an estimated magnitude of 7.5. Trajan, then visiting the city, crawled to safety through a window of his collapsing palace. For several days, as aftershocks rattled the ruins, the emperor and his retinue camped on the racetrack of the Hippodrome. Four centuries later, during the reign of Justinian, an even more devastating earthquake struck Antioch, reportedly killing 250,000 people. Fires raged over the rubble, destroying almost everything spared by the tremors. The city's octagonal cathedral, built by Constantine, was one of the last buildings to burn.[6]

The effectiveness of ancient disaster relief depended on the ability and willingness of local authorities to mobilize resources. In

---

* The historian Ammianus describes how the sea withdrew from the harbor of Alexandria, allowing people to wander on the seabed and gather fish by hand, before returning to inundate the city.

the wake of the great fire of 64, Nero opened public buildings and his own gardens to those who had lost their homes, set up refugee camps, and lowered the price of grain. Later, he supervised the reconstruction of the burnt districts, clearing away rubble and establishing financial incentives for rebuilding.* After the eruption of Vesuvius, Titus created a senatorial commission to coordinate relief and made funds available for the reconstruction of the devastated cities.[7]

Although cities stricken by earthquakes would receive little immediate assistance, they could appeal for help in rebuilding. When an earthquake destroyed Rhodes in 226 BCE, the citizens received promises of assistance from many quarters, including an offer from Ptolemy III to re-erect the fallen Colossus. Four centuries later, when the city of Smyrna suffered catastrophic earthquake damage, the orator Aelius Aristides sent an appeal to Marcus Aurelius for financial aid. The emperor obliged.[8]

Perhaps the most impressive example of ancient disaster relief followed the earthquake (and subsequent Persian sack) that devastated Antioch under Justinian. The entire city was reconstructed with imperial funds. The walls were rerouted for greater security. The river was diverted to a new channel. Streets were laid out, with sewers, stoas, fountains, and markets. Two great churches rose from the rubble. Hospices were set up for the poor and sick. Finally, in hopes of supplementing the emperor's largesse with divine protection, Antioch was renamed Theopolis—"city of God."[9]

---

* The boats that carried grain up the Tiber from Ostia were filled with rubble for the return trip, dumping the debris in coastal marshes. Nero encouraged the outer walls of new buildings to be made of peperino tufa, which was believed to be fireproof.

· 27 ·

What Do Their Tombstones Tell Us?

$\mathscr{F}$rom the days of Solon to the reign of Alexander, the luminaries of Athens were laid to rest in the Kerameikos Cemetery, just outside the Dipylon Gate.* Some tombs were in the form of elegant marble vases. Others were marked by sculptures of lions, sirens, and—in one case—a life-size bull. The most prominent, however, were sculpted stelae. These are among the masterpieces of classical art: young soldiers in heroic poses; parents bidding farewell to their children; aristocratic ladies in festival dress, gazing out into eternity.

With few exceptions, the epitaphs of the Kerameikos tombs record little more than the name and patronymic of the deceased. That would change during the Hellenistic and imperial eras, when epitaphs across the Greek world became much more detailed. For ease of reference, however, this chapter focuses on Latin epitaphs, which provide a uniquely rich source of evidence for life and death in antiquity.

Not all Romans could afford a tomb. The poor were often buried in reused vases or under loose tiles, with a wooden post or nothing at all to indicate the place. For centuries, a potter's field, tangled with weeds and white with bones, sprawled just outside one of Rome's gates. Even within the affluent families who were most likely to build tombs, patterns of commemoration differed. The graves of infants and young children—especially girls—were frequently

---

* In early days of the Athenian Democracy and again under Demetrius of Phaleron (a distinguished orator turned Macedonian quisling), ostentatious tombs were outlawed. The most impressive gravestones in the Kerameikos were erected between these bans.

The street of tombs outside Pompeii's Herculaneum Gate. *Author's photo*

left unmarked. Women who died soon after marriage, by contrast, were exceptionally likely to receive a monument. Freedmen, eager to demonstrate their status, commissioned tombs more often than the freeborn. Soldiers and veterans are better attested than civilians.[1]

The most common form of tomb in the Roman world was an upright stone slab. Styles, however, varied widely with place and period. Barrel-shaped stelae, for example, often marked tombs in Mauretania, while sculptures of bulls and bears were common in Lusitania. Through the second century, when cremation was standard in Italy and the western provinces, urns containing the ashes of the dead were often placed in small funerary altars or the niches of a columbarium.* As inhumation

---

* Most columbaria were managed by burial clubs. After paying the entry fee (in one instance, one hundred sestertii and an amphora of good wine), each member was assigned a niche. When he died, the club would pay for his funeral and inter his ashes. (There was a bustling trade in secondhand niches and urns, which suggests that some clubs were less than totally committed to the idea of eternal remembrance.) Wealthy families sometimes set aside a columbarium for their slaves and freedmen; one belonging to Livia, the wife of Augustus, had no fewer than three thousand niches. The equally capacious columbarium built for Augustus's freedmen now houses a restaurant.

became more common, sarcophagi were increasingly prominent,* either as stand-alone monuments or as elements of a larger tomb.[2]

Both before and after the transition to inhumation, wealthier Romans were often buried in mausoleums. The most common type, well represented in the necropolis under St. Peter's Basilica, was a rectangular structure with a vaulted ceiling, sometimes surrounded by a courtyard.† Some mausoleums, like the Tomb of the Julii at Glanum or the Tomb of Lucius Poblicius at Cologne, took the form of stylized temples. Others were more idiosyncratic, like the Pyramid of Cestius or the rotunda built by Augustus.‡

The one indispensable element of a Roman epitaph was the name of the deceased.§ Age at death was frequently recorded. Though sometimes given in years, months, and even days, this was more often an approximation, rounded to the nearest multiple of five or ten years and sometimes qualified with the phrase *plus minus*—"more or less."¶ Before the empire became Christian, the date of death was almost never given.

---

* Inhumation became standard for members of the imperial family during the third century. The body of Justinian was so well embalmed that the crusaders, pillaging the emperor's sarcophagus more than six centuries after his death, found it almost perfectly preserved. Empress Galla Placidia was apparently buried in a seated position. According to a Renaissance legend, she could be seen through a crack in her sarcophagus, still dressed in her imperial robes, until a boy stuck a candle into the coffin for a better look and accidentally incinerated the body.

† Because Roman families commemorated the dead at annual festivals, mausoleums were often equipped with facilities for communal dining and even rooftop terraces. During these celebrations, libations were sometimes poured over the ashes or bones of the deceased through purpose-built holes.

‡ Most emperors were interred in mausolea—in the case of the Julio-Claudians, the one built by Augustus. Some, however, never received a formal burial. Vitellius, Elagabalus, and Petronius were flung into the Tiber. Constantine II was dumped into the River Alsa. Justinian II and Alexius II were cast into the sea. So was Constantine V, after being posthumously declared a heretic. All that was mortal of Andronicus I was left to rot in a vault of the Hippodrome at Constantinople. The ashes of Phocas were scattered to the winds.

§ Occasionally, the name of a tomb's occupant would be connected with a visual pun; a man named Leo, for example, might have the image of a lion on his stone. These designs, like the text of the epitaph, would be drawn on papyrus and given to the stonecutter. The illiterate carver of one epitaph, discovered in Hippo Regius, apparently inscribed the placeholder text. It reads, in effect, "Here lies a boy, insert name."

¶ One venerable lady, who lived to ninety-nine, insisted that her age be immortalized in her epitaph. Her tragic antithesis was a baby in North Africa, whose life lasted only nine breaths.

From the first century onward, epitaphs often began with the abbreviation *DM—Dis Manibus*, "To the spirits of the departed." The name of the person who had set up the tomb might be recorded. So might the native place of the deceased, their lineage, and their occupation. Selections from the departed's will were sometimes inscribed, along with such practical details as the size of the tomb plot and the fines that would be levied against anyone who disturbed or defaced the monument. The epitaph might end with the formula *sit tibi terra levis*—"May the earth lie lightly upon you"—or the less evocative abbreviation *HMHNS—hoc monumentum heredibus non sequetur*, "This monument will not pass to my heirs."[3]

Despite their lapidary nature, epitaphs are a treasure trove of historical information. They record careers, for example, that seldom appear in literary sources. We encounter slaughterers of sacrificial animals, aqueduct engineers, oracle interpreters, and professional fanatics (men who specialized in exciting the crowds at sacred rituals). One man is described as a *medicus equarius et venator*—that is, a gladiator with a side hustle as a veterinarian. Another is commemorated as a juggler of glass balls in the baths. A former farm laborer celebrates his rise to city councilor. A former slave, born in Parthia, records how he gained his freedom.[4]

Epitaphs provide insight into the intricacies of the imperial household, with its thousands of slaves and freedmen. A high-ranking slave accountant of Tiberius, for example, had a tomb set up by sixteen of his own slaves, who had jobs ranging from secretary to silver steward. Alongside a manager of inheritances received by the emperor and a librarian of the imperial collections, we find Dorcas the hairdresser; Chia the masseuse; Titus Primitivus, master chef; and Tiberius Claudius Zosimus, supervisor of food tasters.[5]

Epitaphs also shed light on the careers of soldiers. Some were cut short, like that of a teenager who joined the Praetorian Guard and died while accompanying Hadrian on his travels. On the opposite extreme was the grizzled centurion who recorded that he had served with thirteen legions over the course of forty-six years. One detailed inscription records every position that a legionary ever held, including stints as a hospital orderly, prison guard, clerk, and recordkeeper. Another boasts that Soranus, best and bravest of the Batavian Horse Guard, could swim across the Danube in full armor and was such a fast shot that he could transfix one of his own arrows while it was still falling to the ground.[6]

Although their epitaphs record careers ranging from fishmonger to silk merchant, women were usually remembered as wives and mothers.* One grieving husband recorded that he had lived with his wife for forty years "without any cause for complaint." A senator praised his better half for saving him during the proscriptions of the Second Triumvirate. A less conventional eulogy hailed a woman who had lived in apparent harmony with two male lovers.[7]

Occasionally, epitaphs note the cause of death. A soldier died heroically while fighting a fire. A mosaicist fell off his ladder. A boxer died in the ring. A wife was murdered by her husband after twenty-eight years of marriage. A boy was poisoned by his stepmother.[8]

Perhaps the most evocative Roman epitaphs are those written in the voice of the deceased.† Some are curses against anyone who disturbs the tomb: "May he who defecates here be blinded!" or, more creatively, "If anyone disturbs my remains, may he live a long time in agony, and then be turned away by the gods below when he dies." Others are more plaintive: "I raise my hands against the god who carried my life away." Resignation is a common theme: "I was not, I was; I am not, I care not." So is Epicurean indulgence: "Mix the wine, wear garlands, and drink wherever you are—and don't forget to make love to beautiful women!" There are occasional stabs at humor, like the actor who recorded, "I used to die onstage—but never like this!" And there are, finally, expressions of grief that cut across the gulf of two thousand years, like the epitaph written by a plasterer named Pompeius Catussa for his wife: "Go visit the Baths of Apollo, as I used to with my wife. I wish I still could."[9]

---

* In a celebrated speech, the censor Metellus Numidicus urged Romans to marry because "we cannot do without women, although we cannot live comfortably with them." Children, in his view, justified the inconvenience. The man who gave thanks in his wife's epitaph that she was finally dead doubtless sympathized.

† The speaker is not necessarily human. One epitaph from Rome is written in the voice of Margarita, a little white dog who acknowledged "barking more than she needed to."

V
BELIEFS AND CONTROVERSIES

How Different Were the Greek and Roman Gods?

*B*oth the Greeks and the Romans worshipped hundreds of deities. Because classical polytheism was founded on a mass of local traditions, there was little agreement on the exact number or nature of those gods. Cicero complained that there were three different Zeuses, five varieties of Helios, and at least five wholly incompatible Aphrodites. New gods were constantly added to the pantheon. The private chapel of Emperor Severus Alexander supposedly included statues of Jesus, Orpheus, and Abraham. The satirist Lucian imagined Zeus trying to impose order on an increasingly crowded Olympus, where stocks of heavenly nectar were running short and dog-headed Anubis was irritating everyone with his barking.[1]

At the pinnacle of this teeming numinous universe were the Olympians, the twelve gods headed by Zeus and Hera. Since the time of Homer—and, in some cases, since the Bronze Age—they had been the preeminent deities of the Greek world.* Merchants and colonists brought them to Italy in the eighth century BCE, just as Rome was coalescing into a city.

Scholars used to think that the Romans originally worshipped abstractions.† It was suggested that Venus, for example, was nothing

---

* Although many members of the educated elite came to reject the gods of Homer and the myths, the *Iliad* and *Odyssey* remained the foundation of Greek education. Stories and maxims from them were spread to the illiterate majority via media ranging from drama to public art.

† The Romans themselves believed this. In his (mostly lost) survey of Roman religion, Varro claimed that there were no temples or images in early Rome.

more than beauty made manifest before she absorbed the personality and myths of Aphrodite. Although there is probably some truth in this idea, recent research has made it clear that the Greeks influenced Roman religion virtually from the beginning.[2]

By the time Rome emerged into the full light of history, the Roman gods had been assimilated to their Greek counterparts. The Greek Zeus had been equated with the Roman Jupiter; Hera with Juno; Athena with Minerva; and so on. Then or later, there seems to have been little doubt in the Romans' minds that their chief gods were the same as those of the Greeks. The Greeks, for their part, generally accepted that the Romans worshipped the Olympians under different names.* This was a long-standing assumption. In the *Iliad*, the Greeks and Trojans pray to the same gods. A myth claimed that the Egyptian gods were just the Olympians disguised as animals.[3]

In both Greek and Roman thought, the idea that the most important gods had universal power was accompanied by a belief in lesser deities whose authority was limited to a certain place or particular activity. The Romans were much more enthusiastic than the Greeks about worshipping these minor gods. Some belonged to conquered peoples. Although they did not always respect foreign sanctuaries—Pliny tells the story of a legionary who robbed an Armenian temple—the Romans were eager collectors of exotic deities. While on campaign, Roman generals could formally summon the gods of their enemies to join the winning side—a process known as *evocatio*, "calling forth."[4]

In response to a crisis, the senate sometimes invited a powerful foreign god to Rome. Asclepius was brought from Greece to deal with a plague, and Cybele—complete with her self-flagellating eunuch priests—came from Anatolia during the war with Hannibal. "Every people worships its own gods," observed one early Christian author, "but the Romans worship the gods of all." Occasionally,

---

* The identification of the gods with equivalent deities from other cultures was always flexible. In one Roman-era papyrus, Isis is equated with Aphrodite, Persephone, Athena, Hestia, Leto, and Hecate, among others. A similar lack of precision is conveyed by an inscription from Asia Minor that identifies a local goddess with Selene, Artemis, Hecate, Aphrodite, or Demeter. When Hadrian's lover Antinous was declared a god, he was assimilated to Osiris, Dionysus, and Apollo without any apparent friction.

Engraving by Pietro Santi Bartoli (1672) of the rain miracle scene on the Column of Marcus Aurelius. The bearded figure at the center represents the storm. *Public domain*

religious profusion became religious confusion. During the reign of Marcus Aurelius, a legion surrounded by enemy troops and cut off from its water supply was saved by a sudden cloudburst. Most Romans attributed the miracle to Jupiter. Others assigned the storm to the Egyptian gods, evoked by a magician in the emperor's entourage. Christians credited Christ.[5]

Although some Greek gods personified concepts—most famously, Nike (Victory) and Tyche (Fortune)—abstractions were much more prominent in Roman religion. There were important public cults for Concordia (Harmony), Spes (Hope), Virtus (Honor), and Fides (Faith), among many others. The Romans were also distinctive in their willingness to assign gods to highly specific objects and actions. They revered Sterculinus, the god of manuring; Robigo, the god of mildew;* and Vervactor, the god of plowing a fallow field. St. Augustine remarked that no fewer than three Roman gods were responsible for protecting doorways: Cardea presided over hinges;

---

* Ovid describes how the entrails of a dog and a sheep were offered to Robigo, the priest imploring the god to "keep his scaly hands off the harvest."

Limentinus, over the threshold; and Forculus, over the door itself. The goddess Lucina was invoked during childbirth; her counterpart, Statina, guarded the day an infant stood for the first time. None of these deities had Greek equivalents.[6]

Even when gods were shared, as in the case of the Olympians, they were often regarded very differently by the Greeks and Romans. The Romans honored Mars with several important festivals.* The Greeks, by contrast, virtually ignored Ares. The fertility god Saturn presided over Saturnalia, the most famous of all Roman festivals, during which the social order was turned on its head. Although there were broadly similar celebrations in Athens, Cronus—the Greek Titan to whom Saturn was assimilated—was a very different figure. Nor was there any Greek equivalent to the Roman custom of worshipping Jupiter, Juno, and Minerva together.

Ancient authors remarked on the many differences between Greek and Roman religion.† Plutarch produced a lengthy treatise in which he attempted to explain Roman religious customs to Greek readers. Another Greek scholar, Dionysius of Halicarnassus, claimed that the inconsistencies went back to Romulus, who had adopted the Greek gods but rejected their myths. No author, however, attempted to reconcile the systems, in part because the inconsistencies seemed unimportant. Intellectuals of the Roman imperial era insisted that the gods were not the morally ambiguous beings of the myths. They were loftier, more benevolent, further removed from mankind. Only demons—minor divinities who snuffled at sacrificial smoke—moiled in the mortal world.[7]

Such speculations, however, were the preserve of a small, educated elite. Most people, Greek or Roman, continued to worship the

---

* One of these included the curious custom of the October horse. A chariot race was held in the Circus Maximus. The right-hand horse of the winning chariot was sacrificed, and the residents of two neighborhoods staged a mock battle for possession of the head.

† Roman religious ritual tended to be more formal than its Greek counterpart. Close attention was paid to the phrasing of prayers, on the assumption that the gods would respond only if every word was correct. Roman ritual was also strikingly conservative, as witnessed by the continued prominence of the Arval Brethren, a priesthood dedicated to the obscure agricultural goddess Dea Dia. Their hymns, unchanged for nearly a millennium, gradually became unintelligible.

gods as they always had. They cared less about the nature of divinity than about the rituals and prayers that had protected their farms and families since time immemorial. The statues in the local shrine, the charms of the midwife, the hymns sung at festivals—these defined the gods. And because local traditions, in all their variety and inconsistency, lay at the heart of classical religion, no Roman deity could ever be completely identical to his or her Greek counterpart. The gods were too close, and too far away.

Did the Romans Believe That Their Emperors Were Divine?

*R*oman emperors were worshipped as gods. Their statues appeared in household shrines. Their birthdays were celebrated as religious holidays by the legions. In sanctuaries throughout the provinces, priests with gilded crowns offered sacrifice at the feet of their images. Yet emperors, as plagues and assassins repeatedly demonstrated, were all too mortal. Nor, even by the loose standards of the Olympians, did they often exhibit godlike qualities. The emperors themselves were conscious of their ambiguous divinity. As he lay dying, Vespasian joked, "Alas—I think I'm becoming a god." The Romans laughed— and then declared him a god.[1]

The Roman imperial cult had distinguished antecedents. The Greeks had long revered heroes, mortals whose lives or deaths had set them apart. Heracles, the greatest hero, had gone on to join the Olympians. Alexander the Great received divine honors from many Greek cities. The Hellenistic kings, following his example, were revered as gods in their domains. At the Ptolemaic court at Alexandria, there were priests for Alexander, for the reigning king and queen, and for each of their deified predecessors.

There was no precedent for divine kingship in Rome. But in the final years of the Republic, as the traditional restrictions broke down, Julius Caesar appears to have taken tentative steps toward a Hellenistic-style royal cult, complete with an altar and priests. Although he was assassinated before these plans could come to fruition, his political allies—headed by Octavian, the future

Augustus—compelled the senate to recognize Caesar as a god. A temple of the deified Caesar was built beside the Forum, its pediment glittering with a gilded image of the comet* said to have carried the dictator's soul to the heavens.[2]

Augustus presided over the creation of his own imperial cult. In Rome and the western provinces, where there was no tradition of deification, he was carefully distinguished from the gods. Instead of being worshipped directly, he was associated with the goddess Roma or the senate. Alternatively, he was revered through the proxies of his Lares and Genius (guardian spirits) or his Numen (divine power). But in the eastern provinces, where the great generals of the Roman Republic had already been granted divine honors, he was openly worshipped as a god.

After his death, Augustus was formally deified by the senate. He was granted a temple and a college of priests at Rome.† In this, as in so much else, he set the pattern for the next three centuries. Although living emperors continued to be worshipped in the Greek east, they were only recognized as gods in Rome and the western provinces after their deaths. Deification came to be seen as a seal of approval. Only emperors who had ruled well—who were, in other words, politically useful to their successors and retrospectively acceptable to the senate—were worthy of inclusion in the pantheon.[3]

Augustus's immediate successors did not rule well. Tiberius antagonized the senate too often to be apotheosized. Caligula proclaimed himself a living god,‡ but the senate denied his divinity once he was safely dead. Claudius returned to the Augustan model and

---

* This comet—the "Julian Star"—seems to have appeared in the summer of 44 BCE and was visible in the evening sky over Rome for seven consecutive days. It is most often identified with C/-43 K1, observed by astronomers in Han dynasty China. The comet may have been as bright as the planet Venus (the goddess, coincidentally, from whom Caesar claimed descent). The only brighter classical comet was "Aristotle's comet," which rivaled the moon.

† After the funeral of Augustus, a senior senator declared that he had seen the emperor's soul ascending. Cassius, one of Caesar's assassins, reportedly saw a ghostly figure of the dictator during the Battle of Philippi.

‡ Caligula connected the imperial palace with the Temple of Castor and Pollux in the Forum and liked to sit between the statues of the twin gods, receiving homage from his subjects. He also established a temple for himself, complete with a golden cult image, where peacocks, flamingoes, and pheasants were offered in his honor.

was duly deified.* The practice of posthumously deifying worthy emperors had been institutionalized by the beginning of the second century, when—in a speech praising Trajan—Pliny the Younger piously anticipated the time when the emperor would join the gods. It was still important, however, for emperors to avoid seeming eager for divine honors. In response to one of Pliny's letters, Trajan professed reluctance to associate even his statues with those of his deified predecessors.[4]

That the emperors, living and dead, were worshipped by millions of Romans is clear. Whether they were believed to be gods in the same sense as the Olympians is less apparent. Some sources attribute miraculous powers to living emperors. Vespasian was said to have healed a blind man and a cripple in Alexandria, Hadrian was credited with ending a drought in Africa, and Marcus Aurelius reportedly called lightning down on barbarian siege engines. Similar or greater feats, however, were ascribed to traveling sages and magicians like Apollonius of Tyana.[5]

The emperors did not owe their divinity to supernatural abilities, but rather to the simple fact of their power over the lives of millions. Both the emperors and their subjects recognized the political functions of the imperial cult. In parts of the western provinces, the emperors actively promoted the cult to encourage both adherence to Rome and cooperation among local elites. Provincial notables, for their part, saw the advantages of playing along. Especially in the densely urbanized Greek East, they were eager disciples of the cult, recognizing its temples, festivals, and priesthoods as means of winning the approval of their fellow citizens.

Although the rituals of the imperial cult were modeled on those of the traditional gods, emperors were seldom worshipped on precisely the same terms. In more or less subtle ways—ranging from

---

* The philosopher and courtier Seneca wrote a satirical sketch called the *Apocolocyntosis* ("pumpkinification") shortly after Claudius's deification. Attempting to gain entry into Olympus, the emperor's soul is rebuffed on the advice of the deified Augustus. Instead, Claudius is sent to Hades and condemned to shake dice in a bottomless cup for all eternity. Despite such musings, Claudius was honored with temples at Rome and throughout the empire. One of his sanctuaries was the final refuge of the Roman settlers besieged by Boudica's hordes at Colchester.

the position of their statues to the prepositions used in prayer—they were set apart, honored with the same ceremonial but not regarded or revered in quite the same light.

Roman religion was not founded on belief. That the gods existed was taken for granted. What mattered was addressing them properly. The Romans had a contractual view of religion, encapsulated by the phrase *do ut des*—"I give so that you will give." The gods would bestow their blessings if, and only if, they received the proper sacrifices and prayers, regardless of what the men making those sacrifices and prayers thought about them. Emperors, living and dead, could be counted on to behave in the same way, responding to the familiar language of religion.

The cult, however, was never simply political. When Hadrian's young lover Antinous drowned in the Nile, the grieving emperor declared him a god. Statues and shrines sprouted in the provinces, as local elites competed to catch the emperor's favor. But long after Hadrian was gone, Antinous, often associated with Osiris or another god, continued to be invoked in hymns, pictured on amulets, and honored with games. He was worshipped until late antiquity.[6]

The imperial cult was ultimately about addressing power—but so was traditional Roman religion. If not a god himself, the emperor had much in common with the gods, especially for the millions of Romans without direct access to him. Though remote, he possessed great power to help or harm. He had only to be reached with the proper prayer.

A statue of Antinous in the guise of Osiris, now in the Vatican Museums. *Author's photo*

Why Did the Romans
Persecute the Christians?

$\mathcal{G}$reco-Roman religion was focused on the plenty, prosperity, and health that the gods could grant their worshippers. It relied on the accumulated weight of tradition, which enshrined the rituals by which mortals pleased the gods and gained their blessings. Although private devotion was important—some Romans carried statuettes of patron deities—religious practice was always centered on public sacrifices and festivals meant to guarantee the gods' gifts. From these rituals, Christians were conspicuously absent. By ignoring the rites owed to the gods, Christians earned the distrust of their neighbors. And by refusing to pray or sacrifice for the safety of the empire, they exposed themselves to accusations of treason.[1]

Christians tried to explain themselves. A series of Christian authors produced treatises explaining the tenets of their faith; one attempt, addressed to Marcus Aurelius, described Christianity in the terms of Platonic philosophy. Few pagan Romans were convinced. Traditional polytheists felt no hesitation about adding Mithras* or

---

* Although worshippers claimed that Mithras came from Persia, his cult seems to have been a product of the Roman world. (According to one theory, it was invented by an unknown Roman "religious genius" around the turn of the second century.) Mithraism was founded on small cells of male worshippers, who met for ritual meals in cave-like sanctuaries dominated by an image of Mithras slaying the primordial bull. The cult made extensive use of cosmic symbolism. The seven grades of initiation were associated with the seven planets, and the signs of the Zodiac often appeared on the ceilings of sanctuaries. (It has been theorized that the whole iconography of Mithraism, including the slaying of the bull, was inspired by a group of constellations.) Mithraism included elements, such as a sacramental meal, that were reminiscent of Christianity. Early Christian authors dismissed these parallels as Satanic plagiarism and mocked Mithraists for worshipping the sun in dark caves.

Sol Invictus* to their pantheon. But the Christian God, who forbade the worship of all others, was different.† A pagan intellectual named Celsus penned a stinging critique of Christianity, in which he accused Jesus of being a magician and criticized his followers as antisocial cultists. A century later, the philosopher Porphyry attacked the Bible on textual and historical grounds.[2]

Persecutions of the Christians, however, were local and sporadic for more than two hundred years. Tacitus recorded Nero's execution of Christians after the great fire of 64. His contemporary Pliny the Younger wrote to Trajan for advice regarding how to deal with a small Christian community in Bithynia-Pontus. During the reign of Marcus Aurelius, a brutal anti-Christian pogrom took place at Lyon. Two decades later, another local outburst claimed the life of Perpetua, a young woman who left an account of her time in prison.[3]

It was only in the mid-third century, during the reign of Decius, that the first systematic persecution took place.‡ Decius ordered every inhabitant of the empire to offer sacrifice for the safety of the Roman state and its rulers. Though not intended to do so, this measure set the stage for a Christian witch hunt. Anyone who refused to sacrifice was taken into custody. Many Christians were exiled; some were executed. Not long after, Emperor Valerian instituted a campaign explicitly targeting the Christian clergy.[4]

---

* Over the course of the third century, the Roman god Sol gained the title Invictus—"unconquered." (The epithet had originally been applied to Jupiter and Hercules.) The significance of Sol Invictus in Roman religious life was enhanced by the emperor Aurelian, who elevated the priests of the sun to the rank of pontifex, founded a major festival, and constructed an opulent temple for the god. It used to be thought that the Sol Invictus worshipped in Aurelian's sanctuary was imported from Syria and that Aurelian, like some Roman Akhenaten, sought to make Sol the dominant god of the pantheon. Most scholars now believe, however, that Sol Invictus was just the traditional Roman sun god, elevated to greater prominence by the personal devotion of the emperor. The emperors of the Tetrarchic period continued to revere Sol Invictus. For nearly two decades, even after his conversion to Christianity, Constantine issued coins bearing the likeness of the sun.

† The Jewish God insisted on the same prerogatives, but Judaism was protected from persecution by being an ancient and familiar religion associated with a single ethnic group. Although the ethical precepts of Judaism attracted pagan sympathizers (known as "God fearers"), most stopped short of full conversion, not least because it required circumcision.

‡ By one estimate, the number of Christians grew from only around a quarter-million at the beginning of the third century to several million by its end—which helps to explain why the emperors were increasingly concerned about the new religion.

The full might of the Roman state was hurled against the Christians a generation later. Diocletian, founder of the tetrarchy, had always emphasized Roman tradition. One of his edicts, for example, banned the Egyptian practice of sibling marriage as "fit only for barbarians and beasts." Another condemned the new religion associated with the Persian prophet Mani because "it was utmost depravity to change the religious doctrines set down by our ancestors."[5]

Initially, Diocletian seems to have been wary of attacking the Christians, not least because he understood the dangers of creating martyrs. Urged to move against the new religion by his junior coruler Galerius, he consulted an oracle of Apollo for advice. The god's response convinced him to act. On February 23, 303—the festival of Terminus, god of endings—Diocletian proclaimed that every church in the empire was to be closed and all Bibles were to be burned. Christians of rank would be demoted; any Christian freedman could be enslaved. By the day's end, the great church of Nicomedia, Diocletian's capital, had been demolished. Within months, churches were burning in Palestine, and Christians were being interrogated outside Carthage.[6]

At Nicomedia, Diocletian presided personally over the trial and execution of Christians in the imperial service. He issued another edict ordering the arrest of priests and bishops, who were tortured until they agreed to sacrifice to the traditional gods. The following spring, yet another imperial edict went out through the eastern provinces ordering the inhabitants of every city and village to sacrifice.[7]

Two years after the persecution began, Diocletian retired.* Galerius took his place as senior emperor and appointed his nephew Maximinus junior emperor in the east. A devout worshipper of the old gods, Maximinus tried to create a pagan religious hierarchy with a professional high priest overseeing the temples of every province. To discredit Christianity, he distributed the *Acts of Pilate*, which portrayed Jesus as a common criminal.[8]

---

* In retirement, Diocletian became an avid gardener. He was especially proud of his cabbages. The walls of his enormous retirement villa—roughly the size of Philip II's Escorial—later sheltered an entire medieval town (now Split, Croatia). Ironically, Diocletian's mausoleum was converted into the cathedral.

Besides organizing new rounds of universal sacrifices in the provinces under his control, Maximinus ordered items for sale in the markets to be sprinkled with sacrificial blood so that Christians could not touch them. Anyone who entered the public baths was also to be spattered with blood and wine from temple rituals. The barrage of anti-Christian measures began to exhaust even believers in the traditional gods. In some cities, there was growing sympathy for the victims of the persecution, to the point that local officials were compelled to move executions of Christians into the countryside.[9]

The persecution ground on until the spring of 311, when Galerius—now dying of cancer—issued an edict of toleration. He did not apologize to the Christians, who had "abandoned the ways of their ancestors." But having shown themselves so unwilling to return to the traditional gods, they would be permitted to assemble and worship, "as long as they did nothing to disturb the peace." He concluded, plaintively, by asking the Christians to pray for him. Maximinus issued his own edict of toleration soon after.[10]

Little more than a year after the persecution ended, Constantine had his vision at the Milvian Bridge, which set Christianity on the path to becoming the majority religion of the Roman world. Although Constantine undoubtedly regarded himself as a sincere Christian, his political agenda mirrored Diocletian's. He sought unity, and he saw religion as a means of attaining it. In that sense, the Council of Nicaea was a mirror image of the Great Persecution.

31

How "Good" Were the Five Good Emperors?

In the first volume of his *Decline and Fall of the Roman Empire*, Edward Gibbon famously opines, "If a man were called to fix the period in the history of the world, during which the condition of the human race was most happy and prosperous, he would, without hesitation, name that which elapsed from the death of Domitian to the accession of Commodus." Although few modern historians would venture anything quite so sententious, the period Gibbon describes—from 98 to 180 CE—is generally considered the apogee of the Roman Empire. It coincided with the reigns of the "Five Good Emperors." Nerva, the first, restored balance to the government after the tyranny of Domitian. Trajan waged a series of wars that pushed the empire's frontiers to their greatest extent. Hadrian traveled tirelessly through the provinces, dispensing justice and instituting reforms. Antoninus Pius presided over a generation of uninterrupted peace. Marcus Aurelius applied the principles of Stoic philosophy to the problems of ruling a world empire.

Though far from perfect—Hadrian, for example, had a bad habit of executing senators—the Five Good Emperors were, as a group, effective and responsible rulers. Under their stewardship, the Pax Romana extended from Scotland to Sudan, Roman coins circulated in Sweden and Sri Lanka, and Roman merchants reached China. Although conditions didn't change profoundly for the subsistence farmers who made up the bulk of the empire's population, new goods, such as mass-produced pottery and roof tiles, made life a bit

Reverse of a denarius struck under Hadrian, with
the legend "ADOPTIO" (adoption). The figures
represent Trajan and Hadrian. *Public domain*

more comfortable. So did an extensive trade network, which blunted
the impacts of local famines.*

The real beneficiaries of the Roman peace, however, were members of the elite. Both at Rome and in the provinces, aristocrats had
never been wealthier. Men like Herodes Atticus—an orator and senator who divided his time between vast estates in Greece and Italy—
dominated the imperial bureaucracy, governing provinces and leading
legions before retiring to the manicured gardens of their villas.† With
war banished to distant frontiers, cities thrived as never before. Most
of the theaters, fountains, forums, and baths that dominate Roman

---

* The population of the Roman Empire rose to its highest level in this period—by most
estimates, around seventy million, perhaps ten to fifteen million more than in the reign
of Augustus. The economy also reached its apogee. Ancient economies generally grew in
tandem with the population because few inventions or innovations affected the efficiency
of labor. It has been convincingly argued, however, that the second century witnessed a
modest economic boom, driven by the cultivation of new land, economies of scale, and
the growth of cities.

† Among much else, the awesomely wealthy Herodes built the Odeon that still graces
the Athenian Acropolis, the all-marble Panathenaic Stadium (used for the 1896 and 2004
Athens Olympics), and a colossal fountain at Olympia.

ruins from Spain to Syria were built under the Five Good Emperors. Perhaps the most emblematic product of the building boom was Hadrian's villa at Tivoli, where replicas of places the emperor had visited stood among artificial groves and rivers.

Although the reign of Marcus Aurelius witnessed the brutal Marcomannic Wars, the golden age—according to Cassius Dio and many historians since—ended only when Marcus was succeeded by his ineffectual son Commodus. Despite a period of stability under the Severan Dynasty and a golden autumn in the mid-fourth century, the Roman Empire would never again be as peaceful or prosperous as it had been under the Five Good Emperors. That fact raises two questions. First, what—from the perspective of our ancient sources— made an emperor good? And second, how much did the emperor's quality really matter for the success of the Roman Empire?

In the eyes of ancient authors, good emperors played by the political rules established by Augustus. They waged successful wars against Rome's enemies, refrained from levying onerous new taxes, beautified the city of Rome, and treated the elite (as embodied by the senate) with respect. This last criterion was especially impor- tant because Roman historians were, almost without exception, members of the elite themselves. They tended to assume that what was good for their class was good for the empire as a whole. Though not necessarily misleading—rulers who worked well with their officials, after all, tended to be effective administrators—an emperor who never antagonized the senate was not guaranteed to be a great leader.*

That brings us to the larger question: How much did the quality of an emperor really matter for the success of the Roman Empire? The system created by Augustus had significant weaknesses; its pseudo-republicanism, for example, precluded a clear law of succes- sion. It was, however, far more stable than the anarchic Late Repub- lic. It satisfied the ambitions of the aristocracy by employing them

---

* A good example is Severus Alexander, an amiable youth who respected the senate, lis- tened to his mother, and got himself killed by his own troops the first time he campaigned on the northern frontier.

as officials. It ensured a modicum of responsible management in the provinces. And in the person of the emperor, it had a symbolic center.

Arguably, the most important thing an emperor did was simply exist. Under normal circumstances, his primary role was to receive delegations and petitions from his subjects. He spent—or was supposed to spend—most of his time passing judgment and issuing edicts. The basic machinery of government, however, could function without him. Neither Caligula nor Nero caused the empire any obvious distress.

How good, then, were the Five Good Emperors? Or, to put that a different way, was the Roman Empire so successful during the second century because of its leaders or in spite of them? Though that's not a question that can be answered succinctly or neatly, a few factors are worth pointing out. The second century appears to have coincided with the Roman warm period, a climatic anomaly that brought exceptionally benign weather to the Mediterranean Basin.* The empire managed to avoid major pandemics until the Antonine

---

* The Roman warm period lasted from the early second century BCE to the mid-second century CE. The most precise evidence is provided by dendrochronology. Using wood preserved in bogs and other saturated environments, scholars have created ring sequences that reveal a long period of warm summer temperatures in the Alps and northern Europe, peaking in the first century CE. Corroborating evidence comes from the Greenland ice cap, where ratios of oxygen isotopes and chloride levels suggest several protracted periods of low sea ice in the first two centuries CE. Careful study of glaciers in the Swiss and Austrian Alps has revealed a long period of retreat in the same era, which may have reduced some glaciers to their late twentieth-century size.

Evidence continues to accumulate. Until recent decades, the cold-sensitive nettle bug was found only in southern Britain. But during the Roman era, it scurried happily about the north, which suggests summer temperatures at least a degree Celsius warmer than mid-twentieth-century averages. Levels of atmospheric mercury in a Spanish bog have been interpreted as evidence that the peak of the Roman warm period there was up to two degrees Celsius warmer than twentieth-century averages. An analysis of plankton remains in the central Mediterranean suggests local sea-surface temperatures substantially warmer than today's. Near the Roman city of Sagalassus, in the hills of what is now southwestern Turkey, archaeologists have discovered olive presses and olive pollen in areas too cold for olive trees today. Like Roman olive-crushing installations found in the mountains of Greece, their existence may indicate average temperatures at least two degrees Celsius warmer than today's.

Some regions, in short, must have been exceptionally balmy, at least for a few decades. But the degree of warming varied considerably over both time and space. Regarding the Roman world as a whole, mean temperatures at any point in the warm period were probably more or less comparable to late twentieth-century averages.

Plague. Thanks to new conquests and newly productive mines, the precious metals on which the imperial economy depended were in ample supply. The Parthian Empire along the eastern frontier was weak, and the Germanic tribes to the north were disorganized. Before Marcus Aurelius, finally, none of the Five Good Emperors had a natural son, leaving them free to choose their successors.

All Five Good Emperors were competent. At least two have a fair claim to be called great. But if they were good, they were also lucky.

32

Did Mosquitoes and Rats
Cause the Fall of Rome?

*M*alaria was endemic throughout Italy until the early twentieth century. The most dangerous form, caused by the *Plasmodium falciparum* parasite, was especially prevalent in and around Rome.* Both falciparum malaria and the mosquitoes of the *Anopheles* genus that carry it were established in Italy by the beginning of Roman history. Under the emperors, however, the mosquitoes' range expanded, exposing more and more people to the threat of disease. Mosquitoes were spread by human agency—insects stowed away on ships, and their larvae were carried in water casks. But the environment seems to have also become increasingly favorable to them, both around Rome and in many coastal cities.[1]

The Roman warm period—the exceptionally balmy and moist climatic regime that graced much of the Mediterranean during the imperial apogee—was accompanied by regionally higher rainfall. We have accounts of terrible floods in Rome, even during the normally dry summer months. The pools left by each inundation allowed mosquito populations and malaria to flourish. A more systemic problem was widespread deforestation. As Rome and other Italian cities expanded, the trees that had mantled the hills above the coastal plains were cut, both for fuel and to clear new land for farming. Erosion on the exposed slopes washed huge quantities of sediment into

---

* The hum of mosquitoes can be heard in classical literature. Horace complains about the insects that tormented him as he traveled along the Appian Way, and a humorous poem attributed to Virgil begins with a shepherd swatting a mosquito on his face.

the rivers, choking their channels and producing marshy deltas. The building of Roman roads through marshes and along hillsides interrupted natural drainages, creating additional mosquito habitats. The aqueducts fed hundreds of fountains and countless puddles.

As mosquito habitats expanded, malaria became an increasingly dire problem. It has been suggested that the decline of the ancient Greek cities of southern Italy—almost all located on marshy coasts—was at least partly caused by debilitating levels of malaria. Around Rome, silting created a pestilential marsh at the mouth of the Tiber, and changes in local drainage patterns engorged the Pontine Marshes. Falciparum malaria was already hyperendemic in Rome by the time of Galen, who described the symptoms of what he called "tertian fever" with clinical precision. The scourge may have become even worse in late antiquity, when epitaphs from the catacombs reveal huge malaria-driven mortality spikes in late summer and early fall.*

Malaria reshaped settlement patterns across Italy, as people moved to escape the "evil air" of the lowlands. Some cities were abandoned. The Roman Campagna—once a region of lush gardens and sprawling villas—became the lonely wasteland it would remain until the nineteenth century. Yet it would be excessive to claim, as some scholars have, that malaria played a significant role in the decline and fall of the Roman Empire. Although it robbed the Romans of human resources they could ill afford to lose, it did not sap the basic vitality of the imperial system. A better claim, in that regard, can be made for another disease and a different pest.

Rattus rattus—the black or ship rat—is native to Southeast Asia. It gradually expanded westward, following trade routes. By the end of the Roman Republic, it had reached the Mediterranean.† Rats breed prolifically. Females produce up to five litters a year, and newborns reach maturity within a few months. The only factor that limits population growth is the availability of nutrients—and

---

* Scientists have found traces of falciparum malaria DNA in skeletons from the catacombs.

† The movements of rats are difficult to date archaeologically, both because rat bones are fragile and because excavators have historically paid little attention to the remains of rodents. Literature is of little help; both Greek and Latin used the same word for *rat* and *mouse*.

throughout the Roman world, rats found one of their favorite foods in massive quantities. Each city and military camp had granaries, and almost every substantial port was visited by grain barges. Trade routes became rodent superhighways, carrying rats from Egypt and other grain-exporting regions to destinations throughout the Mediterranean. By late antiquity, rats had reached northern Britain* and the Rhine frontier.

Yersinia pestis, the bacterium responsible for bubonic plague, inhabits the guts of fleas that prey on rodents. During a flare-up of the plague, infected fleas bite rats, who sicken and die. As the rat population dwindles, the fleas seek out other mammals—including humans. The modern form of *Yersinia pestis* seems to have evolved around three thousand years ago among the gerbils and marmots of Central Asia.† At some point, it made the leap to rats, moving with them into the Mediterranean Basin. By the first century, isolated plague outbreaks were beginning to erupt in Rome's eastern provinces. Secondhand reports came to the attention of a few medical authors, who cataloged the symptoms—swollen lymph nodes, gangrene, vomiting—as a curiosity. Plague never reached the capital and appears nowhere in the voluminous works of Galen. But as the years passed and rats multiplied, the danger of a pandemic grew.

The storm broke during the reign of Justinian. Plague appeared in Pelusium, near Alexandria, and spread rapidly through Egypt and along the coasts. Within a matter of months, thousands were dying daily in Constantinople. The pestilence reached Rome the following year and Britain by the year after. Levels of mortality seem to have approached those of the Black Death, which claimed nearly half the population of Europe.

This is sometimes described as a disaster from which the Romans never recovered. Before the plague, Justinian had reconquered North Africa and Italy, codified Roman law, and built Hagia Sophia. Afterward, he seemed able to do little more than cling grimly

---

* The Romans introduced both rats and cockroaches to Britain, probably via Londinium.
† An earlier strain of the plague—apparently not transmitted by fleas—appears to have swept across Europe during the Bronze Age.

to his conquests. But as in the case of malaria, it shouldn't be assumed that the plague made Roman recovery impossible. It just made the lives of the Romans—and the job of the emperor—harder. The continued survival of the empire, despite recurrences of the plague and the many disasters of the seventh century, is a standing rebuttal to any simple theory of decline and fall.

VI

LEGACIES

33

How Did Roman Cities Get Their Modern Names?

*H*undreds of Roman cities are still inhabited today. Especially in countries that speak Romance languages, their modern names often reflect their Roman roots. Roman Olisipo is modern Lisbon. Toletum is Toledo. Massilia is Marseille. Bononia is Bologna. And Roma, of course, is still Roma. The names of many other Roman cities, however, have changed radically. In Sardinia, for example, Forum Traiani became Fordongianus. In Slovenia, Poetovio became Ptuj. In Algeria, Igilgili became Jijel. Arausio, in France, became Arausione, Aurasice, Aurengie, Aurenga, and finally Orange.* Borbetomagus, in Germany, became Vormatia, Wormazia, and then Worms.

Identical names sometimes evolved in different directions. Both Nice, France, and Iznik, Turkey, were originally Nicaea. Napoli, Italy, and Nablus in the West Bank were both Neapolis. Fréjus, France, and Friuli, Italy, are variations of Forum Iulii. Aosta, Augst, and Augsburg were all Augusta. Kayseri, Turkey; Cherchell, Algeria; and Zaragoza, Spain, are variations of Caesarea. Lajjun, Israel; Leon, Spain; and Caerleon, Wales, derive their names from *legio*, "legion."† The French towns Aix and Dax are descendants of the Latin *aquae*, "springs." (The same word, literally translated, is behind Baden-Baden,

---

* The name of the orange fruit has an entirely separate etymology, having come into Europe (via Arabic) as the Spanish *naranj*. In France, this became *orange*, possibly influenced by the fact that the city of Orange was a center of the orange trade.

† There are variations on all of these. Forum Livi became Forlì; Forum Populi, Forlimpopoli. Augustodunum evolved into Autun; Augusta Taurinorum, into Turin. Niksar, Turkey, began as Neocaesarea.

Germany, and Bath, England.) Constantine, Algeria, and Constanța, Romania, are both named after Constantine, while Konstanz, Germany, and Coutances, France, are named for his father, Constantius.*

There were regional patterns in the preservation and transformation of names. In Britain, almost every Roman city was at least briefly abandoned during the empire's collapse. Although many sites were reoccupied, they received new names from their Anglo-Saxon settlers. Sometimes those names had Roman origins. Lindum Colonia, for example, came to be known as Lindocolina, which became Lincylene and then Lincoln. Eboracum became Eoforwic, which was eventually shortened—via the Danish Jorvik—to York. Londinium was reborn as the Anglo-Saxon settlement of Lundenwic, later rebuilt as Lundenburg, and finally shortened to London. Because Roman cities were often surrounded by walls, the Anglo-Saxons called them castles, using a word—*ceaster*—derived from the Latin *castrum*, "camp." Thus the Roman town of Venta Belgarum was renamed Venta Castle—that is, Wintanceaster (modern Winchester). Roman Mamucio became Anglo-Saxon Mamecestre, now Manchester. Glevum became Glowecestre and then Gloucester. The legionary fort of Deva was simply called the castle—Chester.

In what are now southern and western Germany, the replacement of Latin by Germanic dialects was reflected in the shifting names of former Roman cities. Mogontiacum became Maguntia, Meginze, and finally Mainz. Castra Regina, built near the Celtic settlement of Radasbona, came to be known as Radaspona, which gradually became Regensburg. Augusta Treverorum was abbreviated to Treveris and then Trier. Colonia Agrippina came to be known simply as Colonia, which evolved into Köln.

To the west, in modern France, the population continued to speak Latin.† Especially in southern France, where the collapse of the Roman Empire was relatively gentle, the modern names of many

---

* Orléans was Civitas Aurelianorum, after Emperor Aurelian. One wonders how that austere ruler would feel about being the namesake of New Orleans.

† The French names for Germany's Roman cities are correspondingly closer to the Latin originals. In French, Köln is Cologne, Trier is Trèves, Regensburg is Ratisbonne, and Mainz is Mayence.

cities are direct descendants of their ancient predecessors. Arelate became Arles, Nemausus became Nîmes, Lugdunum became Lyon, and Burdigala became Bordeaux. Although the classical name of Paris was Lutetia, the city was already known by the name of a local tribe—the Parisii—by late antiquity.

The names of Spain's major Roman cities are still recognizable. Corduba has become Córdoba, Gades is Cádiz, Valentia is Valencia, Emerita Augusta is Mérida, and Hispalis—via the Arabic Ishbiliyah—is Sevilla (Seville). The names of Italy's Roman cities have changed even less. In the north, Mediolanum is Milano (Milan), Brixia is Bresica, and Verona is still Verona. Florentia has become Firenze (Florence), Saena has become Siena, and Pisae has become Pisa. South of Rome, Beneventum is Benevento, Tarentum is Taranto, Surrentum is Sorrento, and Brundisium is Brindisi.

East of the Adriatic, where Slavic languages replaced Latin in the Early Middle Ages, relatively few modern cities preserve their ancient names. Many of these are along the Croatian coast, such as Pula, Roman Pola; Zadar, Roman Iader; and Split, Roman Spalatum. But there are scattered survivors inland. Naissus became Niš, Serbia. Scupi became Skopje, North Macedonia. Philippopolis became Plovdiv, Bulgaria.

Farther south, in Greece, Greek has been the predominant language for three millennia, and the names of the major cities have changed little, despite shifts in pronunciation. The classical name of Athens—Athenai—became Athena in the Byzantine period and has remained so since.*

The names of some ancient cities in modern Turkey are still recognizable. Prusa is Bursa, Smyrna is İzmir, Attaleia is Antalya, Iconium is Konya, and Ancyra is Ankara. Other transformations are less obvious. Nicomedia, for example, became İznikmid in Turkish, later shortened to İznik. Germanicopolis became Ermenek. Claudiopolis

---

* Through the mid-twentieth century, advocates of classicizing *katharevousa* Greek insisted on Athenai instead of Athena. The case of Thessaloniki is even more complicated. The classical name Thessalonike (Thessalonica in Latin) was shortened to Saloniki in the Middle Ages, and the city is still called variations of Saloniki in Turkish and the South Slavic languages. Officially, however, it resumed its ancient name after becoming part of Greece in 1912.

was shortened to Bolu. Istanbul seems to be a Turkish rendering of the Greek phrase *eis ten polin* ("into the city").

Across North Africa and the Levant, where Arabic is the dominant language, the names of former Roman cities are often difficult to spot.* Homs, for example, is the Arabic form of ancient Emesa. Ancient Berytus is modern Beirut. Damascus is Dimašq in Arabic, though the conventional English name is the same as the Roman one. The name of Luxor, Egypt, is derived from Qasr, the Arabic rendering of the Latin *castra*, "camps." On the other side of the Mediterranean, in what is now Morocco, the Roman city of Tingis became the Arabic Ṭanjah; the English name—via the French—is Tangier. In Algeria, Hippo Regius became Ubbo and finally Bon.

Some Roman cities are still known by nicknames they acquired during the Middle Ages. In England, for example, the Roman town of Verulamium came to be called Saint Albans after the Roman martyr buried there. In France, likewise, Glanum was renamed Saint-Rémy from the abbey that owned the land around it. When a church dedicated to a martyred Roman soldier was built near Colonia Ulpia Traiana† on the German frontier, the local settlement came to be known as Ad Sanctos—"by the saints"—which gradually metamorphosed into Xanten. In Turkey, the city of Aphrodisias became synonymous with Caria, the province it governed. The modern village beside the ruins is still known as Geyre.‡

The names of some Roman cities were reclassicized in the modern era.§ Agrigentum in Sicily, for example, was known as Girgenti

---

* After the Arab conquest of the Near East, many cities reverted to the Semitic names locals had always used, which often long predated the arrival of the Romans. Harran, now in Turkey, has had the same name since at least the second millennium BCE. The Greeks and Romans, however, called it Carrhae—a Hellenization of the Assyrian name. The modern name of Urfa, another city in southeastern Turkey, is derived from its ancient Syriac name. Under the Hellenistic kings and their Roman successors, the official name was Edessa, after a city in Macedonia. Amman, the capital of Jordan, returned to its original (and modern) name after a thousand years as Philadelphia.

† The town was also known as Tricensimae—"Thirty-ville"—after the number of the legion stationed there.

‡ Both El-Kantara, Algeria, and Alcántara, Spain, are named for Roman bridges, via the Arabic *al-Qanṭarah* ("bridge").

§ In 1865, the French village of Merdogne successfully petitioned Napoleon III to change its name to Gergovie, after the ancient Gallic town that had resisted Caesar. (The villagers also objected to the fact that their town's name sounded more than a little like *merde*, "dung.")

from the Middle Ages until 1927, when Benito Mussolini ordered it changed to the ancient-sounding Agrigento.* Corneto became Tarquinia. Aglar was reclassicized to Aquileia. As recently as 1969, Resina—built over the ruins of Herculaneum—became Ercolano. In 1974, the Romanian city of Cluj—on the site of Roman Napoca—was formally renamed Cluj-Napoca to emphasize its ancient heritage. Over the course of the nineteenth and early twentieth centuries, successive Greek governments gave classical names to hundreds of settlements. The city of Edessa, for example, reverted to its ancient name after a millennium as Vodena, and the village of Kastri was renamed after the neighboring site of Delphi.

Some ancient-sounding cities are later foundations. To take two English examples, Chew Magna gained its *Magna* only in the early modern period, and the *Regis* in Bognor Regis wasn't tacked on until 1929. Under Catherine the Great, the Russian Empire planted dozens of cities with classical names on the shores of the Black Sea, including Sevastopol (from Sebastopolis, "city of Augustus") and Odessa (named after the nearby Greco-Roman city of Odessus).

Perhaps the most evocative modern names are those assigned to the ruins of Roman cities that were never reoccupied. For centuries, Alexandria Troas in Turkey was called Eski Istanbul, "Old Istanbul." The Villa of the Quintilii on the Via Appia came to be known as Roma Vecchia, "Old Rome." Other ruins were associated with legendary kings. The Turkish village beside Miletus was named Balat, from Palatium, "palace." The settlement that grew up around the colossal Villa Romana del Casale in Sicily was also called Palatium, which evolved into Piazza Armerina, the modern name of the neighboring town. And the hilltop city of Justiniana Prima, now in Serbia, came to be known as Caričin Grad, "city of the queen." Just who that queen had been, however, nobody knew.

---

* The ancient city of Samos—which came to be known during the Middle Ages as Tigani (literally "frying pan," but probably a corruption of the Italian *dogana*, "customhouse")—renamed itself Pythagoreio in 1955 after its most famous ancient resident.

34

How Did the Romans
Forget Hieroglyphs?

*E*gyptian hieroglyphs emerged in the thirty-third century BCE, two and a half millennia before Rome was founded. They survived until the final decades of the Western Roman Empire. Of the writing systems in use today, only Chinese characters approach such longevity. Our own alphabet falls a thousand years short.

Hieroglyphs were used primarily in religious and funerary contexts.* They were meant to be monumental, eternal; each sign was a miniature work of art. By the time Egypt became a Roman province, the form of the Egyptian language encoded in hieroglyphs was nearly two thousand years old. The script, however, was still evolving. Over the course of the Hellenistic period, the number of signs had grown from roughly 750 to several thousand. Signs were associated with more phonetic values than ever before and used in increasingly elaborate ways. The culmination of these trends can be seen at Esna Temple, where one Roman-era hymn is written entirely in crocodile signs.

Cornelius Gallus, the first Roman governor of Egypt, commemorated his suppression of a revolt with an inscription written in Latin, Greek, and hieroglyphs. Hieroglyphic texts were inscribed on

---

* Over the millennia, five writing systems have been associated with the Egyptian language. Hieroglyphs, the oldest, were almost immediately supplemented by the cursive Hieratic script, which became standard for administrative and literary texts. After the seventh century BCE, Hieratic gave way to the more streamlined Demotic script. Demotic was replaced in late antiquity by the Coptic alphabet, which combined the Greek letters with six Demotic signs. Coptic, finally, was replaced by the Arabic alphabet.

obelisks commissioned by Domitian and Hadrian.* During the reign of Trajan, there were no fewer than five professional hieroglyph cutters working in the town of Oxyrhynchus. The majority of Roman Egypt's hieroglyphic texts, however, were written in temples—hymns for the gods, descriptions of festival rituals, retellings of myths. They could be quite lengthy: The modern publication of the hieroglyphs in the Temple of Hathor at Dendera runs to nearly two thousand pages; those of Esna Temple fill well over one thousand.[1]

Like the Ptolemaic kings before them, the Roman emperors were patrons of the temples, supporting major construction projects at Esna, Philae, and many other sanctuaries. They appeared in temple reliefs as pharaohs, performing the time-honored rituals that ensured the preservation of Egypt. Popular devotion remained strong: The catacombs at Saqqara contain more than four million mummified ibises and a half-million mummified falcons, all sold as offerings to Roman-era worshippers in the temples of Memphis.

Despite soaring falcon sales, the temples of Roman Egypt were a shadow of the economic powerhouses they had once been. During the reign of Ramesses III, the great Temple of Amun at Karnak owned nearly 700,000 acres of fertile land; 421,000 cattle; and 65 towns, among much else. Although no temple of the Hellenistic period could boast such resources, the Ptolemies had at least granted sanctuaries financial and administrative autonomy. The Romans, by contrast, systematically brought temples under government control, confiscating most of their estates and forcing them to rely on state stipends. The social privileges of priests were also curtailed.[2]

Imperial support for the temples ended after Constantine became a Christian. By then, Luxor Temple had already been

---

* Roman emperors brought thirteen large obelisks and a similar number of smaller obelisks to Rome. At least eight of the smaller obelisks stood near the Temple of Isis and Serapis in the Campus Martius. One of these—now atop Bernini's Fountain of the Four Rivers—features hieroglyphs praising Domitian. There was another obelisk in Hadrian's villa at Tivoli, set up to commemorate the emperor's lover Antinous. The hieroglyphs of that obelisk seem to have been composed by an Egyptian priest. Roman craftsmen with no knowledge of the Egyptian language, however, were probably responsible for an obelisk carved around the same time, now in the Florence Archaeological Museum, which is decorated with hieroglyphs seemingly chosen at random. A similar artifact, the so-called Bembine Tablet, features symbols only distantly related to hieroglyphs.

The crocodile hymn in the Temple of Khnum at Esna. *Author's photo*

converted into a legionary fort, and a village—complete with a church—was starting to grow up inside the mortuary temple of Ramesses III. The decay of the temples dealt a fatal blow to hiero-glyphs.* Even in the pharaonic period, less than 1 percent of the population had been able to read and write them. This tiny minority had always been concentrated in the temples, where the script was taught. After Greek replaced Egyptian as the administrative lan-guage, only priests had any incentive to learn the ancient signs—and now the priests were disappearing.

Many Romans were intrigued by hieroglyphs.† An ostracon found at Medinet Madi seems to describe Hadrian questioning Egyptian priests about the meanings of signs. Plutarch was famil-iar with the meanings of at least a few hieroglyphs. Chaeremon of Alexandria, one of Nero's tutors, wrote a lost treatise on the topic. Someone with at least an elementary understanding of hieroglyphs made a Greek translation of the inscriptions on an obelisk in the Circus Maximus.[3]

Yet no extant Greek or Roman author claimed the ability to read hieroglyphs. They tended to assume that hieroglyphic signs were emblems of sacred wisdom and had to be understood allegori-cally. There were Greek-speaking priests in Egypt who could have corrected this error‡ and Egyptian teaching manuals that could have been translated for their benefit. But these opportunities were missed. The only Egyptian work on hieroglyphs that appeared in a classical language was written too late. *Hieroglyphica*, attributed to a priest named Horapollo, probably dates to the mid-fifth century. Although

---

* The Egyptian language, it should be emphasized, continued to thrive. Although Greek was widely spoken, Egyptian remained predominant well into the Middle Ages, when it began to be replaced by Arabic. The language of the pharaohs was used in a few parts of Upper Egypt through the early twentieth century. It remains the liturgical lan-guage of the Coptic Church.

† Like many observers in later centuries, the Romans were ambivalent about Egypt. Although they were fascinated by the ancient monuments, they tended to stereotype Egyptians of their own time as fanatics and criminals, and they regarded the animal-headed Egyptian gods with contempt.

‡ During the reigns of Ptolemy I and Ptolemy II, a Greek-speaking Egyptian priest named Manetho produced a detailed history of Egypt. His work, however, remained obscure until late antiquity, when Christian authors mined it for chronological references. Only fragments survive today.

the author knew the meanings of some signs, he interpreted many others incorrectly and seems to have had no idea how they could be combined into sentences.

By the time Horapollo wrote, there was probably no one in Egypt who knew much more about hieroglyphs.* The only temples still in operation were at Philae, left open to appease the pagan tribes of the southern desert. It was at Philae, on August 24, 394, that the last known hieroglyphic inscription was written. It reads,

> Before Mandulis, son of Horus, by the hand of Nesmeterakhem, son of Nesmeter, Second Priest of Isis, for all time and eternity. Words spoken by Mandulis, lord of the Abaton, great god.[4]

Beside the inscription was a relief of the god Mandulis. Sometime in late antiquity, the god's image was defaced. But the hieroglyphs—mysterious or simply powerless—were left alone.

---

* By this time, the Hieratic script was already dead. The last Demotic inscription would be carved at Philae in 452.

The last known hieroglyphic inscription. *Author's photo*

Did the Early Christians Destroy Pagan Temples?

*W*hen Constantine converted to Christianity, there were—by one count—424 temples in the city of Rome.* Tens of thousands more were scattered across the provinces. They soared heavenward, like the towering Temple of Jupiter at Baalbek. They crouched beneath the earth, like the Oracle of the Dead at Ephyra. They housed flocks of doves and sacred fish, mammoth tusks and meteorites, shapeless idols of age-black wood and chryselephantine statues with glowing eyes. They were the most spectacular, most expensive, most famous buildings in the known world. And within two centuries of Constantine's reign, virtually every one had been abandoned or destroyed.

Some temples were attacked by Christians. Martin of Tours burned shrines and felled sacred groves in the Gallic countryside. On the other side of the empire, Bishop Porphyrius demolished the Temple of Zeus in Gaza, and Abbot Shenoute led squads of monks against the pagan sanctuaries of Upper Egypt. The violence came to a crescendo during the reign of Theodosius I, when a mob sacked the Serapeum of Alexandria and the orator Libanius begged for an end to the rampant destruction of pagan sanctuaries around Antioch.[1]

The vast majority of Roman temples, however, were not destroyed violently. The imperial government discouraged indiscriminate

---

* The most famous was the golden-roofed Temple of Jupiter Optimus Maximus, finished in the first year of the Republic. Among the many other remarkable temples in Rome were the subterranean Porta Maggiore Basilica, apparently used by a neo-Pythagorean cult; the sanctuary of Isis and Serapis on the Campus Martius, with its sacred wells and forest of obelisks; and a shrine of the Palmyrene gods, filled with Aramaic dedications, in Trastevere.

destruction. Even after public worship of the old gods was prohibited, temples remained public monuments. A series of decrees stipulated that they were to remain open and forbade their demolition for building material.* Elite Christians were generally sympathetic: A bishop of Ilion gave Julian a tour of his city's temples.[2]

Christian ire tended to focus less on temple buildings than on the cult images they contained. (Pope Gregory I, writing centuries later, would urge missionaries in Anglo-Saxon England to preserve shrines but destroy their idols.) At Ephesus, for example, statues of the deified Augustus and Livia were mutilated and had crosses cut into their foreheads. Nearby, a wealthy citizen named Demeas set up an inscription commemorating his replacement of a likeness of Artemis with a cross. The most famous statues of the gods, however, were respected as works of art. Phidias's Olympian Zeus was moved intact to Constantinople. So was the colossal bronze image of Athena Promachos, which would guard the Forum of Constantine until the time of the Fourth Crusade.[3]

Many temples were maintained for decades after being closed for worship. In most cases, they were finally ruined by some combination of earthquakes and pillaging. As early as the mid-fourth century, only a generation after Constantine, Libanius complained that the citizens of Antioch were stripping stone from pagan sanctuaries for reuse in their homes. Eventually, the emperors condoned the practice; it was rumored that Justinian built columns from the Temple of Artemis at Ephesus† into Hagia Sophia.[4]

Only a small minority of temples were converted into churches. This was partly a matter of incompatibility. Churches needed to house congregations of worshipers.‡ Temples—designed to shelter

---

* Admiration for the beauty of temples continued into the Middle Ages. The Tempietto del Clitunno, a chapel in Umbria with a Roman-style Corinthian porch, may have been built as late as the eighth century. Even the inscription on its facade, written in square capitals, imitates the monuments of a half-millennium before.

† The Temple of Artemis seems to have been dismantled piecemeal over the course of the fifth and sixth centuries. Stone from the temple was built into a series of local churches, and a small basilica was constructed inside the cella of the temple itself.

‡ After the reign of Constantine—who presided over the construction of the first monumental Christian buildings—most churches in the Roman world were basilicas. Inspired by the civil basilicas that had long been a fixture of Roman forums, churches of this type were long and narrow, with a central nave culminating in the apse that framed the main altar. The other standard design was the martyrium, a centrally planned building originally modeled on pagan hero shrines and mausoleums. The most famous early example was the rotunda in Constantine's Church of the Holy Sepulcher.

The Duomo of Syracuse, originally a temple of Athena. *Author's photo*

only the statue and possessions of a god—tended to be too dark and cramped for services. An additional problem was the belief that temples were haunted. Christians assumed that the pagan gods were demons sent by Satan to mislead mankind. These beings lurked in the strongholds of the old religion, waiting to tempt or possess the unwary. To be rid of them, a temple had to be thoroughly purified—ideally by a resident holy man.[5]

In most Roman cities, the first monumental churches were built on the outskirts, often near a martyr's tomb. It was only later, from the mid-fifth century, that they began to appear in city centers. The first temples were converted around the same time. In Rome, no temple seems to have become a church before the Pantheon, consecrated in 609. With its huge, open rotunda, the Pantheon needed few architectural modifications. Most converted temples, however, were more like the Parthenon, which was substantially altered when it became a church around the end of the fifth century: An entrance was punched through what had been the back wall, an apse was built into the former pronaos, and some of the mythological sculptures were defaced.[6]

In the massive Temple of Apollo at Didyma, a church was simply inserted into the cella, which had been left open to the sky. A basilica, likewise, rose in what had been the second court of Ramesses III's mortuary temple.* The most common method of converting a temple into a church, however, was to fill the spaces between the colonnades and partially or wholly dismantle the cella within, creating a three-aisled basilica. The best-preserved Greek temples—the Temple of Hephaestus at Athens and the Temple of Concordia at Agrigento—were both remodeled in this way.†

Other temples underwent more radical adaptations. In Rome, the medieval church of San Nicola in Carcere was built over three adjoining temples. The central temple became the nave; the outer walls engulfed the colonnades of the temples on either side. A circular shrine of Isis is embedded in the seven chapels that make up Bologna's Basilica of Santo Stefano. The Temple of Aphrodite at Aphrodisias was almost completely disassembled; only the lateral colonnades were left in place, to form the nave of a new cathedral.

A few buildings underwent the double conversion from temple to church to mosque. The Duomo of Syracuse, initially a temple of Athena, became a church, then a mosque, and finally a church again. The Great Mosque of Damascus replaced a church of John the Baptist that had been built into a Roman temple of Zeus. At the Parthenon, the Muslim call to prayer was heard for centuries over the Christian frescoes clinging, ever more precariously, to the walls of Athena's temple.

---

* Another church was built into the first courtyard of Luxor Temple; it was later replaced by the Mosque of Abu Haggag, still functioning today.

† In the Roman Forum, the porch of the Temple of Antoninus and Faustina—which became a church in the Early Middle Ages—was filled in to make more room for chapels. The ancient portico was restored in 1536 as part of a whirlwind campaign to clean up Rome's ruins for a visit of Holy Roman Emperor Charles V.

What Happened to the Colosseum After Rome Fell?

In 1532, Benvenuto Cellini, goldsmith to the pope, watched a necromancer summon demons in the Colosseum. The necromancer—a Sicilian priest—stood at the center of the arena and traced a circle in the earth. Reading a Latin incantation, he cast perfume onto a blazing fire. Then, Cellini claims, the ruins were filled with countless demons, who whirled around them in clouds. With some difficulty, the necromancer managed to dismiss all the demons but two, which followed Cellini back to his house, leaping from rooftop to rooftop overhead.

The Colosseum Cellini knew was a gutted ruin. All the seats were gone, half the outer wall had collapsed, and heaps of fallen stone choked the arches. The only sign of life was a small chapel at the east end of the arena, where passion plays were performed on Good Friday. The vaults and passageways, however, were filled with the debris of earlier centuries, when the Colosseum had been a palace, a castle, a bullring, a den of thieves, and a bustling neighborhood.

Thanks to a combination of rising costs and Christian disapproval, gladiators last fought at the Colosseum sometime in the early fifth century. The final beast hunt was held in 523. Soon even the Colosseum's function was forgotten. Some medieval authors claimed that the amphitheater had been a temple of the sun, crowned by a vast golden dome. Others thought that it had been a temple dedicated to all the gods, with a gigantic statue of Jupiter or Apollo in the arena.* The

---

* The Theater of Marcellus, a short distance from the Colosseum, was also thought to have been a temple.

A painting by Maarten van Heemskerck (1552) showing a ruined arena modeled on the Colosseum, with a statue of Jupiter in the center. *Wikimedia Commons*

strangest legends revolved around the Roman poet Virgil, who was said to have built the Colosseum with the help of demons and used it as a theater for sorcery.

At first, the Colosseum was boarded up, with fences in the arcades to prevent entry. But within a few decades of Justinian's catastrophic Gothic Wars, squatters were living inside. The cavernous corridors, drier and better constructed than most of the era's houses, were roomy enough to accommodate hundreds of people and animals. Storage lofts, stables, and a chapel were built into the vaults, and busy roads crossed the packed rubble of the arena.*

Most of the Colosseum's new inhabitants were involved in the lucrative business of recycling stone. The outer walls were made of the fine limestone known as travertine, and the seats were marble. Besides being easy to reuse, both marble and travertine could be burned in kilns to make lime for mortar. Even before the final

---

* The hypogeum—the labyrinth of tunnels and chambers under the area—was filled in late antiquity after clogged sewers left it prone to flooding. When the hypogeum was excavated in the nineteenth century, the archaeologists found fragments of marble decoration from the upper levels, wooden floorboards preserved by the saturated soil, and the bones of beasts slain in the last hunts.

games were staged in the arena, Theodoric authorized the pillaging of the Colosseum's most decayed parts.* By the ninth century, the building was being mined on an industrial scale, with tunnels driven through the massive concrete foundations to harvest the travertine blocks of the hypogeum.

The settlement inside the Colosseum, concentrated in areas that were not being dismantled, grew steadily. By the eleventh century, two-story houses lined the arena. A contemporary document describes one as a structure of brick and wood, with marble front steps, a garden on one side, and an apple orchard behind. Along with all the others in the Colosseum, this house was destroyed during the Norman Sack of 1084. Soon after, the aristocratic Frangipani family incorporated the amphitheater into their vast castle. A palace rose on the east side, and knights issued from the gates to battle rival clans or attack the pope in the Lateran.† In 1332, after the Frangipani had been evicted from their stronghold, a bullfight was held in the Colosseum to welcome the Holy Roman Emperor Ludwig of Bavaria.‡ By this period, the ruins were notorious as a nest of bandits. Nineteenth-century excavators found the bones of murder victims hidden in the arcades.

The south side of the Colosseum, built over waterlogged sediment, had always been susceptible to seismic damage. In 1349, one of the worst earthquakes in Rome's history caused the entire southern perimeter wall to collapse. The gigantic heap of rubble—known locally as the *coxa*, the "juicy thigh"—would be mined for the next four centuries. A single busy contractor carried off more than 2,500 cartloads of stone in 1452.§ Blocks from the Colosseum were used in

---

* Until the nineteenth century, inscriptions could be seen along the south side of the Colosseum, marking the boundaries of the "quarries" allotted to late Roman senators.

† The Roman amphitheater at Nimes also became a medieval castle, complete with a knightly order known as the Soldiers of the Arena. Later a neighborhood grew up inside it, with a population of two thousand and a distinctive dialect.

‡ To judge from the fact that eighteen men (but only eleven bulls) were killed, the would-be matadors were more enthusiastic than skilled.

§ Pope Paul III authorized his nephew, Cardinal Farnese, to take as much stone from the Colosseum as he could remove in twelve hours. On the appointed day, the cardinal had four thousand men ready to attack the ruins.

the Palazzo Farnese, the Palazzo Barberini, Sant'Agostino, the Ponte Sisto, and many other structures. The balcony in St. Peter's Basilica from which the pope gives his Urbi et Orbi blessing was fashioned from Colosseum travertine.

The amphitheater was saved from complete destruction by the fact that it was jointly owned, from the fourteenth century onward, by a local religious order, the city of Rome, and the popes. Although all three profited from the sale of stone, none could authorize wholesale demolition. The popes, who took the leading role in the Colosseum's management, were not always sympathetic stewards. Pius V proposed demolishing the building for its pagan associations, Sixtus V attempted to install a wool mill inside, and a later pontiff allowed manure to be dumped under the arcades. In general, however, the popes tried to limit pillaging, authorizing only the removal of stone that had already fallen from the walls. They seem to have been especially concerned with maintaining the north side of the Colosseum, which formed a monumental backdrop for papal processions between the Lateran Palace and the Vatican.

Gradually, the Colosseum came to be regarded as a Christian monument.* The little church of Santa Maria della Pieta was built next to the arena. A hermit lived inside, selling the grass that grew among the ruins.† Pope Clement X commissioned Gian Lorenzo Bernini to design a grand baroque church that would have filled the interior of the Colosseum. Although this church was never built, a crucifix was erected in the center of the arena, and Stations of the Cross were set up around the perimeter.

By Bernini's time, the Colosseum had become a major tourist destination. Johann Wolfgang von Goethe, who visited by moonlight in 1786, was astonished by its scale. Lord Byron devoted several

---

* According to tradition, St. Ignatius was devoured by lions in the Colosseum during the reign of Trajan, and Saints Abdon and Sennen were executed in the arena under Decius. All extant accounts of their martyrdoms, however, are much later than the events they purport to describe. It is very likely that Christians died in the Colosseum; we just don't know when or how.

† In 1741, the hermit was assaulted by thieves, who stabbed him seven times and left him for dead.

stanzas of *Childe Harold's Pilgrimage* to it. Artists sold paintings of the overgrown ruins to visitors. Efforts to excavate and stabilize the building began in the early nineteenth century.* Since then, with the exception of a brief period as a German arsenal during the Second World War, the Colosseum has been what it is today: the most famous of all ancient ruins and the definitive symbol of Roman grandeur and decadence.

---

* When Pius VII decided to buttress the collapsing outer wall, the work was deemed so hazardous that only convicts were employed. The pope reduced the sentences of those who survived.

Are There Roman Ruins Under Vatican City?

In 1574, workmen accidentally broke through the floor of St. Peter's Basilica. A torch dropped into the void revealed an ancient mausoleum walled with gold mosaics and carpeted with bones. A few decades later, an elaborate marble sarcophagus was discovered under another part of the basilica.* But it was only after 1939, when Pope Pius XII started to renovate the Vatican grottoes, that the extent of the Roman necropolis under St. Peter's became clear.[1]

Two thousand years ago, the future site of St. Peter's Basilica lay on the suburban fringe of Rome. Above it rose the Mons Vaticanus, whose slopes—now crowned by the Apostolic Palace—were mantled with scraggly vineyards and pockmarked by clay pits. In the direction of the river lay several imperial estates. Besides gardens, they contained a practice track for charioteers, a pool for naval combats, and a circus completed by Nero. The circus boasted a granite obelisk† brought by barge from Alexandria.[2]

Over the course of the second and third centuries, a necropolis developed around the Circus of Nero.‡ Most of the tombs were small

---

* The epitaph—which encouraged passersby to sample the pleasures of wine and women—so horrified Vatican authorities that they smashed the inscription and threw the pieces into the Tiber. The lid of the sarcophagus survived. It can now be found in the Indianapolis Museum of Art.

† The obelisk remained in place through the Middle Ages, when it became customary for pilgrims to crawl through the narrow space between its supports as a sign of penitence. It was moved to its current position at the center of St. Peter's Square in 1586.

‡ The necropolis must have already been substantial by the reign of Elagabalus, who reportedly had to destroy a number of tombs to make room for the elephant-drawn chariot he wanted to drive in Nero's Circus.

mausoleums. Built of brick-faced concrete trimmed with terra-cotta, they stood in neat rows by the roadside. Their interiors were richly decorated, some with mosaics, others with figured stucco. The walls shone with frescoes—scenes from Greek myth, personifications of the stars, even a portrait of the Egyptian god Horus.[3]

Each mausoleum remained in use for generations, and some received burials for more than a century. Many of those interred within had been functionaries in the imperial bureaucracy. A considerable number were either freedmen or their descendants. A few were Christian, apparently attracted by a small monument in the heart of the necropolis. That monument consisted of three niches cut into a red-painted wall. The bottom niche, beneath the surface of the surrounding pavement, was covered by a perforated lid. The two above were framed by miniature columns. This was the structure described by a Roman priest named Gaius as the Trophy—memorial or tomb—of the apostle Peter, who had been executed in Nero's Circus.[4]

After his conversion to Christianity, Constantine decided to build a church of unprecedented scale and grandeur over the tomb of the first apostle. The emperor's workmen cut deep into the Mons Vaticanus and dumped the spoil—more than a million cubic feet—over the base of the hill. In the process, the upper part of the necropolis around Nero's Circus was obliterated. The tombs on the lower slopes, however, were buried and preserved beneath the colossal foundations of the basilica.

At the focal point of Constantine's church stood the once-humble Trophy of Gaius, now encased in precious marble and crowned by a canopy with spiraling columns. Early in the Middle Ages, Pope Gregory I built an altar directly above the apostle's memorial. With various embellishments, this structure remained intact until the Renaissance, when old St. Peter's was torn down to make room for the modern basilica, and a new high altar was erected on top of Gregory's. The finishing touch was Bernini's Baldacchino, which unwittingly mirrored the canopy Constantine had set up over the Trophy of Gaius.

Three centuries later, when Pius XII's archaeologists reached the area beneath the high altar, they discovered Gregory's altar,

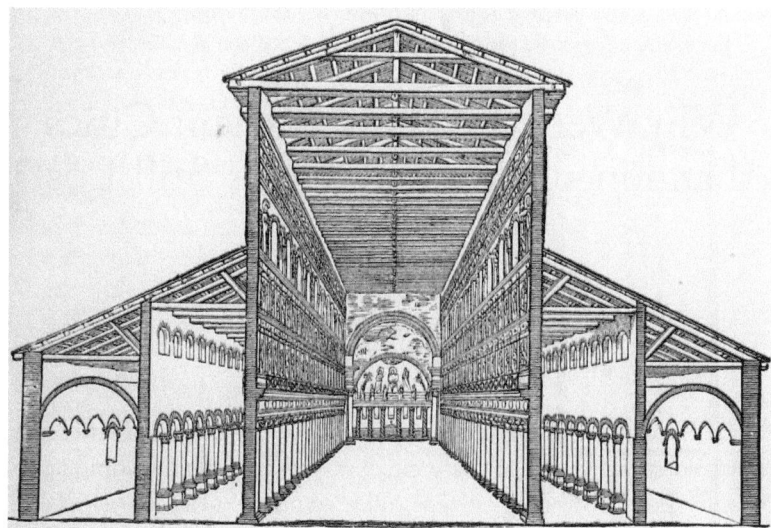

A nineteenth-century cutaway drawing of old St. Peter's Basilica.
Wikimedia Commons

Constantine's shrine, and the Trophy of Gaius superimposed on one another, all more or less intact. They also discovered part of the wall—its plaster still red—against which the Trophy of Gaius had been built. Behind the trophy, the foundations of the red wall bent upward; here, in a recess, the excavators found the bones of an elderly man with a powerful physique. These, according to the church, are the remains of Peter.*

Whenever I visit St. Peter's Basilica, I make my way to the foot of the Baldacchino, where marble steps descend to a chapel paneled with semiprecious stones. In the rear wall are doors of gilded bronze. Behind, sheathed in medieval mosaics, is the Trophy of Gaius, rooted in the Roman necropolis beneath St. Peter's Basilica.

---

* The excavators conjectured that the builders of the red wall had stumbled on the bones and identified them with the apostle Peter. About half the skeleton—including the skull—was missing. This seems to accord with the tradition that Peter's head was moved to St. John Lateran. Secular scholars are less sure about the identity of the bones. It seems clear, however, that the site has been associated with Peter since at least the second century. Constantine, at least, had no doubt that he was building his basilica over the apostle's tomb.

Why Were So Many Ancient Cities Abandoned? Are Any Cities Still Lost?

The Roman Empire was organized as a confederation of cities two thousand strong. Each of these cities was responsible for administering a territory. Its leading citizens collected taxes on Rome's behalf and kept order in the countryside. In return, they received all the benefits of the Pax Romana, with its unprecedented opportunities for political advancement. To consolidate and commemorate their position, civic elites poured vast sums into public buildings, creating the monumental cityscapes that still define our image of Roman civilization.

The golden age ended amid the invasions and economic crises of the third century. Along the frontiers, barbarian incursions damaged or destroyed hundreds of cities. Even places spared by the marauders were compelled to cobble walls together from disassembled monuments.* Although stability returned in the fourth century, long-term social changes slowed the process of recovery. The later Roman emperors had difficulty convincing local notables to manage their cities. The wealthiest magnates often left for well-paid positions in the imperial administration. Those who remained were increasingly impoverished, less able and less willing to govern.

Cities with important roles in the government of the empire thrived as long as the empire did. Arles, Milan, and Trier, for example, grew larger than ever before in late antiquity. But in most parts

---

* Rome's Aurelian Walls, twelve miles in circumference and eventually more than fifty feet tall, are the most famous example. The Athenians built a wall around the same time using the stone of buildings ruined during a destructive barbarian raid.

of the northwestern provinces, where the urban tradition had shallow roots, cities contracted. Londinium began to lose inhabitants in the late second century and seems to have been completely abandoned—like most British cities—after the empire fell.

In general, cities near the Mediterranean were likelier to survive the collapse of the Western Roman Empire than those on the frontiers. (The prosperous cities of the Rhineland were a partial exception.) Besides being closer to still-vital trade routes, Mediterranean cities had a better chance of being peacefully incorporated into one of the barbarian kingdoms that replaced the empire.* In later centuries, however, coastal cities became subject to pirate attack. Even St. Peter's Basilica was looted by Saracen raiders in the ninth century. To escape the danger, the inhabitants of some coastal settlements moved en masse to the nearest defensible hill.

Cities in many parts of the Eastern Roman Empire remained vital until the early seventh century. Then the Avars and Slavs overran the Balkans; even the Spartans fled to the impregnable stronghold of Monemvasia. During the cataclysmic war with Shah Khosrow II, Persian armies sacked and burned their way across Asia Minor.† The cities of Syria and Palestine—close to the center of the Umayyad caliphate—fared better, surviving and even flourishing after the Arab conquests.‡ Eventually, however, almost every region was subjected to raids and invasions. Arab horsemen ravaged the Anatolian Plateau, driving the inhabitants into castles and caves. In the Maghreb, the migrating Banu Hilal tribe destroyed so many cities during the eleventh century that regions cultivated since the Carthaginian period reverted to pastoralism.

---

* The cities of southern Gaul, which passed directly into the control of a well-organized Visigothic kingdom, were especially fortunate. So, until Justinian's Gothic Wars, were the cities of Italy. The cities of Britain, by contrast, were largely destroyed by generations of invasion and civil war. The Anglo-Saxon chieftains, whose power was based on control of the countryside, had no reason to rebuild them.

† Cities near the Syrian frontier had long suffered from Persian raids. Sassanid armies twice took tens of thousands of prisoners from Antioch and settled them in the Persian heartland—most memorably in a newly built city called Wēh Antīōk Khosrow ("Khosrow's Better Antioch").

‡ The monumental colonnaded streets of Anjar, founded by Caliph al-Walid in the early eighth century, recall those built by Roman provincial elites more than a half-millennium before.

Invaders were far from the only problem cities faced. The plagues in the reigns of Marcus Aurelius and Justinian caused considerable depopulation.* As the climate cooled in late antiquity, mountain cities withered. The irrigated fields of Egypt's Fayyum Basin were ruined by salination. The harbors of Ephesus, Miletus, and many other ports silted up. Earthquakes caused much of Alexandria and Baiae to sink into the sea. Malaria† depopulated marshy regions.[1]

Even where invasions were infrequent and the landscape remained healthy, the disappearance of the Roman Empire was accompanied by profound economic changes. These were most dramatic along the former frontiers, where many cities had depended, directly or indirectly, on military spending. Cities everywhere, however, relied on dense networks of exchange. On the Limestone Massif of northern Syria, dozens of large villages had emerged in late antiquity, supplying olive oil to Antioch and its environs. But after trade routes changed in the wake of the Arab conquests, the villages were abandoned. Their gaunt ruins, never again inhabited, came to be known as the "Dead Cities."‡

It can be easy to forget how fragile cities are. They rely on sprawling networks of trade and transport, delicate webs of infrastructure, and critical masses of people and resources. Although invasions and natural disasters played their part, most ancient cities were doomed by subtler changes that slowly unraveled their reasons for being.

Many ancient cities have vanished beneath modern buildings and modern names. But only a few have truly disappeared from human knowledge. The most famous examples are Herculaneum and Pompeii, buried by Vesuvius. Local farmers had been uncovering artifacts

---

* To judge from papyri, many Egyptian villages lost a third or more of their populations during the Antonine Plague. Whether these losses permanently weakened their viability is unclear.

† The unfortunate residents of Kaunos, now on the south coast of Turkey, caught malaria so frequently that their skin was said to be tinged green.

‡ The population of the Limestone Massif has never recovered to its Roman apogee. Until at least the early twentieth century, parts of the Italian Mezzogiorno, most of Turkey's Mediterranean coast, the Hauran in Syria and Jordan, the Negev Desert, Egypt's Fayyum Basin, and many parts of coastal North Africa were less populous than they had been under Roman rule.

The baths of Serjilla, one of Syria's "Dead Cities." *Wikimedia Commons*

above the site of Pompeii for centuries, calling the area around the half-buried amphitheater *la civitò*—"the city." But it was only in 1709, when well diggers struck the marble seats of Herculaneum's theater, that the first excavations under Vesuvius began.*

Other lost cities were hidden, at least from European scholars, by their remoteness. A famous case is Petra, forgotten until 1812, when the intrepid Swiss explorer Johann Burckhardt reached the place that the local Bedouin called Wadi Musa—"the Valley of Moses." Timgad, the "African Pompeii," had been abandoned for a millennium by the time James Bruce, a wandering Scottish nobleman, stumbled on its ruins in 1765. His description of a well-preserved Roman city on the edge of the Sahara was disbelieved until the late nineteenth century, when a new generation of explorers surveyed and photographed the ruins.

---

* At the end of the sixteenth century, a canal was cut through the middle of Pompeii. Although the workmen must have discovered many ruins, the discovery was not announced—possibly to avoid attracting the attention of the Inquisition. Excavators at Herculaneum have found medieval pottery in backfilled tunnels, suggesting that the buried city was rediscovered long before 1709.

In 1963, a man in the Turkish town of Derinkuyu found a mysterious void behind the wall of his cellar. This proved to be an entrance to a vast subterranean city, constructed and enlarged during the Roman and Byzantine periods. Its eighteen levels, capacious enough to hold twenty thousand people, featured a wine press, stables, and several churches.

A handful of ancient cities are still lost. Herculaneum and Pompeii are only partly excavated, and the suburbs, villages, and villas that surrounded them remain largely unexplored. Over the past three centuries, chance discoveries have revealed dozens of elaborate Roman villas in the districts of Boscoreale and Boscotrecase, just north of Pompeii. One of these—excavated and reburied in the late nineteenth century—produced the Boscoreale Treasure, which contained some of the greatest masterpieces of Roman silverwork ever discovered.* The nearby villa of Publius Fannius Synistor was decorated with a series of spectacular frescoes, now a highlight of the Metropolitan Museum of Art. In 1906, shortly after the frescoes were removed, Vesuvius buried the villa beneath a fresh blanket of volcanic debris.

Many other villas in the vicinity await rediscovery. So does Murecine, a suburb of Pompeii. A few mansions were discovered there in the eighteenth century and then reburied and lost. In the years since, sporadic discoveries have produced such marvels as the archive of the Sulpicii—the most detailed set of financial records to survive from the Roman world. We can only guess at what else is hidden under the ashes.

Across the Bay of Naples from Vesuvius are the fumaroles of the Phlegraean Fields, another volcanic hot spot. Here, beside a series of hot springs, the Romans built elaborate baths, domed and vaulted with concrete, which survived to be drawn by Renaissance architects. But on the morning of September 29, 1538, a crack opened beside Tripergole, a town that had grown up among the ancient baths. Smoke rose from the fissure, followed by surging fountains of lava. In less than a day, a volcano more than four hundred feet high came

---

* About a thousand aurei were discovered with the silver, their gold given a reddish tint by the heat of the eruption.

into being, covering Tripergole and its Roman baths. Nobody knows where or how deeply the ruins are buried.

Equally dramatic disasters claimed other ancient settlements. On a winter night in 373 BCE, the Greek city of Helike was struck by a severe earthquake. The ground liquified, tsunamis roared over the harbor, and the whole town—walls, temples, and people—sank beneath the waves. Not even a Spartan fleet anchored offshore escaped. The submerged ruins, eventually covered by mud, were rediscovered only in 2001. Other sunken cities remain lost. According to the Greek geographer Pausanias, a city on the slopes of Mount Sipylus, in what is now Turkey, disappeared into a vast chasm during an earthquake.* A lake formed in the basin, and the ruins could long be seen at the bottom. If it ever existed, this city has not been located.[2]

Other lost cities were destroyed by war. Tigranocerta, a capital of ancient Armenia, was captured by the Roman general Lucullus in 69 BCE. Some 8,000 talents—more than 400,000 pounds—of silver were seized during the sack. The city was burned, and its inhabitants were dispersed. The site has never been found.

Remote outposts of the classical world often disappeared when the trade that sustained them vanished. Ptolemais Theron†—an important Hellenistic trading center on the coast of the Red Sea—has never been found. Nor, probably, has Muziris, the rich settlement on the Malabar Coast that served as the center of Rome's Indian trade. Muziris may have been destroyed by a medieval cyclone. But most lost ancient cities vanished because their inhabitants did—driven or drifting away, taking their traditions and memories with them. Then, unless some record survives to be read, silence descends.

---

* In his commentary on Pausanias, James Frazer suggested that this story originated from the presence of a deep natural canyon on one side of the mountain, which looks like the result of a great earthquake.

† *Theron* means "of the hunts"; the Ptolemies hunted elephants in the vicinity.

· 39 ·

Does Any Country Still
Use Roman Law?

$\mathcal{R}$oman law has led a double life. For a thousand years, it grew and developed with the Roman state. Then, more than a half-millennium after the Western Roman Empire fell, it reemerged as the legal framework of medieval and early modern Europe and went on to inspire the civil codes used across two-thirds of the globe today. The pivot that connects these two careers is the *Digest*, the culmination of the most ambitious project in the history of Roman law.

It took three years to compile the *Digest*—three years, during which a commission set up by Emperor Justinian sifted through more than three million lines of legal commentary and condensed them into the definitive compilation of the opinions of the Roman jurists. The finished work, with 9,123 extracts in 50 books, was proclaimed on December 16, 533. It was free, the emperor declared, of errors or contradictions; it would be observed for all time.[1]

Roman law had first been formalized nearly a thousand years before, in the code known as the Twelve Tables. From those origins, it had ramified and proliferated, enriched by the edicts of magistrates, the decrees of emperors, and the treatises of jurists. The first attempts at codification coincided with the reign of Diocletian,* but it was only under Theodosius II, in the fifth century, that an imperially sponsored

---

* A precondition was the gradual replacement of scrolls with codices (books), which made works of reference vastly easier to create and use. The sheer bulk of accumulated commentary, however, continued to cause confusion. A rule arose that, if the writings of the greatest jurists disagreed, the majority view should always prevail.

collection of laws appeared. Justinian sponsored the definitive codification a century later. Besides the *Digest*, Justinian's compilers assembled the *Institutes* (an elementary textbook for law students*) and the
Code (a collection of legislation by emperors from Hadrian onward).
Together with the *Novels*—laws issued later in Justinian's reign—the
Digest, the *Institutes*, and the *Code* came to be collectively known as
the *Corpus Juris Civilis*.[2]

Before considering how the *Corpus*—and especially the
Digest—shaped modern law, it might be helpful to briefly discuss
how civil law operated in ancient Rome.[†] During the early imperial era, a case between citizens began at the court of the praetor.
(There were, by then, sixteen praetors, two of whom presided over
the main civil jurisdictions.) Some cases proceeded no further. A
praetor could declare a plaintiff's suit invalid, or the defendant
could admit that it was just. Normally, however, it was the praetor's
task to define the case with a statement known as a formula and to
appoint a judge. The judge need not be an official or even a Roman
citizen; he could be almost anyone whose arbitration was acceptable
to both parties. Plaintiff or defendant might suggest a candidate;
alternatively, the praetor could select someone. Sometimes three
or five judges were appointed. An especially prominent case, particularly one dealing with a disputed inheritance, might be brought
before the Court of One Hundred.

Whatever the arrangement, the judge or judges set a time and
location for the trial. On the appointed day, the plaintiff and the
defendant appeared with their advocates. The lawyers orated; wit-
nesses and written testimonies were adduced. When the dust had
settled, the judge (who was usually not a legal expert himself) might
consult with one or more men known to be learned in the law. Then

---

* The most important law schools in Justinian's empire were at Constantinople and
Beirut. Justinian specified a five-year course of study, with the first year dedicated to the
Institutes, the next three to the *Digest*, and the last to the *Code*. With no false modesty, he
decreed that freshmen should be known as *Iustiniani novi*—"New Justinianites."

† The following focuses on private or civil law—the law, in other words, that governed
interactions between citizens—because this was always the heart of the Roman legal tradition. No fewer than forty-six of the *Digest*'s fifty books deal with it.

he rendered his decision. The state would not enforce the verdict,* but if the plaintiff did not receive his due, he was entitled to personally imprison the defendant and sell his property.[3]

Especially later in Roman history, when more scope was given for appeal, the wheels of justice turned very slowly; Theoderic once ended a suit that had dragged on for thirty years by threatening to execute both lawyers. In all periods, the law favored the rich. Besides having the resources to weather the legal process and the social capital to influence judges, the elite were formally categorized, from the second century onward, as *honestiores*—the "better sort," exempt from the worst punishments. The laws themselves, however, were remarkably sophisticated. Nearly a quarter of the *Digest*, for example, was taken up with the legal intricacies surrounding wills and succession. Contract law was also impressively nuanced. In itself, of course, complexity is no guarantee of quality, but it at least conveys a determination to apply the law to every contingency.[4]

In the Byzantine Empire, the *Corpus Juris Civilis* was condensed and translated into the Greek code known as the *Basilika*. But in western Europe, where Justinian's laws had never been widely used,† the *Corpus* was virtually forgotten until the mid-eleventh century, when a manuscript of the *Digest* surfaced in Italy.‡ Within a few decades, scholars at the recently established University of Bologna had begun to study and teach Roman law. Aside from the prestige of its association with the ancient emperors, Roman law had considerable practical appeal. Merchants appreciated its provisions for the enforcement of contracts. The Catholic Church used it to streamline procedure in ecclesiastical courts. And lawyers, presented with a

---

* The punishments for criminal cases, by contrast, were often ferocious. Theodosius I decreed that anyone who married a first cousin was to be burned alive. Constantine ordered molten lead to be poured down the throat of any nurse who corrupted a girl in her charge.

† Italy and southern Spain were the only parts of western Europe under Justinian's authority. Other Roman-influenced systems, mostly abridgements of the Theodosian Code, were used in early medieval Italy and France.

‡ This 1,800-page manuscript seems to have been written at Constantinople soon after the completion of the *Digest*. Supposedly taken from Amalfi as a prize of war, the manuscript has been in Florence's Laurentian Library since the Renaissance.

system so complex that it could be used to argue almost any position, found Roman law very much to their liking.

Roman law came to be accepted through much of medieval Europe. Although local practice continued to vary, the *Digest* provided a common framework for legal decisions. This was especially important in politically fragmented Germany, where the supreme tribunal of the Holy Roman Empire settled all cases in accordance with Roman law. In England, by contrast, the power of the king and the royal courts had consolidated relatively early. As a result, by the time Roman law swept across Europe, England already had a well-established common-law tradition, which it maintains to this day.

On the Continent, Roman law was gradually displaced by national civil codes. The most influential of these appeared in 1804, when France adopted the Code Napoléon. Over the course of the nineteenth century, this system provided a model for the national codes of the Netherlands, Spain, Italy, Belgium, and much of South America. The newly unified German Empire continued to use Roman law until 1900, when the German Civil Code was promulgated. This, in turn, was imitated by many countries, including Japan and Brazil.

Some countries resisted the tide of codification. Until 1946, Greek law was based on the *Hexabiblos*, a late Byzantine abridgement of the Code of Justinian. The Ethiopian Law of Kings, also inspired by the Byzantine incarnation of Roman law, remained in effect through 1960. Versions of "common" Roman law—Roman law shaped by local custom—are still used in the microstates of San Marino and Andorra. Vatican City follows Catholic canon law, modeled on but independent of Roman law. The law of Scotland, though heavily influenced by common law, contains many Roman elements. Roman law also remains in effect in several former Dutch colonies, notably Sri Lanka, Guyana, and (to a lesser degree) South Africa.

More generally, all the national civil codes created in the nineteenth and twentieth centuries are descended from the *Corpus Juris Civilis*. The French code imported many concepts from the *Corpus*, as refracted through the lens of natural law. The German code, likewise, can be understood as a systematic rationalization of the *Digest*. In this sense, the basic elements of Roman law still serve as a shared frame of reference. England and many former British colonies, of course, follow the common-law tradition. So, with the partial exception of Louisiana, does the United States.* But even in common-law jurisdictions, law is defined in basically Roman terms—as the *Digest* puts it, *ars boni et aequi*—the "art of integrity and equity."

---

* The Civil Code of Louisiana, first enacted in 1808, was not based on the Napoleonic Code but on a fusion of pre-Napoleonic French and Spanish traditions, all ultimately rooted in Roman law.

• *40* •

Have Roman Beliefs Survived in Italian Folklore?

*E*choes of ancient Rome are everywhere in Italian folklore and popular religion. Santa Venere, widely revered in southern Italy, may have originated as the goddess Venus. Shrines of saints and the Madonna at crossroads are successors of the ancient Lares Compitales. The figurines of monks and priests traditionally believed to protect houses around Naples are analogs of the Penates found in Pompeii's household shrines.

None of these, however, are straightforward survivals from antiquity. In the seventeen centuries since Constantine, Christianity has infused every aspect of Italian life. Even when folk practices or beliefs seem identical to their Roman counterparts, the rationale behind them has changed. They are not survivals but fossils—the original matter has decayed, leaving only a shape or impression. Or, to use another analogy, they are words in different languages that happen to rhyme. But languages can be related to one another, as Italian is to Latin; though no aspect of ancient Rome has survived unchanged in modern Italy, lines of descent can sometimes be traced.*

At first glance, an Italian Catholic wedding is profoundly different from anything in ancient Rome. Neither Roman law nor

---

* I describe Italy as a unity here, when of course Italy is really a patchwork of cities, regions, dialects, and histories only notionally unified by a dysfunctional and frequently disregarded national government. Folk practices in Naples had little to do with those in Milan, and vice versa. Additionally, though many of the customs I discuss here can still be found in parts of Italy, my discussion focuses on the early twentieth century, before the country was transformed by mass migration from south to north, the modernization of agriculture, and the influence of mass media.

Roman custom required a marriage ceremony. If a man and woman declared their intention of forming a union and then cohabited, they were married in the eyes of the law.* Especially among upper- and middle-class families, however, a public ceremony was common. Well in advance of a wedding, a formal betrothal took place, at which the groom gave the bride a pledge of engagement. This was usually a ring, placed on the third finger of the left hand. Though traditionally made of iron, gold rings were common by the imperial era. It came to be believed that a vein or nerve connected the left ring finger to the heart. The early Christians maintained the custom of engagement rings, which has endured to this day.[1]

Another Roman legacy is the tradition that weddings in May are unlucky.† The Romans regarded roughly a third of the year as unsuitable for marriage ceremonies, usually because the days in question were ill omened or associated with a festival. The month of May was stigmatized by Lemuria, a festival meant to propitiate the restless dead. Widows, however, were free to marry in May or whenever else they liked.[2]

A Roman bride wore a long white robe with an elaborately tied girdle. Her head was covered by the *flammeum*, a gauzy saffron veil. Early Christian brides were similarly dressed, though they preferred purple and white veils. Many other elements of the Roman wedding ceremony outlasted the transition to Christianity, such as the signing of a marriage contract and the solemn joining of the bride and groom's right hands. Although these vanished over time, the bridal veil‡ survived—as, in the Orthodox Church, did the ancient custom of crowning the bride. After the ceremony, a Roman bride was carried over the threshold of her husband's house. Plutarch and other ancient authors debated the origins of this custom, speculating that it commemorated the abduction of the Sabines by Romulus. It's more

---

* This convention survived the Christianization of Europe by several centuries; only under Charlemagne did it become legally necessary for marriages to be conducted by a priest.

† As Ovid put it, *mense maio malae nubunt* ("they marry badly, who marry in May"). Technically, however, only Lent was off-limits for Catholic weddings.

‡ The ceremony of "taking the veil" for a nun is still imagined as a mystical marriage to Christ. In parts of Europe, the late Roman/early Christian custom of spreading a large veil over both bride and groom survived into the twentieth century.

likely to have begun as a precautionary measure against the evil omen of a bride stumbling as she entered her new home. However it began, the superstition still exists.[3]

From weddings, we proceed to funerals. To judge from the inscriptions on their tombs, few Romans hoped for a meaningful life after death. Christians, by contrast, believe that the dead are born into a new life with God. In theory, then, a Christian funeral should be a celebration—and this seems to have indeed been the custom in the early church, when the mourners dressed in festive clothes and carried the palm of victory. By late antiquity, however, Christians, like their pagan neighbors, wore black to funerals.[4]

When a Roman died, his eyes and mouth were closed by a relative.* Trained slaves washed the body, anointed it, and dressed it in fine clothes. A small coin to pay the ferryman over the Styx was often placed in the mouth. The body was then carried to the atrium and laid on a couch, feet toward the door. Almost all these customs survived until quite recently. Before the advent of modern medicine, most people died at home. Funeral parlors were seldom involved in the preparations for burial before the twentieth century. Like their Roman and early Christian ancestors, Italians closed the eyes of the newly deceased. The tasks of washing and dressing the body were performed by family members or local specialists, as they had been since slave undertakers vanished with the Roman Empire. The body was laid out at home in its Sunday best. In parts of southern Italy, a coin was placed in the mouth.[5]

Every Roman family that could afford it staged a funeral procession. At the head were musicians. Then came hired mourners, women paid to weep and sing praises of the dead. Next, slaves freed by the deceased, all wearing the cap of liberty. After them, a line of relatives wearing the wax masks of eminent ancestors. Finally, the body, carried on an elaborate couch. The immediate family walked behind, lamenting.† Although the advent of Christianity added a funeral service, the custom of processing to the grave endured. The

---

* The eyes were reopened when the body was laid on its funeral pyre.

† Originally, Roman funerals took place only at night. By the imperial era, however, only families too poor to pay for a procession followed the old custom.

freedmen and wax masks disappeared, but professional mourners could be hired in parts of Italy until the nineteenth century. The torches carried in Roman funeral processions survived as candles.*

Perhaps the most persistent classical artifact in modern Italian folklore is the evil eye. Most Romans seem to have believed that certain people could cause harm with the power of their gaze. Although the means by which this result was achieved remained mysterious—Plutarch speculated about maleficent effluvia—the underlying cause was understood to be envy, which withers anything it touches. Children were especially susceptible, though livestock could also be harmed.[6]

There were several methods of warding off the evil eye. Apotropaic images, such as the gorgon heads often found on breastplates and temple pediments, were thought to deflect it. So were paintings or mosaics of eyes being attacked by weapons and poisonous creatures. For personal protection, Romans wore amulets, often in the shape of a phallus. These amulets, known as *fascina*—the origin of our word *fascinate*—were hung around the necks of children, incorporated into the signs of shops, and slung beneath the chariots of triumphant generals. If exposed without the protection of an amulet, a victim of the evil eye might avert disaster by extending his middle finger (the *digitus infamis*) or wedging his thumb between two fingers.† Alternatively, he could spit into a fold of his tunic.[7]

Belief in the evil eye is still widespread in Italy. Babies, new mothers, and young animals are thought to be most vulnerable, but anyone can be harmed. Well into the twentieth century, phallic amulets were frequently worn for protection; other symbols of male fertility, such as a horn, snake, or coral, are more common now. A remedy for exposure to the evil eye is pretending to spit three times. Hand gestures can also be used. The most famous of these is the

---

* During the consecration of a Catholic church, the relic that will be interred in the altar is carried forward like the body in a Roman funeral procession—on a litter, surrounded by attendants bearing incense. The nine days of mourning observed during the funeral of a pope also derive from ancient Roman practice.

† This is the Italian *mano fica*, a sign of insult in the Roman period. The *digitus infamis* was also known as the *digitus impudicus*—the "indecent finger"—and it meant more or less what it does today.

A mosaic from Antioch, showing an evil eye being attacked from all sides. The Greek caption over the figure on the left means, in effect, "back at you." *Public domain*

manu cornuta: a fist with the index and little fingers extended. You may recognize this as the "devil horns" of heavy metal, popularized by Ronnie James Dio. But as Dio explained in interviews, he had learned the sign from his Italian grandmother, who used it to ward off the evil eye. The same gesture can be seen on a Roman tombstone dating to the first century BCE—another example of continuity across religions and over millennia.

• *41* •

How Much Has Latin Influenced English?

*E*nglish is a Germanic language. It is a sister of Frisian and Low German, a close relation of Dutch, and a variously distant cousin of Icelandic, Swedish, and Yiddish. But thanks to fifteen centuries of invasion, invention, and pedantry, nearly two-thirds of the modern English vocabulary derives from Latin.

English was born when tribal groups from what are now Denmark and northern Germany—including the Angles and Saxons—overran the former Roman province of Britain.* The dialects spoken by the invaders, which would evolve into Old English, were Germanic. From the beginning, however, Latin words were present. Long before they came to Britain, the Angles and Saxons had dealt with Roman merchants, from whom they learned such words as *wine*, from the Latin *vinum*; *pound*, from *pondus*; *cheap*, from *caupo*; and *monger*, from *mango*. Other Latin words entered Old English via interactions with the Romano-British and Christian missionaries.

The latinization of English truly began, however, with the Norman Conquest. For more than three hundred years, Norman French—based on vulgar Latin—was the language of government and law in England. Latinate French words pertaining to these spheres flooded

---

* After three and a half centuries of Roman rule, Latin was widespread in Britain, especially in the southeast and along the heavily militarized northern frontier. Many of the island's inhabitants, however, still spoke some form of Brittonic, the Celtic language used before the Roman conquest. But even in the far west, where Roman influence had been lightest, a fair amount of Latin seems to have crept in. Modern Welsh, a direct descendant of Brittonic, still preserves such Latin loanwords as *ffenestr* (from *fenestra*, "window") and *llyfr* (*liber*, "book").

the English vocabulary: *sovereign* and *parliament, justice* and *jury, duke* and *prince.* Later in the Middle Ages, as the influence of French waned, more words were imported directly from Latin. Some, like *requiem* and *limbo,* were religious. Others related to scholarship: *allegory, library, desk, scribe.* Growing interest in Roman law inspired the coinage of *client, conviction,* and *prosecutor.*

The Renaissance witnessed an explosion of learned borrowings from Latin. In keeping with Latin's status as the language of scholarship, notable additions were made in the fields of medicine (*rabies, forceps, lumbago*), physics (*lens, pendulum, inertia*), and mathematics (*radius, series, formula*). The most remarkable Renaissance coinages, however, were literary. Many of the 1,700 or so words invented by Shakespeare had Latin roots, including *summit, submerged, excellent, castigate,* and *obscene.* Ben Jonson is responsible for *defunct* and *strenuous.* Sir Thomas Elyot produced *animate, exhaust,* and *modesty.* Not all the Latinate terms concocted by Renaissance wordsmiths persisted: *lapidificial, obstupefact,* and *vadimonial* were too beautiful for this world. But *arbiter, omen, equilibrium, stimulus,* and thousands more are still with us.

Borrowing from Latin continued at a more restrained rate until the nineteenth century, when new sciences and new concepts elicited another generation of Latinate words: *aquarium, bonus, consensus, deficit, extra, et cetera.* The twentieth century added thousands more (*computer, molecule, satellite*) and countless compounds crafted with Latin prefixes (*re-, de-*) and suffixes (*-ize, -ment, -tion, -able*).

In addition to its vast influence on vocabulary, Latin is responsible for some quirks of English spelling.* Particularly in the seventeenth century, classically educated authors and editors altered numerous words to resemble Latin ancestors and analogs. Sometimes a new Latinate spelling changed a word's pronunciation: *aventure* became *adventure, perfit* became *perfect,* and *verdit* became *verdict.* More often, the changes were silent, like the *p* added to *receipt,* the *c* stuck in *scissors,* the *b* inserted into *doubt,* and the *s* in *island.*

Generations of English teachers instructed their students to carefully avoid splitting infinitives and compose sentences that no

---

* Latin is only partially responsible for English spelling becoming a minefield. The worst culprit was probably the Great Vowel Shift, a series of major changes in pronunciation that had the misfortune to coincide with the advent of printing.

prepositions dangled from. Both of these "rules" originated in (or were at least argued by false analogy with) Latin. Such pedantry has sometimes given Latin a bad name. So does the fact that Latinate vocabulary, liberally deployed, degenerates into sesquipedalian super-fluity.* In reaction, some advocated greater use of Germanic words. The nineteenth-century author William Barnes wrote an *Outline of English Speech-Craft*, in which he urged such alternatives as *kin-elder* for *ancestor*, *forcarve* for *amputate*, and *waterlode* for *aqueduct*.†

Most writers, however, appreciate the unparalleled expressive-ness made possible by the complex heritage of English. Consider, for example, the slightly different connotations of these pairs of Germanic and Latinate adjectives: *earthly* and *terrestrial, hidden* and *latent, timely* and *temporal*. There are whole clusters of English words borrowed directly and indirectly from the same Latin root: *amiable* and *amicable*; *frail* and *fragile*; *poor, pauper,* and *impoverished*. English allows you to *get* or *obtain*, to *hug* or *embrace*, to have *freedom* or *liberty*.‡

A famous example of these expressive possibilities appears in the second act of *Macbeth*. Wracked with guilt over his murder of Duncan, Macbeth fixates on the blood staining his hands:

> Will all great Neptune's ocean wash this blood
> Clean from my hand? No, this my hand will rather
> The multitudinous seas incarnadine,
> Making the green one red.[1]

The polysyllabic Latinate phrase *multitudinous seas incarnadine* means much the same thing as the Germanic *making the green one red*. Yet there is no redundancy here: The power of the passage con-sists in playing the phrases off one another. English, in short, would have been much simpler without Latin. But it would also have been immeasurably poorer.

---

* The saying "A rolling stone gathers no moss" was once humorously paraphrased,

Cryptogamous concretion never grows
On mineral fragments that decline repose.

† Barnes was equally ungracious to words of Greek origin, substituting *folkdom* for *democracy*, *welkin-fire* for *meteor*, *bird-lore* for *ornithology*, and *sun-print* for *photograph*.
‡ English frequently assigns a Latinate adjective to a common Anglo-Saxon noun: *water* and *aquatic*, *book* and *literary*, *moon* and *lunar*, *mouth* and *oral*, *house* and *domestic*.

· *42* ·

How Roman Is the Times New Roman Font?

*T*he Latin alphabet, the modern world's dominant writing system, evolved from the Greek alphabet adopted by the Etruscans.* When the Romans began using it in the seventh century BCE, it had only twenty-one letters.† *Y* and *Z* were added later to express the sounds of Greek words. The scholarly emperor Claudius contributed three more letters—a replacement of *Y*, an equivalent of *U*, and a counterpart of the Greek letter *psi*—that disappeared after his reign. Our *U* and *W* are medieval; *J* was distinguished from *I* in the early modern period.

At first, the letters of the Latin alphabet closely resembled their Greek models. Their shapes became more distinctive over the course of the republican era, developing by the reign of Augustus into the majestic square capitals (known as *scriptura monumentalis* or *litterae quadratae*) that still grace many Roman monuments. The letters of late antique inscriptions tended to be taller, narrower, and less regular.

The angular letter forms of inscriptions were imitated on paper in the script known as rustic capitals. Because they were written

---

* The Greek alphabet, adapted from the Phoenician alphabet around 800 BCE, arrived in Italy with the first Greek colonists. (The oldest extant Greek inscription was found in Italy, not far from Rome.) The Greek alphabet adopted by the Etruscans and Romans was a "western" variant, substantially different from the East Ionic alphabet that eventually became standard throughout the Greek world.

† At first, there were effectively twenty letters in the Latin alphabet, since the Romans used "C" to represent the sounds of both C and G—a habit that persisted in the case of the names Gaius and Gnaeus, always abbreviated C and CN. The letter K was seldom used in later centuries, save in a few abbreviations (most notably, K for the kalends, the first day of the month). A few learned Romans regarded Q as superfluous and refused to use it.

The dedicatory inscription of Trajan's Column, written in square capitals. *Wikimedia Commons*

rather than carved, rustic capitals were more fluid, with curves and serifs absent on stone. Though impressive on the page, they were so time consuming to produce that they tended to be used only for luxury texts. Less formal documents were written in flowing cursive.*

After the collapse of the Western Roman Empire, the production of secular manuscripts virtually ceased. Religious texts, however, continued to be copied, most often in a new rounded script called uncial. Versions of uncial were used widely for nearly a half-millennium. The script persisted longest in Ireland, where Gaelic was written in a typeset version until the mid-twentieth century.

Elsewhere, uncial was displaced by Carolingian miniscule. Miniscule letters—simplified and compressed versions of capitals—had been around for centuries. But the miniscule that evolved from uncial in the late eighth century was clearer, more elegant, and ultimately more popular than any of its predecessors. It came to be associated with the brief but brilliant renaissance centered on the court of Charlemagne, during which secular texts were copied in large numbers for the first time since the fall of Rome. This was the era, and the script, that saved classical Latin literature from oblivion.

From the twelfth century onward, however, Carolingian miniscule began to be replaced by the compressed and angular script

---

* The Romans also employed a form of shorthand, reportedly invented by Cicero's secretary Tiro. This intricate system of symbols and abbreviations survived into the Middle Ages; the sign ⁊ (*et*—"and" in Latin) is still sometimes used in Irish and Scottish Gaelic.

known as Gothic or black letter. Though now associated with Germany, where the Gothic Fraktur was common until the Second World War,* it was used throughout Europe. During the Late Middle Ages, thanks to the rise of the universities and a growing literate class, more books were being produced than at any time since the fall of Rome. Gothic was adapted to different genres: a cramped variant for scholastic treatises, a large and rounded form for ecclesiastical books, and the intricate bastarda for vernacular texts.

The invention of printing changed surprisingly little. The first printed books were designed to resemble contemporary manuscripts. The font of Gutenberg's forty-two-line Bible, for example, imitated a local Gothic script. Religious texts were typically printed in typeset versions of the familiar scholastic black letter. Printed editions of the classics, however, used the script that was destined to replace all the others. It was known as *littera antiqua*—the ancient (or Roman) script.

Littera antiqua was born early in the fifteenth century, when a group of Italian humanists developed a tidy, elegant hand modeled on Carolingian miniscule. They thought they were imitating the handwriting of the ancient Romans. That assumption, combined with easy legibility, made the humanist script popular in manuscripts of classical texts. When printers adopted it, they maintained the convention of pairing humanist miniscule lowercase letters with capitals inspired by ancient inscriptions. This is essentially the system still used by all "Roman" fonts today.

At the turn of the sixteenth century, when Venice was the center of European printing, the premier printer of classical texts was Aldus Manutius, otherwise famous for his role in standardizing the use of the comma and semicolon. Aldus produced both expensive folio editions of Greek and Latin authors for scholars and more modestly

---

* In the nineteenth and early twentieth centuries, the Gothic black-letter typeface known as Fraktur came to be closely associated with German nationalism. Intense controversies erupted over whether Germany should transition—like the rest of Europe—to Roman fonts. The Nazis initially promoted Fraktur as "authentically German." Hitler, however, despised it, and in 1941, Germany officially abandoned the Gothic script. It survives today primarily in religious texts of the Amish and other German-speaking Christian fundamentalists.

priced octavo "handbooks" for the educated public. All were printed in a beautifully designed humanist typeface.*

Thanks in part to Aldus's influence, Roman fonts steadily displaced their Gothic predecessors everywhere outside the Germanic countries. The Aldine designs were imitated and refined, most famously by Claude Garamond and Robert Granjon, whose fonts were the most popular in Europe for nearly two hundred years.

Times New Roman, designed by Stanley Morison in 1931, was modeled on the Roman fonts of Robert Granjon. Compact but clear, distinctive without being jarring, it was meant to subtly recall the grand tradition of Renaissance Roman fonts. In the sense that none of its lowercase letters and only twenty-three of its capitals are directly modeled on ancient forms, Times New Roman is not quite half-Roman. But more broadly, it's all Roman—a direct descendant of the original Latin alphabet.

---

* For his handbooks, Aldus and his assistant Francesco Griffo designed the first italic font, modeled on the cursive of the humanist Niccolò Niccoli.

VII

WHAT IF?

Could Potatoes Have Saved
the Roman Empire?

Consider the potato. *Solanum tuberosum. La pomme de terre.* The tuber. The spud. The bakeable, fry-able, mash-able marvel we all know and love. What might the historical consequences have been if this delicious, nutritious Peruvian paragon had reached the Roman Empire?

The Columbian exchange—the transfer of plants, animals, and microbes between the Old World and the New—transformed the diet and destiny of Europe. Hungary embraced paprika. Italy began a torrid affair with the tomato. Chocolate overtook the continent. But perhaps the most transformative transatlantic transplant was the potato. At first, potatoes were curiosities. Some speculated that they had aphrodisiac properties. Others voiced concerns about their leprous appearance. But gradually, and with gathering speed in the eighteenth and nineteenth centuries, the potato was adopted as a field crop throughout northern Europe.

Land planted with potatoes produces several times as much food per acre as wheat or any other grain. Potatoes can be cultivated in poor soil and will grow in almost any temperate climate. If supplemented with milk, they provide all the nutrients needed by the human body. Potatoes, in short, meant food security, and food security swiftly translated into more Europeans. It has been estimated that potatoes were responsible for a quarter of Europe's population growth between 1700 and 1900. In Ireland, the number of inhabitants more than doubled. Potato eaters were also healthier: People from potato-rich regions grew, on average, a half-inch taller than their potato-forlorn forebears. Some scholars have suggested that, by fueling the rise of a new industrial working class, the potato made possible the global ascendancy of northwestern Europe.

So how would history have been different if the Romans had potatoes? The scenario isn't as far-fetched as you might think. Sweet potatoes reached Polynesia centuries before Columbus, carried in canoes from the coast of South America. Potato seeds could have crossed the Pacific by similar means and been caught up in Rome's Indian Ocean trade. The Romans were enthusiastic adopters of new crops; if the potato had reached Rome, its merits might have been quickly recognized.

Because potatoes grow best in cool and damp environments, they have never flourished on the coasts of the Mediterranean. They thrive, however, north of the Alps. This part of the Roman world had relatively few inhabitants. The potato could have changed that. Historically, the population of the Roman Empire rose from around 60 million during the reign of Augustus to 75 million in the mid-second century. Widespread cultivation of the potato over the same period could have dramatically enhanced the rate of growth.

Let's imagine a Roman Empire of 100 million people, with almost all the added population in the potato belt north of the Alps. In the classical world, where technological change was limited, population growth was the primary driver of economic growth. Within Malthusian limits, more people meant more taxes, more trade, and more prosperity. Thanks to the diffusion of existing technologies and increasingly sophisticated trade networks, the growth of the early imperial Roman economy seems to have outpaced that of the population. In theory, then, a steep rise in the Roman population could have massively expanded the empire's economy. Perhaps the greatest beneficiaries would have been the Rhine and Danube borderlands, which likely would have become both more prosperous and—if the emperors responded to the population surge by creating more military units—better defended. Potatoes, in short, might have created frontiers that were harder for barbarians to breach.

Alternatively, potatoes could have made everything worse. With the exception of the regions around military camps, the northwestern provinces were not well integrated into the Roman economy. It's possible that an additional twenty or thirty million inhabitants in this part of the empire would have created a crisis. In Qing-dynasty China, for example, the introduction of New World crops—especially the sweet potato—allowed the population to more than double in less than a century. The resultant social and economic pressures caused widespread turmoil and set the stage for the bloody White Lotus Rebellion.

In any case, the cultivation of potatoes would not have stopped at the Roman frontier. The peoples east of the Rhine and north of the Danube were also farmers. It's reasonable to assume that their populations would have grown as quickly as the empire's and that an increase in the number of Roman soldiers and civilians would have been balanced by multiplying tribes and raiding parties.

Perhaps, in the long term, potatoes wouldn't have made a fundamental difference. The underlying strength and resilience of the Roman Empire derived from political and social structures, not the size of the population. Food security might have made life easier for farmers in the northern provinces. But politically and economically, the spud could have been a dud.

• *44* •

What Languages Would Europeans Speak If Latin Never Existed?

*K*ing Pyrrhus surveyed the battlefield. Corpses carpeted the ground as far as the eye could see. The Romans had fought well; thousands of his own men lay among them. But he had won. Finally, he had won. The last Roman army had been crushed, and Italy lay open before him. A brilliant future awaited—in which he, Pyrrhus, would be the Alexander of the west. Smiling, he spurred his horse toward the gates of Rome . . .

In hindsight, the rise of Rome seems irresistible. From the beginning of the third century BCE, when the Republic broke the power of the Samnites, the Roman system of alliances and way of war achieved a momentum that even Hannibal failed to check. The Romans came to dominate the whole Mediterranean world with astonishing speed. Even more remarkably, they kept their hold on power for more than a half-millennium. Nothing about this situation, of course, was inevitable. If the Romans had lost the Battle of Lake Regillus against the Latin League, the Battle of Sentinum against the Samnites, or the Battle of the Metaurus against the Carthaginians—to mention only a few potential turning points—the Republic's expansion could easily have been reversed.

In 280 BCE, King Pyrrhus of Epirus, a talented general, invaded Italy at the head of a seasoned army. After winning two hard-fought battles, he moved his base of operations to Sicily, which he briefly conquered. Returning to Italy for a final confrontation with the Romans, he was decisively defeated at the Battle of Beneventum. If he had been victorious, Pyrrhus would have been in a position to dictate terms to the Republic. Although he probably would not have tried to subjugate Rome itself, he almost certainly would have disassembled the alliances on which Roman power relied. Many cities and peoples in southern Italy had defected to him after his first victory. Many more would have followed if he had landed a decisive blow. Had this occurred, and especially if Pyrrhus had managed to establish himself permanently in southern Italy and Sicily, Rome would have been reduced to the status of a minor regional power. Without the Roman Empire, the history of the world would have been profoundly different. To focus on one aspect of many, Latin would never have spread across Europe.

At the time of Pyrrhus's invasion, Latin was spoken only in central Italy. Greek was common in the south. The so-called Sabellic languages—most prominently, Oscan and Umbrian—dominated the center of the peninsula; Pompeii was an Oscan-speaking city until Sulla settled a veteran colony there. North of Rome, Etruscan was spoken as far as the Apennines.* Cisalpine Gaul belonged to the Celtic world. Celtic languages were spoken across a vast swath of central and northern Europe, from the British Isles to the lower Danube. In Spain, they mingled with Iberian, Tartessian, and Punic. In southern Gaul, they coexisted with Greek; the coins issued by Gallic chieftains often used the Greek alphabet.[1]

Farther north, Celts lived among Germanic tribes. German speakers spread gradually southward over the course of the Iron Age, reaching the vicinity of the Rhine and Danube by the third century BCE. In eastern Europe, they encountered speakers of the Scythian

---

* The origins of Etruscan—which, unlike Latin, Greek, and the Sabellic languages, was not Indo-European—have puzzled scholars since antiquity. Herodotus was told that the Etruscans were immigrants from Lydia, but this story is now believed to have been Lydian propaganda, invented to strengthen trade ties with the Etruscans. Archaeological evidence indicates that Etruscan culture, if not the Etruscan language, emerged in Italy. The little-known Raetic language seems to have been related to Etruscan, as (possibly) was the Pelasgian language spoken on the island of Lemnos. Although it has sometimes been theorized that the Etruscans either originated in or had connections with these regions, it's more likely that Raetic and Lemnian were cousins of Etruscan and that they—like Etruscan—were isolated by the arrival of the Indo-European languages long before the dawn of classical history.

languages and the Dacians, who used a form of Thracian. Thracian was also spoken south of the Danube, alongside Illyrian. The various dialects of Greek, already converging on Koine,* were universal in Greece proper and served as a lingua franca throughout the Balkans.[2]

The expansion of Latin in the provinces was occasionally promoted by Roman officials. Agricola, governor of Britain under Domitian, set up a school where the sons of chieftains could learn the language. In general, however, Latin spread organically. Provincial elites were motivated to learn the language by the benefits of alignment with the ruling power. The cities in which elites tended to congregate, connected with the commerce of the larger empire, became engines of linguistic diffusion. The Roman army taught Latin to millions of recruits and settled veterans in farms and colonies near the frontiers. Roman merchants imported millions of slaves into Italy and the western provinces, where they were compelled to learn their masters' tongue. During late antiquity, the Vulgate Bible and Latin Mass spread to every corner of the western empire.[3]

In the eastern provinces,† however, Greek was too well established and too prestigious to replace. Roman officials in the east simply spoke Greek: It was in Greek that Antony wooed Cleopatra and Pilate interrogated Jesus.‡ Even in the Latin-speaking western prov-

---

* Koine Greek—the "common" Greek based ultimately on the Attic dialect—was a product of the Hellenistic world. In Egypt and Syria, Greek became the language of the cities and their elites; the surrounding countryside remained Coptic and Aramaic speaking. In Asia Minor, Greek gradually became the language of both city and countryside. The process may have been accelerated by the region's extreme linguistic diversity. Mithridates VI of Pontus, whose kingdom lay in northeastern Asia Minor, reportedly spoke all twenty-two of his subjects' languages.

† The boundary between the Greek- and Latin-speaking parts of the Roman Empire—often known as the Jireček Line, after the Czech scholar who proposed it—bisected the Balkans, running diagonally from the Greek cities on the coast of the Black Sea to a point near the modern border between Albania and Montenegro. North and west of that line, Latin predominated; south and east, Greek. (In North Africa, the Latin/Greek divide fell somewhere along the coast of Libya's Gulf of Sidra.) The most prominent western exceptions were the ancient Greek colonies of Sicily and southern Italy; the inhabitants of a few villages in Calabria and Puglia still speak Greek dialects. Caesar and Augustus scattered colonies of Latin-speaking veterans across Greece and Asia Minor. Most assimilated fairly quickly to their Greek environs. The last bastion of Latin in the east was Constantinople, where the imperial court switched to Greek only in the seventh century.

‡ The education of a Roman aristocrat began with Homer and often ended with a few years in Athens. Both Claudius's *Etruscan History* and the *Meditations* of Marcus Aurelius were written in Greek.

inces, local languages persisted well into late antiquity. A quarter-millennium after Caesar's conquest of Gaul, Irenaeus of Lyon had to learn Celtic to communicate with his flock. A half-millennium after the fall of Carthage, the young St. Augustine spoke Punic with his friends. Brittonic, the Celtic dialect most common in Britain before the Romans arrived, was still the majority language when the Romans withdrew four centuries later. Welsh is a direct descendant. Basque survived the onslaught of Latin, just as it had outlasted the arrival of the Indo-European languages two thousand years before.[4]

In Britain, Latin vanished amid the chaos of the Anglo-Saxon conquest. The Slavic invasions drove Latin from the Balkans. Arabic displaced it in North Africa. The most populous and prosperous parts of the former western empire, however, continued to speak Latin, and they use Romance languages today.

But if—to return to our premise—the Romans had never left Italy, then Europe's political, and thus linguistic, history would have followed a very different course. Without Roman intervention, the Hellenistic Greek kingdoms would likely have remained viable. The biggest success story might have been the Seleucid Empire. If the legions had not defeated Antiochus III, Parthia might have remained a minor kingdom in northeastern Iran. Philip V, never crushed by Rome, would have been left free to consolidate Macedonian hegemony over the Balkans.

Without the Punic Wars, Carthage could have expanded unchecked. Despite periodic conflicts with the Greeks of Sicily, the Carthaginians would likely have created an increasingly complex network of colonies and outposts in Spain and southern Gaul. The flag might have followed trade into these regions, cementing Carthaginian dominance over the coasts of the western Mediterranean.

Without the conquests of Caesar and the emperors, finally, the Celtic kingdoms of central and northern Europe would have continued to thrive. Although some regions would have been unsettled by Germanic migrations, Celtic culture would have likely remained dominant across much of the continent.

On the basis of those assumptions, let's imagine the languages of Europe after a few Rome-less centuries. Greek would become the lingua franca of the Mediterranean, used throughout Italy and in the ports of the Carthaginian Empire.* Greek would also be the prestige language of the Celtic world, employed by chieftains and aristocrats as a sign of status. Punic would be firmly established in Spain. Migrations would have scattered pockets of German speakers from Gaul to the Balkans. Farther east, the lower Danube might be dominated by an ascendant Macedonia or an expansionist Dacian kingdom. Either way, the language of commerce and culture would be Greek.[5]

Adding another twenty centuries to that scenario compounds unknowns on unknowns. But I think that Celtic languages would still be used across much of Europe, with Greek serving—like modern English—as the continent's default second language. A few geographically isolated languages, like Basque and Albanian, might occupy much the same places they do today. And perhaps, around the backwater Italian town of Rome, a few people would still speak some sort of Latin.

---

* Greek was the traditional second language of the Carthaginian elite. Hannibal was fluent.

What Would a Time Traveler Need
to Survive in Ancient Rome?

*M*aybe you built a time machine. Maybe you found some sort of glowing portal. Maybe you just know a helpful wizard. It's none of my business how you're getting to ancient Rome. My job is to keep you from dying or being otherwise inconvenienced while you're there. Some people seem to think that time travel is all fun and games— that you can just zip back to Rome, high five Caesar, and zip back. It's not that easy. You can't simply stroll into antiquity with an iPhone in one hand and an AK-47 in the other. You have to fit in.*

Step 1 is choosing a date. Some periods are much more congenial to time travelers than others. The heroic era of the Roman Republic—Scipio, Hannibal, and all that jazz—is exciting in theory, but Rome itself was an unprepossessing heap of mud-brick, and the Latin was deeply weird. Those inclined to watch Cicero speak or Caesar triumph will likely be interested in the late Republic. This, however, was an era of street gangs, rampant political violence, and mayhem on a scale that dismayed even the Romans. And unless you're a devotee of decadence who doesn't mind barbarian hordes, I can't recommend late antiquity.

Try to arrive in the early imperial era, when the city and empire of Rome were at their apogee. Avoid the Year of the Four Emperors—lots of riots, very unpleasant. Unless you have the smallpox

---

* Depending on your chosen method of time travel, historical continuity may be an issue. But even if you've done what science fiction assures us is most probable and created an alternate timeline with no causal relation to the present, it's just gauche to explore Rome in sweatpants.

vaccine and a strong stomach, don't show up during the Antonine Plague. And think twice about the reigns of Caligula, Nero, and Domitian, if only because your travel insurance rates will skyrocket. Whichever year you select, don't come in late summer, when Rome was overrun by malaria-carrying mosquitoes. The most congenial time for a visit, in my opinion, would be a lengthy and debauched festival—say, Saturnalia or Floralia—when the presence of a time traveler will be least likely to attract attention.

Because you're trying to experience Rome as the Romans did, the goal of your visit should be to see as much as possible without standing out. You therefore need to create a persona that will explain your ignorance of local customs. The best bet is to claim that you're a foreigner visiting Rome for the first time. Male time travelers can choose from a range of exotic occupations. Astrologer is a solid choice, as it gives you immediate access to the horoscope-obsessed Roman elite. There is, however, a slight risk that you'll be accused of sorcery and executed. Another enticing possibility is spice merchant. This persona will give you an unimpeachable reason to carry lots of valuable spice around. On the downside, you're likely to be targeted by thieves. Finally, there's the default mode: the wealthy tourist. The big advantage here is low expectations. Visitors were always trickling into ancient Rome, and most of them had no idea what they were doing. The disadvantage, of course, is that you'll be cheated by more or less everybody you meet.

Because the lives of ancient women were so circumscribed, female time travelers have fewer options. Your best bet is the wealthy tourist persona. Very few women traveled alone, so you'll be less conspicuous if you travel with a male acquaintance.

As the saying goes, clothes maketh the man (or woman, as the case may be). If you're male, don't even think about wearing a toga. Wearing a toga correctly is difficult, and you're going to get it wrong. In any case, only Roman citizens wear togas; you're trying to pass yourself off as a foreigner. Instead of a toga, wear a tunic. A basic tunic is just a wool tube with sleeves. I suggest wearing one made of fine linen; you'll get much further in Rome if people think you're important. Avoid anything dyed purple. Some emperors take offense at that sort of thing. Feel free, however, to dabble in other stylish hues.

You should also avoid togas if you're a woman (the only female toga wearers in Rome are prostitutes), and steer clear of the stola and palla worn by Roman matrons. The safest bet will be a full-length tunic made of fine linen or silk. The brighter the colors, the better. Layer tunics of different hues for best effect and complement them with the flashiest jewelry you can find. Think cubic zirconia, in bulk. Both men and women usually wore leather sandals when outdoors and kept valuables in a discreet money belt or pouch.

Next, language prep. The more Latin you know, the better.* At a bare minimum, you'll have to learn some essential phrases:

English	Latin
Where is the bathroom?	*Ubi est latrina?*
How much for this naked statue?	*Quanti constat haec statua nuda?*
You are mistaken. I did not assassinate Caesar.	*Erratis. Caesarem non occidi.*

Be sure that all your shots are up to date: chickenpox, mumps, tuberculosis, typhoid fever, polio, and whooping cough were all prevalent in Rome. You might want to also try one of the new malaria vaccines. Finally—though it isn't easy to find these days—be sure to get inoculated for smallpox if you visit during or after the Antonine Plague.†

Last but not least: what to bring. I'm going to assume that you will spend one week in Rome. I'm also going to assume that you can only bring around a single backpack's worth of items with you. You will, of course, need money. The most obvious solution would be to bring Roman coins. Unless your budget is unlimited, however, this will be cost prohibitive. High-value Roman coins, and especially

---

* There's quite a bit of Greek spoken on the streets of Rome too, thanks to a large immigrant community (slave and free) from the eastern provinces. If you know modern Greek, most of the vocabulary will be familiar, though the pronunciation will be quite different.

† If you're planning a particularly adventurous visit, you might also inquire into treatments for chlamydia and herpes, the only STDs known to have been prevalent in antiquity.

golden aurei, are very expensive these days.* You could try to just bring unworked silver or gold and sell it in Rome, but this will raise a lot of questions and sorely test your language skills. I recommend bringing substances that are much cheaper now, relatively speaking, than they were in the Roman era. Spices are probably your best bet. Some that are now very affordable, such as pepper and cinnamon, were worth almost their weight in gold in antiquity.

You should bring several changes of clothes. Rome's streets are very dirty, and you want to make a good impression. You could always get your clothes cleaned while in Rome, of course, but that would mean taking them to a fuller, who will douse them in a solution of human urine. Even if you aren't dismayed by that, the treatment takes more time than you have, so I suggest two changes of street clothes and a formal dinner outfit.

Contrary to what you might think, you won't need a water-purification kit. Rome's water doesn't always taste good, but it's quite safe. Although many water mains are lead, dissolved limestone in the water coats the insides of the pipes, neutralizing any ill effects. Roman food, however, is often riddled with parasites. Bring loperamide, and hope for the best. For serious medical emergencies, your only real hope is to stagger back to your time machine. It would be wise to bring a basic first aid kit with antiseptic cream for lesser wounds. An artemisinin derivative (and a can-do attitude!) will help if malaria strikes.

For a guidebook, this volume or either of its scintillating predecessors will serve handsomely. Finally, because nobody will believe that you're important if you haul your own gear, bring a friend along to ancient Rome. But perhaps not an especially close friend. Scapegoats, after all, are always useful.

Good luck, and *vale.*

---

* You could always have modern replicas made, of course, but that might get you into trouble with modern governments convinced that you're trying to scam people on eBay.

Notes

A NOTE ABOUT THE NOTES

These citations follow the conventions of the *Oxford Classical Diction-ary*, which are listed online: https://oxfordre.com/classics/page/3993. All primary sources not included in that list are cited by their standard Latin titles.

CHAPTER 1

1. Five thousand birds: Varro, *Rust.* 3.7.2. Severus Alexander: SHA, *Alex. Sev.* 41.7.

2. Two hundred sestertii: Varro, *Rust.* 3.7.10. Forty thousand sestertii: Columella, *Rust.* 8.8.10; cf. Plin., *HN* 10.110. Pigeon poem: Mart. 1.7. Tombstones: e.g., Petron., *Sat.* 71. Mausoleum dovecote: *Epigr. Gr.* 452.

3. Decimus Brutus: Frontin., *Str.* 3.13.8; cf. Plin., *HN* 10.110.

4. Pliny: Plin., *HN* 10.104. Doves of Venus: e.g., Ov., *Met.* 9.708.

5. Juvenal: Juv. 3.201–2. Dove as term of endearment: e.g., Plaut., *Cas.* 1.1.50. Gladiator: Suet., *Claud.* 21.5.

CHAPTER 2

1. Sulla: Plut., *Vit. Sull.* 1.4. Augustus: Suet., *Aug.* 78. Ptolemy: Diod. Sic. 31.18.

2. Maximum height: Suet., *Aug.* 89; Aur. Vict., *Caes.* 13. *Insula Felicula*: Tert., *Adv. Valent.* 100.7.

3. On the layout of this kind of apartment, see *Dig.* 9.3.5.2.

4. Shake hands: Mart. 1.86. The practice (of building cantilevered upper floors, not shaking hands) was banned in late antiquity: Amm. Marc. 27.9.8; *Cod. Iust.* 8.10.11.

5. Seductive water carriers: Juv. 6.314f. Chamber pots: Juv. 3.269f; cf. *Dig.* 9.3.5.1–2.

6. Subletting: *Dig.* 19.2.30. July 1: e.g., Cic., *Fam.* 13.2; Suet., *Tib.* 35.2. Quality apartments in the Praedia of Julia Felix in Pompeii were leased for five years (Dessau, *ILS* 5732). *Insula Arriana Polliana*: ibid. 6035. Caesar's debt relief: Suet., *Caes.* 38.2; we know, incidentally, that the annual rent of a fullery in Pompeii was 1,652 sestertii (*CIL* IV.3340.142). Two thousand sestertii: Suet., *Iul.* 38. Senator who paid six thousand: Vell. Pat. 2.10.1. Thirty thousand sestertii: Cic., *Cael.* 17.

7. Juvenal: Juv. 3.190f. Martial's apartment: 1.118. Noise: ibid. 12.57. Seneca: Sen., *Ep.* 56.1–2. Cicero: Cic., *Att.* 14.9.1.

8. Arsonists burned: *Dig.* 48.19.28.12. Upper stories: Sen., *Ep.* 91.13. Hesitated to invest: Gell., *NA* 15.1. Burning properties for insurance money: Mart. 3.52. Eviction: ibid. 3.38.5, 12.32.3; cf. Petron., *Sat.* 62.

CHAPTER 3

1. The Elephant: *CIL* IV.581. Price list: ibid. XII.5732.

2. Other men's wives: ibid. IV.7698.

3. Accused of adding water: Mart. 1.56, 3.57; *CIL* IV.3948. Falernian: ibid. IV.1679; cf. *AE* 1989:182; in a fresco at the Caupona of the Via de Mercurio, a customer asks for another cup of Setian wine (*CIL* IV.1292). Never changes the flavor: Petron., *Sat.* 50.

4. Fried pike: Auson., *Mos.* 123f. Greasy food: Hor., *Epist.* 1.14.21. Roaches: SHA, *Hadr.* 16.4.

5. Local gossip: e.g., Juv. 9.102–10; Apul., *Met.* 1.7, 1.21. Open all night: e.g., Cic., *Pis.* 13. Prefect: Amm. Marc. 28.4.4.

6. Regarded as promiscuous: e.g., *Dig.* 23.2.43; 23.2.43.9. Lucius Callidius Eroticus and Fannia Voluptas: Dessau, *ILS* 7478. Compare the erotic fresco in the main room of the Caupona on the Via di Mercurio.

7. Juvenal: Juv. 8.171–78. Ammianus: Amm. Marc. 14.6.25. Murder of the praetor: App., *B Civ.* 1.54. Emperors slumming in bars: Tac., *Ann.* 13.25; Suet., *Ner.* 26.1; SHA, *Verus* 4.6f.

8. Criminal offense: *Dig.* 47.10.26. Emperors limiting foods: Suet., *Tib.* 34; Suet., *Ner.* 16; Cass. Dio 60.6, 62.14, 66.10.

9. Tavern keeper from Tivoli: *CIL* XIV.1309.

CHAPTER 4

1. Muddy streets: Juv. 3.247. Feral dogs: Suet., *Vesp.* 5.4. Alley pigs: Hor., *Epist.* 2.2.72–75.
2. *Koprologoi*: Arist., [*Ath. Pol.*] 50.2. Dung-collection cart: Tac., *Ann.* 11.32. Cesspits in Greek cities: e.g., *OGI* 483.79–84.
3. Boundary stones: *CIL* VI.31614–15; Dessau, *ILS* 6082.
4. Rode his horse: SHA, *Sev.* 10.8. Destructive Spanish rabbits: Strabo 3.2.6.
5. Sabine farm: Hor., *Sat.* 2.7.118; Hor., *Epist.* 1.14.1–3.
6. Olive oil every month: SHA, *Sev.* 18.3.
7. 150 tons: Dion. Hal., *Ant. Rom.* 3.44.

CHAPTER 5

1. Ovid banned: Ov., *Tr.* 3.1.59–72. Sejanus presided: Tac., *Ann.* 4.34–35. Valens: Amm. Marc. 29.2.
2. Martial: Mart. 1.2.7–8.
3. Atticus: Cic., *Att.* 4.8. Shop of Atrectus: Mart. 1.117.
4. Cicero: e.g., Cic., *Att.* 12.6a. Wealthy orator: Plin., *Ep.* 4.7.
5. Tryphon: Quint., *Inst.* praef.; Mart. 4.72.
6. Few sestertii: Mart. 13.3. Five denarii: ibid. 1.117. Gellius: Gell., *NA* 9.4, 5.4, 2.3.
7. Pliny: e.g., Plin., *Ep.* 9.34; cf. Mart. 3.50. Parthians: Plut., *Vit. Crass.* 32.3.

CHAPTER 6

1. Rickets: Sor., *Gyn.* 2.43–44.
2. Lucian: Lucian, *Navigium* 5. Generous terms: Suet., *Claud.* 18–19; eventually, grain transport became compulsory: *Cod. Theod.* 13.5. Paul: *Acts* 27–28.
3. Puteoli: Sen., *Ep.* 77. Olive lees in mortar: Plin., *HN* 15.8.
4. Clodius: Cass. Dio 39.24. Caesar: Suet., *Iul.* 41.3. Additions: SHA, *Sev.* 18.3; SHA, *Aurel.* 35.2, 48.1.
5. Window 39: Dessau, *ILS* 6069.
6. Times of crisis: Tac., *Ann.* 2.87, 15.39; Cass. Dio 55.26. Supervising bakers: Aur. Vict., *Caes.* 13.5.
7. Lynch the consuls: Sall., *Hist.* 2.45M. Stale crusts: Suet., *Claud.* 18.2. Augustus: Macrob., *Sat.* 2.28.
8. Justinian: Constantine Porphyrogenitus, *De Ceremoniis* 2.51.

CHAPTER 8

1. Quadrans: e.g., Juv. 2.152; Sen., *Ep.* 86.9. Children free: *CIL* II.5181.22f.
2. Hot to cold: Galen, *De Methodo medendi* X.10 708–9K; cf. Celsus, *Med.* 1.4. Seven or eight times a day: e.g., SHA, *Comm.* 11.5.
3. Sculptures moved to baths: e.g., *CIL* VIII.20963. Baths of Neptune: ibid. XIV.98 (this inscription may actually refer to the Baths of the Marine Gate).
4. Emperor Severus Alexander reportedly assigned tracts of woodland to individual baths (SHA, *Alex. Sev.* 24.5).
5. Orata: Plin., *HN* 9.168. Darnel grass: ibid. 18.156.
6. Facing south or west: Vitr., *De arch.* 5.10.1; cf. Lucian, *Hippias* 7. Tanning in the pools: Sen., *Ep.* 86.8. Ceiling of bronze: SHA, *M. Ant.* 9.4–5.
7. Public troughs: Frontin., *Aq.* 94; even during the imperial era, bathwater was often muddy after a heavy rain (ibid. 89). Marcus Aurelius: M. Aur., *Med.* 8.24. The poet Martial wrote epigrams about communal bathwater being dirtied by contact with pathics and gigolos (Mart. 2.42, 2.70, 6.81). Gangrene: Celsus, *Med.* 5.26. Wound plasters: Scribonius Largus, *Compositiones* 214. Hadrian: SHA, *Hadr.* 22.7.
8. Reserved for criminals: Plin., *Ep.* 10.32.2. Roaches: Plin., *HN* 11.99.

CHAPTER 9

1. Colossal rollers: Vitr., *De arch.* 10.2.11–12.
2. Sandbags: Plin., *HN* 36.96. On cranes, see Vitr., *De arch.* 10.2.1–10.
3. Building inscription of the Temple of Asclepius: *IG* IV² 102.

CHAPTER 10

1. Death of Apollodorus: Cass. Dio 69.4. Six or seven years: Janet DeLaine, "The Pantheon Builders: Estimating Manpower for Construction," in *The Pantheon from Antiquity to the Present*, ed. Tod Marder and Mark Wilson Jones, 160–92 (Cambridge University Press, 2015).

CHAPTER 11

1. Nail prohibition: Dion. Hal., *Ant. Rom.* 3.45.2.
2. On the construction of cofferdams, see Vitr., *De arch.* 5.12.5–6. The work was sometimes done by professional divers (Symm., *Relat.* 26.4).

CHAPTER 12

1. Camp for Hadrian: Dessau, *ILS* 2487.
2. Building pontoon bridges: Veg., *Mil.* 3.7; Cass. Dio 71.3. Wine barrels: Hdn. 8.4.4. Caligula's bridge: Suet., *Calig.* 19.
3. Caesar's Bridge: Caes., *BGall.* 4.17–18.
4. Avaricum: ibid. 7.24. Alesia: ibid. 7.69f. Masada: Joseph., *BJ* 7.304f.
5. Rhine canal: Tac., *Ann.* 11.20. Antioch canal: Sherk, *Hadrian* 85a.
6. Canal: *Ep.* 10.42. Aqueduct: ibid. 10.37. Moving from legion to legion: e.g., *CIL* VI.2725.
7. Nonius Datus: Dessau, *ILS* 5795.

CHAPTER 13

1. Janet DeLaine, "Bricks and Mortar: Exploring the Economics of Building Techniques at Rome and Ostia," in *Economies Beyond Agriculture in the Classical World*, ed. D. J. Mattingly & J. Salmon, 230–68 (Routledge, 2000).

CHAPTER 14

1. Pyramids megalomaniacal: Plin., *HN* 36.75; Frontin., *Aq.* 16. Nearly a half-millennium later, Procopius (Procop., *Aed.* 2.1.3) repeated the same criticism.
2. Herodotus: Hdt. 2.125. Diodorus: Diod. Sic. 1.63. Pliny: Plin., *HN* 36.81. 330 days: *CIL* VI.1375.

CHAPTER 15

1. Pliny the Elder provides the most detailed ancient description of the mausoleum (Plin., *HN* 36.30). Unfortunately—as so often—he was careless with his sources, creating endless headaches for future archaeologists.

CHAPTER 16

1. Parade armor: e.g., Arr., *Tact.* 34.
2. Pliny the Younger: Plin., *Ep.* 6.25.3–4. Armor shops: e.g., Dessau, *ILS* 2472.

3. Octavian's arsehole: *CIL* XI.6721.5.
4. Scipio: Livy 26.47. Made in military camps: e.g., Veg., *Mil.* 2.11.
5. *PBerol.* 6765.
6. Every five days: *Cod. Theod.* 10.22.1. Wicker helmet covers: Caes.,
BCiv. 3.62. Summarily executed: Amm. Marc. 29.3.4.

CHAPTER 17

1. Head of Crassus: Plut., *Crass.* 33.1–4.
2. Transfix two men: Plut., *Vit. Crass.* 27. Arrian: *Acies contra Alanos.*
3. Lucullus: Plut., *Luc.* 32.1–2. Antony: Plut., *Ant.* 50–51. Frostbite: Tac.,
Ann. 13.35. Crassus: Plut., *Vit. Crass.* 22.1–2. Hatra: Cass. Dio 68.31.
4. Supply line: Tac., *Ann.* 13.39. Corbulo: ibid. 14.23–26.
5. Limited conquest: Cass. Dio 68.30; cf. Mattingly-Sydenham, *RIC* II
667–68.
6. Two eyes of the world: Theophylact Simocatta 4.11.2.

CHAPTER 18

1. Status of slave gladiators: Plin., *Ep.* 10.40. Titus: Mart., *Spect.* 29.
2. Claudius: Suet., *Claud.* 21.5. Spiculus: Suet., *Ner.* 30.2. Wives and
children: e.g., *CIL* VI.10176, 10177. Four sons: Suet., *Claud.* 21.5. Secundus:
CIL VI.10168.
3. On legal limitations, see *Dig.* 28.3.6.5–6. Tiberius: Suet., *Tib.* 7.1.
4. Diodorus: Reinhold Merkelbach and Josef Stauber, *Steinepigramme aus
dem griechischen Osten* (Teubner, 2001), no. 11/02/01. *Summa rudis* who lived
to sixty: *CIL* VIII.10983.
5. Clodius and Milo: e.g., Cass. Dio 39.7–8. Nero: Tac., *Ann.* 13.25. Aristocratic ladies: e.g., *Corpus Inscriptionum Graecarum* 2164. Private armies:
AE 1985.816.
6. Caesar's gladiators: Caes., *BCiv.* 1.14. Otho: Tac., *Hist.* 2.11. Marcus
Aurelius: SHA, *Marc.* 21, 23. Caligula: Suet., *Calig.* 55.2.
7. Horace: Hor., *Epist.* 1.1.1–6.
8. Banned from office: e.g., Tert., *De spect.* 22. Seven cities: Louis Robert,
Les gladiateurs dans l'Orient grec (Champion, 1940), no. 90. Gladiator ambas-
sador: *Dig.* 50.7.5.1 (my thanks to Michael Carter for that reference). Vitellius: Suet., *Vit.* 12. Marcus Aurelius: SHA, *Marc.* 12.3. Juvenal: Juv. 3.158.
Macrinus: SHA, *Opellius Macrinus* 4.

9. Celadus: *CIL* IV.4342, 4345. Wives of senators: e.g., Juv. 6.78–113. Messalina: Cass. Dio 60.28. Faustina and the gladiator: SHA, *Marc.* 19.2–7.

CHAPTER 19

1. Pompey's elephants: Plin., *HN* 8.20.
2. Fence in Nero's amphitheater: Calp., *Ecl.* 7.47f. Amber: Plin., *HN* 37.45.
3. Sun hats: Cass. Dio 59.7.8. Leopard: Plin., *HN* 36.40. Python: ibid. 8.37.
4. Fidenae: Tac., *Ann.* 4.62. Pompeii: ibid. 14.17.
5. Valerius Maximus: Val. Max. 1.7.8.
6. Domitian: Suet., *Dom.* 10.1. Lion at Alban villa: Cass. Dio 67.14. Commodus: ibid. 73.20.

CHAPTER 20

1. The "Cryptoporticus of Commodus" is discussed by Irene Iacopi, "Il Passaggio Sotterraneo Cosiddetto di Commodo," in *Sangue e Arena*, ed. Adriano La Regina, 79–87 (Electa, 2001). For Elkins's views, see Nathan T. Elkins, "The Procession and Placement of Imperial Cult Images in the Colosseum," *Papers of the British School at Rome* 82 (2014): 73–107.
2. Augustus: *Mon. Anc.* 23. Nero's naumachiae: Cass. Dio 61.9.5., 62.15.1–5.
3. Mart., *Spect.* 24; Cass. Dio 66.25.3; cf. Suet., *Dom.* 4.1.
4. Titus's naumachia at the Stagnum of Augustus: Mart., *Spect.* 34; Suet., *Tit.* 7.3; Cass. Dio 66.25.4.

CHAPTER 21

1. Recent estimate: Walter Scheidel and Steven J. Friesen, "The Size of the Economy and the Distribution of Income in the Roman Empire," *Journal of Roman Studies* 99 (2009): 61–91.
2. Horace's education: Hor., *Sat.* 1.6.75. Quintus Sulpicius Maximus: *Inscriptiones graecae urbis Romae* III.1336. Petronius: Petron., *Sat.* 46; cf. Mart. 5.56.
3. Elite investment in commerce: e.g., Plut., *Vit. Cat. Mai.* 21; Plut., *Vit. Crass.* 1–2. Denied a place in the senate: Libanius, *Orationes* 42.21. Vulgar professions: Cic., *Off.* 1.150–51.

4. Scaurus: *AE* 1992.278a.
5. Reaper of Mactaris: Dessau, *ILS* 7457. Good farmer: *ILAlg.* I.1362.
6. Juvenal: Juv. 1.104–6. Petronius: Petron., *Sat.* 76. Dealer of goat skins: *CIL* X.4796. Doctor and surgeon: Dessau, *ILS* 7812.
7. Herculaneum citizens: *CIL* X.1403. Selling swords or pottery: Dessau, *ILS* 2472, 7531. Dozen tenants: *POxy* 1459. Gifts and bribes: B. P. Grenfell, A. S. Hunt, and D. G. Hogarth (eds.), *Fayum Towns and Their Papyri* (Egypt Exploration Fund, 1900), 91, 1171–78.
8. Pannonian *primipilus*: *CIL* III.14426. Gilded statue: ibid. X.3903. Lucius Gavius Fronto: *SEG* 17.584.

CHAPTER 22

1. Sybarite in Athens: Diod. Sic. 8.19. Repeal of the sumptuary law: Livy 34.1–7.
2. Four-pound mullet: Mart. 10.31. Three large mullets: Suet., *Tib.* 34. Songbirds: Plin., *HN* 10.141. Lucullus: Plut., *Vit. Luc.* 41.5. Roses: Suet., *Ner.* 27.
3. Lucullus: Plut., *Vit. Luc.* 41.5. Roses: Suet., *Ner.* 27. Pearl: Plin., *HN* 9.122; Val. Max. 9.1.2. Apicius: Plin., *HN* 19.143.
4. Worth its weight in gold: SHA, *Aurel.* 45. Opal ring: Plin., *HN* 37.81. Caesar: Suet., *Iul.* 50.
5. Candelabra: Plin., *HN* 34.11. Nibbled cup: ibid. 37.18. Dipper, Nero's cup: ibid. 37.20. Nero's coverlets: ibid. 8.196. Citrus wood: ibid. 13.91. Lamp and staff: Lucian, *Adversus Indoctum* 13.
6. Lotus trees: Plin., *HN* 36.7. Considered small: Val. Max. 4.4. Villa of the Gordians: SHA, *Gordiani Tres* 32.
7. Three hills: Mart. 7.73.
8. Hortensius: Varro, *Rust.* 3.13. Lakeside villa: Stat., *Silv.* 2.2. Lucullus: e.g., Plut., *Vit. Luc.* 39.3. Fish: Plin., *HN* 9.170. Baths: Juv. 7.178f. Pompey: Cass. Dio 48.36.5. Marius's villa: Plut., *Vit. Mar.* 34. Gardens of Lucullus: Tac., *Ann.* 11.3. Caesar's forum: Suet., *Iul.* 38.
9. Caesar: Plut., *Vit. Caes.* 5. Amphitheater: Plin., *HN* 36.117. Scaurus: ibid. 36.5.
10. Sulla: Plut., *Vit. Sull.* 38. Nero: Plin., *HN* 12.83. Funerary games: Suet., *Tib.* 37. Wealthy freedman: Plin., *HN* 33.35.
11. Four groundskeepers: *CIL* VI.13830.

CHAPTER 23

1. Susa dye: Plut., *Vit. Alex.* 36.
2. Strengthen the stomach: Ath. 86C. Toothache and blisters: Dioscorides, *De materia medica* 2.4.
3. Pliny on dye making: Plin., *HN* 9.133–35. Pungency of Tyre: Strabo 16.2.23. Executed for substandard dye: *Cod. Iust.* 11.8.2.
4. Nymphs: Hom., *Od.* 13.108. Agamemnon: Aesch., *Ag.* 958f. Arena: e.g., Tert., *De anim.* 2; Tert., *De pallio* 40. Dinner guests: Mart. 2.57. Luxury editions: Stat., *Silv.* 4.9.7. Funerals: ibid. 5.1.225. Sheep: Plin., *HN* 8.197.
5. Persian kings: Xen., *Cyr.* 8.3. Alexander: Arr., *Anab.* 7.9.9. Ptolemies: Ath. 197B. Jesus: *Mark* 15.17; *Matt.* 27.28. Marcus Aurelius: SHA, *Marc.* 17.4–5, 21.9; cf. SHA, *Pert.* 8. Aurelian's pallium: SHA, *Aurel.* 29. Purple ink: *Cod. Iust.* 1.23.6. Caligula: Suet., *Calig.* 35.1. Nero's dye sting: Suet., *Ner.* 32. Late antique emperors: *Cod. Theod.* 10.21.3. Ambitious deacon: Amm. Marc. 14.9.7; cf. 16.8.8. Illegal private commissions: *Cod. Theod.* 10.20.18.
6. Three minas: Plut., *Mor. De tranq. anim.* 10; cf. Dio Chrys., *Or.* 66.4. Worth its weight in silver: Ath. 526C. Two talents: Theophr., *Char.* 23. Dyestuff: Plin., *HN* 9.137. Second-rate cloak: Mart. 4.61, 8.101. Finer garment: ibid. 10.41.5.
7. For comparison, a pound of undyed wool was worth between 25 and 175 denarii, and the maximum that could be charged for a pound of undyed silk was 12,000.

CHAPTER 24

1. Critiques of democracy: e.g., Xen., [*Ath. pol.*] 1.2–9; Arist., *Pol.* 3.1279–80.
2. Trial after Arginusae: Xen., *Hell.* 1.7.
3. Polybius's description: Polyb. 6.11–15, 57.
4. The authorship of Quintus's letter, the so-called *Commentariolum Petitionis*, is disputed. It may be nothing more than a learned first-century rhetorical exercise.
5. Nasica: Val. Max. 7.5.2. Stingy senator: ibid. 7.5.1. Bribery: Cass. Dio 36.38.3; Cic., *Sull.* 88.
6. May he fall ill: Dessau, *ILS* 6409. Tomb warning: ibid. 8207. Get up and vote: *CIL* IV.2993t. Praised in verse: Dessau, *ILS* 6422b, 7201. Promises: ibid. 6405, 6421e. Parodies: *CIL* IV.7389; Dessau, *ILS* 6418d.
7. Cicero: Cic., *Leg.* 3.34.

8. Election interference: *Rhet. Her.* 1.21; Cic., *Dom.* 54, 110; Cic., *Sest.* 75–76. The same handwriting: Plut., *Vit. Cat. Min.* 46.2.

9. Cicero's joke: Macrob., *Sat.* 2.3.11. Augustus campaigning: Suet., *Aug.* 56.1. Tiberius: Tac., *Ann.* 1.15.

CHAPTER 25

1. Publicans and sinners: *Luke* 3:12–14.

2. Jewish revolt: Joseph., *BJ* 7.218; Suet., *Dom.* 12.2. Nail tax: Joyce Reynolds, *Aphrodisias and Rome: Documents from the Excavation of the Theatre at Aphrodisias Conducted by Professor Kenan T. Erim, Together with Some Related Texts* (Society for the Promotion of Roman Studies, 1982), no. 115.

3. Cyrene: Plin., *HN* 19.40. Frisians: Tac., *Ann.* 4.72. Land taxes: Hyginus Gromaticus 205L.

4. Like 5 percent: Walter Scheidel and Steven J. Friesen, "The Size of the Economy and the Distribution of Income in the Roman Empire," *Journal of Roman Studies* 99 (2009): 75.

5. Tax fraud: Anna Dolganov et al., "Forgery and Fiscal Fraud in Iudaea and Arabia on the Eve of the Bar Kokhba Revolt: Memorandum and Minutes of a Trial Before a Roman Official (P. Cotton)," *Tyche* 38 (2024): 37–167.

CHAPTER 26

1. Snow drifts: Dion. Hal., *Ant. Rom.* 12.8. The tornadoes (*turbines* in Latin) are recorded in the *Prodigiorum liber* of Julius Obsequens (16, 62, 68).

2. Tempe: Hdt. 7.129.

3. A survey of theories on earthquakes: Arist., *Mete.* 363a–9a.

4. Unflappable Spartan king: Xen., *Hell.* 4.7.4–5.

5. Alexandria earthquake: Amm. Marc. 26.10.16–17.

6. Trajan: Cass. Dio 68.24–25. Justinian: Malalas 17.16.

7. Nero: Tac., *Ann.* 15.39, 43. Titus: Suet., *Tit.* 8.4.

8. Aristides: Aristid., *Or.* 19.

9. Antioch: Procop., *Aed.* 2.10.

CHAPTER 27

1. Potter's field: Hor., *Sat.* 1.8.

2. Speculation in columbarium niches: e.g., Dessau, *ILS* 7892. One hundred sestertii and an amphora: ibid. 7212.

3. Here lies a boy: *AE* 1931.112. Venerable lady: Sen., *Ep.* 77.20. Nine breaths: *ILCV* 4429a.

4. Slaughterer: Dessau, *ILS* 7642. Engineer: *CIL* VI.8495. Interpreter: for the epitaph of Gorgos, "mighty in mind," see C. Schuchhardt, "Kolophon, Notion, und Klaros," *Ath. Mitt.* 11 (1886): 428. Fanatic: Dessau, *ILS* 4181a. *Medicus equarius*: *CIL* VI.9610. Juggler: Dessau, *ILS* 5173. Farm laborer: ibid. 7457. Former slave: ibid. 1980.

5. Slave accountant: Dessau, *ILS* 1514. Manager of inheritances: ibid. 1603. Librarian: ibid. 1589. Dorcas: ibid. 1784. Chia: ibid. 1790. Primitivus: *CIL* VI.7458. Zosimus: ibid. VI.9005.

6. Praetorian: Dessau, *ILS* 7741. Versatile solder: ibid. 2117. Centurion: ibid. 2658. Fast shot: ibid. 2558.

7. Fishmonger: Dessau, *ILS* 7500. Silk merchant: *CIL* VI.9891. Cannot do without them: Gell., *NA* 1.6. Finally dead: *CIL* VI.29149. No cause for complaint: Dessau, *ILS* 8156. Praised wife: ibid. 8393—this is the so-called *Laudatio Turiae*; the senator was probably Q. Lucretius Vespillo. Two male lovers: *CIL* VI.37965.

8. Soldier: Dessau, *ILS* 9494. Mosaicist: ibid. 7671. Boxer: *AE* 1947.187. Wife: Dessau, *ILS* 8512.

9. Margarita: *CIL* VI.29896. Blinded: Dessau, *ILS* 8207b. Refused by the gods: *CIL* VI.36467. Raise hands: Dessau, *ILS* 8498. Resignation: ibid. 8164. Mix the wine: *CIL* VI.17985a. Died on stage: Dessau, *ILS* 5228. Bathe at the Baths of Apollo: ibid. 8158.

CHAPTER 28

1. Cicero: Cic., *Nat. D.* 3.53–60. Alexander Severus: SHA, *Alex. Sev.* 29.2. Anubis barking: Lucian, *Deorum Concilium* 10.

2. Varro on temples: *Antiquitates rerum divinarum* Frag. 38 (Cardauns).

3. Isis: *POxy.* 1380. Inscription from Asia Minor: *Inscriptiones graecae ad res romanas pertinentes* III.903. Antinous: Socrates, *Hist. eccl.* 3.23. Gods fleeing to Egypt: e.g., Ov., *Met.* 5.139f.

4. Armenian temple: Plin., *HN* 33.83. Evocatio: e.g., Livy 5.21.

5. Gods of all peoples: Min. Fel., *Oct.* 6. Rain miracle: e.g., Cass. Dio 71.8–10; SHA, *Marc.* 24.

6. Prayers to Robigo: Ov., *Fast.* 4.905f. Gods of doors: August., *De civ. D.* 4.8. Lucina and Statina: Tert., *De anim.* 39.

7. Plutarch: Plut., *Mor. Quaest. Rom.* Dionysius: Dion. Hal., *Ant. Rom.* 2.18–20.

CHAPTER 29

1. Becoming a god: Suet., *Vesp.* 23.4.
2. Caesar's comet: Suet., *Aug.* 88; Plin., *HN* 2.93–94.
3. Augustus's soul: Suet., *Aug.* 100. Caesar's ghost: Val. Max. 1.8.8.
4. Caligula the god: Suet., *Calig.* 22.
5. Vespasian: Suet., *Vesp.* 7.2–3. Hadrian: SHA, *Hadr.* 20.14. Marcus Aurelius: SHA, *Marc.* 24.
6. Cult statues of Antinous: e.g., Paus. 8.9.7–8.

CHAPTER 30

1. Accusations of treason: e.g., Tert., *Apol.* 24.1.
2. Christianity on the terms of Platonic philosophy: Athenagoras, *Leg. pro Christ.* Mithraism as satanic plagiarism: Clemens Alexandrinus, *Protrepticus* 1.66; Tert., *De err.* 5.2. Dark caves: Firm. Mat., *Err. prof. rel.* 5.2. Aurelian and Sol Invictus: SHA, *Aurel.* 25.5–6; Zos. 1.61. Celsus: Origen, *C. Cels.* 1.6, 8.75. The works of Porphyry were burned on the orders of Theodosius II as late as 448 (*Cod. Iust.* 1.1.3).
3. Nero: Tac., *Ann.* 15.44. Pliny: Plin. *Ep.* 10.96. Martyrs of Lyon: Euseb., *Hist. eccl.* 5.1–2.
4. On the process of offering sacrifice during the persecution: Cyprian, *Epistulae* 8.2.3; 21.3.2. More than forty certificates of sacrifice still survive, preserved in the Egyptian deserts. Number of Christians: Keith Hopkins, "Christian Number and Its Implications," *Journal of Early Christian Studies* 6 (1998): 185–226.
5. Sibling marriage: *Mosaicarum et romanarum legum collatio* 6.4. Manichaeans: ibid. 15.3.
6. Lactantius: Lactant., *De mort. pers.* 11. Palestine: Euseb., *Hist. eccl.* 8.2. Carthage: *Acta Felicis.*
7. Diocletian presided personally: Lactant., *De mort. pers.* 13–14; Euseb., *Hist. eccl.* 8.5–6. Every city and village: Euseb., *De Martyribus Palestinae* 3.1.
8. Acts of Pilate: Euseb., *Hist. eccl.* 9.5; Lactant., *De mort. pers.* 36.4. Maximinus produced a remarkable profession of belief in the old gods: Euseb., *Hist. eccl.* 9.7.
9. Public baths: Euseb., *De Martyribus Palestinae* 9.2.
10. Galerius's edict of toleration: Lactant., *De mort. pers.* 34.

CHAPTER 32

1. Horace: Hor., *Sat.* 1.5.14. Virgil: Verg., *Cul.*

CHAPTER 34

1. Cornelius Gallus: Dessau, *ILS* 8995. Hieroglyph cutters: *POxy* 1029.
2. Ramesses III: *Papyrus Harris* I.
3. Egyptians as fanatics: e.g., Diod. Sic. 1.83. Roman disdain for Egyptian gods: e.g., Juv. 15; Cic., *Nat. D.* 1.16.43. Obelisk in the Circus Maximus: Amm. Marc. 17.4.17–23.
4. This translation is taken from Richard Parkinson, *Cracking Codes: The Rosetta Stone and Its Decipherment* (University of California Press, 1999), 178.

CHAPTER 35

1. Martin: Sulpicius Severus, *Vita sancti Martini* 13–15. Porphyry: Marcus Diaconus, *Vita sancti Porphyrii* 50–51. Serapeum: Rufinus, *Historia Ecclesiastica* 11.22–30. Libanius: *Or.* 30.
2. Temples remaining open: *Cod. Theod.* 16.10.3, 7, 8. Could not be demolished: ibid. 16.10.15, 18. Ilion: Julian., *Ep.* 79.
3. Pope Gregory: *Ep.* 11.76. Demeas inscription: *Die Inschriften von Ephesos* 1351.
4. Libanius: *Or.* 18.126. Emperors condone pillaging: *Cod. Theod.* 15.1.40; 16.10.19, 25.
5. Holy men living in temples: *Vita sancti Danielis Stylitae* 14–15; Gregorius Magnus, *Dialogi* 2.8.11.
6. Pantheon: *Liber Pontificalis* 69.

CHAPTER 37

1. Wine and women: *CIL* VI.17985a.
2. Scraggly vineyards: Mart. 6.92.3, 10.45.5. Swarming mosquitoes: Tac., *Hist.* 2.93. Obelisk: Plin., *HN* 36.74.
3. Elagabalus: SHA, *Heliogab.* 23.
4. Middle class: The tomb of Popilius Heracla (*AE* 1946.136) cost six thousand sestertii—substantial but not extravagant. On Nero's persecution

of the Christians, see Tac., *Ann.* 15.44. By the third century, it was widely accepted that Peter had been crucified upside down in the Circus of Nero and buried nearby (e.g., Euseb., *Hist. eccl.* 2.1).

CHAPTER 38

1. Egyptian villages: e.g., *PMich.* IV.223–25. Kaunos: Strabo 14.2.3 (651–52).
2. Pausanias: Paus. 7.24.13.

CHAPTER 39

1. Three million lines: *Cod. Iust.* 1.17.2.1.
2. Majority should prevail: *Cod. Theod.* 1.4.1.
3. Cousin love: *Cod. Theod.* 3.12.3. Corrupting nurse: ibid. 9.24.2.
4. Theoderic: Malalas 384.

CHAPTER 40

1. Roman engagement rings: Plin., *HN* 33.12; Tert., *Apol.* 6. Nerve: Gell., *NA* 10.10.
2. Ov., *Fast.* 6.225; Plut., *Mor. Quaest. Rom.* 86.
3. Christian veils: Ambrosius, *De Virginitate* 15; Ambrosius, *De institutione virginis* 17. *Tabulae nuptiales* and *dextrarum iunctio*: e.g., August., *Serm.* 51.22; Ambrosius, *Epistulae* 19. Velum spread over couple: Paulinus Nolanus, *Carmina* 25. Plutarch: Plut., *Mor. Quaest. Rom.* 29.
4. Joyous funerals: e.g., Ioannes Chrysostomus *Homilia* 30. Wearing black at pre-Christian funerals: e.g., Juv. 10.245; Servius, *In Vergilii Aeneidem Commentarii* 11.287.
5. Funeral pyre: Plin., *HN* 9.37.
6. Plutrach: *Conv. sept. sap.* 5.7.
7. Remedies for the evil eye: e.g., Plin., *HN* 28.7; Lucian, *Navigium* 15. *Digitus impudicus*: e.g., Mart. 6.70.5.

CHAPTER 41

1. Shakespeare, *Macbeth* 2.2.58–61, in *The Oxford Shakespeare: The Complete Works*, 2nd ed. (Oxford University Press, 2005).

CHAPTER 44

1. Lydian propaganda: Dominique Briquel, "Etruscan Origins and the Ancient Authors," in *The Etruscan World*, ed. Jean MacIntosh Turfa, 36–55 (Routledge, 2013).

2. Mithridates: Val. Max. 9.7; Plin., *HN* 7.88.

3. Agricola: Tac., *Agr.* 21.2; cf. Plut., *Vit. Sert.* 14.3. Provincial elites set up Latin schools for their children: e.g., Tac., *Ann.* 3.43; Suet., *Calig.* 45.2.

4. Irenaeus: *Adversus Haereses* 1. Augustine: August., *Ep.* 17.2.

5. Hannibal: Nep., *Hannibal* 13.2.

Index